# ARTISTS OF AMERICAN FOLK MUSIC

The Legends of Traditional Folk, the Stars of the Sixties,
the Virtuosi of New Acoustic Music

## Edited by Phil Hood

Quill/A *Guitar Player* and *Frets* Book
William Morrow
New York

**GPI Books**

**Art Director/Designer**
Paul Haggard

**Editor: GPI Books**
Helen Casabona

**General Manager: GPI Books**
Judie Eremo

**GPI Corporate Art Director**
Wales Christian Ledgerwood

**Darkroom**
Cheryl Matthews (Director), Joyce Phillips, Joe Verri

**Typesetting**
Leslie K. Bartz (Director), Pat Gates, Lea Milano

**Editor: Frets Magazine**
Phil Hood

**Editor: Guitar Player Magazine**
Tom Wheeler

**President/Publisher: GPI Publications**
Jim Crockett

**Director: GPI Books**
Alan Rinzler

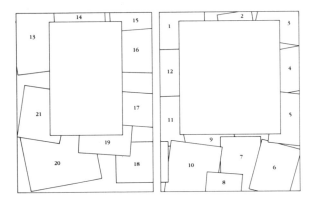

Cover photos: 1: Courtesy Bob Yellin; 2: Jon Sievert; 3: Phil Zimmerman; 4: Jon Sievert; 5: Courtesy Woody Guthrie Publications; 6: John Lee; 7: Jim Marshall; 8: Marshall Freedland; 9: Courtesy Mike Seeger; 10: Doug Rhinehart; 11: Courtesy Pete Seeger; 12: Courtesy Bob Yellin; 13: Mark Mander; 14: Roger Siminoff; 15: Jon Sievert; 16: John Lee; 17: Jon Sievert; 18: Lisa Law; 19: Jon Sievert; 20: Jay Thompson; 21: Bob Kreuger.

## PHOTO CREDITS

Page 5, 6, 19: Courtesy Of University Of Texas At Austin Archives; 7, top, 15, 17: Courtesy Of Woody Guthrie Publications; 7, bottom: Alanna Nash; 8, top, 25, 107, 111, 113, 114: Bob Krueger; 8, bottom, 132: Paul Natkin/Photo Reserve; 9, top, 21, 29, 33, 52, 71, 74, 77, 78, 89, 124, 125, 129, 130, 135, 137, 150: Jon Sievert; 9, bottom, 83, 84, 87: Jim Marshall; 10: Courtesy Of Kentucky Fried Chicken Bluegrass Music Festival; 11, 13: Courtesy Of Country Music Foundation; 12: Bruno; 20: Carl Fleischhauer; 22: Phil Zimmerman; 26: Bud Merritt; 34: Courtesy Of Pete Seeger; 36: Roger Siminoff; 38, 43, 44, 55, 57, 58: John Lee; 41: Johsel Namkung/Courtesy Of Seattle Folklore Society; 47: Marshall Freedland; 50: Courtesy Of Mike Seeger; 59, 61, 62, 68: Jay Thompson; 72: Jerry Jew; 80, 81, 127: Lisa Law; 93: Anders Faergeman; 96: Art Edlestein; 100, 102: Courtesy Of Bob Yellin; 104: Gerald Russell; 108: Catherine Sebastian; 117: Chuck Pulin; 120: Courtesy Of Sire Records; 122: Nick Smacchia; 128: Camilla McGuinn; 139, 142: Gerry Ichikawa; 141: Courtesy Of J. D'Addario & Co., Inc.; 144, 148: Doug Rhinehart; 147: Jon Sievert/Courtesy Of Warner Brothers Records; 152: Jim Hatlo; 154: Eric Levenson; 155: John Hanson.

Copyright © 1986 by GPI Publications

Library of Congress Catalog Card Number: 85-63796

ISBN: 0-688-05916-3

Printed in the United States of America

First Edition

1 2 3 4 5 6 7 8 9 10

# CONTENTS

# INTRODUCTION

FOLK MUSIC, AT ITS MOST BASIC, is the music of the common folk. It's often simple music that reflects the concerns and aspirations of a broad spectrum of people. Folk music's timeless appeal is based on its emotional directness, simplicity, instrumental beauty, and diversity of themes and influences. It's created for self-entertainment, rather than commercial appeal, and is therefore accessible in a way that commercial pop music could never be.

Folk music is the rhythm of ordinary human life—a constant source of inspiration, amusement, and diversion in every race and culture. It is campfire entertainment and religious sacrament, a call to arms, and a witness against injustice. It is a spiritual legacy and connection from one generation and one age to another. It is love songs, and drinking songs, and wedding songs, and nursery rhymes, and gospel hymns, and funeral laments, and patriotic songs that make a whole country sing with one voice. It is stomps, and field hollers, and dirty blues, and gentle waltzes, and that high and lonesome sound. It is the hardy original species of music, from which all the flashier hybrids are cultivated. Or as Bill Broonzy put it, "I guess all songs is folk songs, cause I never heard no horse sing 'em."

American folk music has traditionally been played on acoustic string instruments such as guitars, fiddles, banjos, mandolins, and native-bred equipment like the dulcimer, autoharp, and dobro. Consequently it has usually been performed by individuals or small groups, where the entertainers and audience have a chance to interact. There's never been much distance between folk artists and their audience. In fact, most of the folk audience knows that music well and often can play it themselves.

American folk music evolved from the music brought to this country by immigrants from many lands. The traditional music of Appalachia, for example, borrows from Negro spirituals, minstrel music, blues, Cajun fiddle tunes, and the music of the British Isles, where most of the early Appalachian settlers came from.

In the late '50s and early '60s American folk music went through an unprecedented era of commercial popularity. Before the Beatles, before psychedelic music, the summer of love, or the generation gap, folk music was the voice of protest, rebellion, and self-expression for a generation of young Americans. The folk boom made media heroes and political stars of artists, spurred research into every area of traditional American music and culture, and made owning a guitar a rite of passage for millions of adolescents.

The players and listeners that brought traditional music to the top of the record charts were mainly young, hip, and urban. But, though they were city born and bred, these new musicians had a tremendous respect for their folk music roots, and for the original artists. This new generation was instrumental in helping to rediscover many older musicians who had labored in obscurity for decades, including Doc Watson, Mississippi John Hurt, Sleepy John Estes, and many others.

In the process of becoming commercially successful, folk music, and many of its most dedicated practitioners, were inevitably transmuted into just one more fad to be peddled over the airwaves. And, when the folk boom ended in the mid-'60s, many major record companies quickly abandoned the music for the new electric sounds of the "British Invasion."

Folk music, however, didn't just die away, like last week's dance craze or crash diet. In many respects the rock era appropriated and expanded on the styles and values of folk music. Certainly many of the major rock performers in the '60s and '70s, from Bob Dylan, Joni Mitchell, and Neil Young, to Gordon Lightfoot and The Byrds, either started from folk or had deep roots in the music.

Folk music is very much alive today, not only in its lasting influence on contemporary commercial music, but as currently performed by a vigorous and creative new generation of artists. Like America itself, folk has become thoroughly urbanized. The leading exponents are, more often than not, city kids who grew up to the sounds of the Weavers and Burl Ives, or later, the Kingson Trio and New Lost City Ramblers, themselves urban popularizers of "roots" music.

The seeds for this modern folk era were planted by academics and song collectors, working at the turn of the century. Cecil Sharp, the English collector, mined the Appalachians for ballads in 1917, and two years later published his *English Folk Songs From the Southern Appalachians*. Seven years earlier John A. Lomax, later head of the Archives of Folk songs, at the Library of Congress, had published his *Cowboy Songs And Other Frontier Ballads*. Their work attracted other folklorists and laid the foundation for an ongoing study of folk culture that continues to this day.

Among those drawn to promoting and preserving folk music was Lamar Bascom Lunsford. This singer, fiddler, banjoist, and festival organizer was born in Mars Hill, North Carolina, in 1882. He acquired a large repertoire of traditional folk music while growing up and it remained his avocation for life. Joining folklorist Robert W. Gordon in 1920, he scoured the southern mountains, seeking out performers and collecting songs. Eventually Lunsford went on to found the Mountain Dance and Folk Festival in Asheville, in 1928. It is still the nation's oldest festival of folk music and art.

The Lunsford collection of songs numbered in the thousands, and he himself recorded more than 700 of them in his lifetime. In addition, he started festivals in Kentucky and North Carolina, and performed at the First Interational Folk Music Festival in Venice in 1949.

The spread of folk music, particularly Southern folk music, got its greatest boost from radio. The communications revolution of the '20s brought "old-

(Below) John Avery Lomax (1875-1948) was a major collector of American folk songs. He contributed more than 3,000 recordings to the Archive of Folk Songs in the 1930's.

time" music to listeners around the country, and the best-known, program was the *Grand Ole Opry*. Announcer George D. Hay kicked off the show November 28, 1925, on WSM in Nashville, when he presented an impromptu 60-minute concert by an 80-year old fiddler named "Uncle" Jimmy Thompson. Originally called the WSM Barn Dance, it took the Opry designation a year later.

In 1926 Uncle Dave Macon became the Opry's first singing star, and he performed on the show for fifteen years. Born David Harrison Macon in 1870 in Warren Country, Tennessee, he was a comic and banjoist whose career really did not get underway until he was in his late forties. In the spring of 1927 he recorded 18 cuts under the name Uncle Dave Macon and His Fruit Jar Drinkers. Dave was a songwriter as well, notable for choosing material with political overtones such as "Governor Al Smith," "Farm Relief," and others. His repertoire was extensive and his singing helped preserve many classic songs that might have been lost. At a time when the banjo was being displaced by the guitar in jazz and popular music, Dave's banjo work drew young southern pickers to the instrument, paving the way for its future popularity in bluegrass and country music.

A radio show that was perhaps equal in popularity to the *Grand Ole Opry* was the *National Barn Dance* from Chicago on Station WLS (the call letters stood for "World's Largest Store," after the sponsor, Sears & Roebuck). Beginning in 1924 the National Barn Dance broadcast a variety of country, pop, and folk music, and helped bring attention to many performers including Rex Allen, Gene Autry, Homer and Jethro, Bill Monroe, and Jimmy Osborne.

At about this time, record companies discovered there was a market for traditional music. The Okeh label was particularly active in recording "race" music, songs of black artists primarily intended for a black audience. Ralph Sylvester Peer of Okeh scored big with Mamie Smith and other rhythm and blues artists in the early '20s.

Peer is also credited with coining the term "hillbilly" music. This latter invention occurred while he was recording a group called The Hopkins-Alderman-Rector string band, in 1925. During the session, one of the group's members referred to the band as "just a bunch of hillbillies." Peer decided to release their record under the name, "The Hill Billies." The name stuck, and eventually came to represent the type of music they played.

Peer's greatest discoveries came during a week of field recording he did in August of 1927 in Bristol, Tennessee, on the Virginia border. There he met and recorded Jimmie Rodgers and The Carter Family.

Jimmie, along with Maybelle Carter, was one of the most influential guitarists in traditional music. Prior to the '30s the guitar had been mainly a rhythm instrument in jazz and western music, and in the string band music of the Appalachian mountains. Jimmie Rodgers' guitar phrasing included bass runs

played picking on the neck above the soundhole. He also ended most of his songs with a short bass run "signature," and incorporated many blues figures into his "country" tunes. Maybelle was one of the first to feature the guitar as a solo voice, equal to a mandolin or fiddle.

The '30s witnessed the rise of several other musicians who would have a direct influence on modern folk music. Foremost among them was Huddie Ledbetter, better known as Leadbelly. He was born in Shreveport, Louisiana, around 1885 (the date is disputed). As a young man he worked across the south picking cotton and singing. He got his nickname from co-workers impressed by his stamina. Leadbelly spent the first World War singing in brothels in Shreveport, occasionally foraying into Texas, where he played on street corners with legendary Texas blues singer Blind Lemon Jefferson.

Leadbelly had a violent side to his nature and it played a pivotal role in his life. He was in numerous fights and in 1918 was convicted in Texas for killing a man. This prison stretch figures prominently in the Leadbelly legend, since he sang his way out of jail. His talents attracted attention, even in prison, and they eventually prompted a visit from Governor Pat Neff. After hearing Leadbelly sing, "If I had you, governor/ like you have me/ I'd open the doors/and set you free," the governor pardoned him.

Influential songwriter and blues legend Huddie "Leadbelly" Ledbetter was known for playing his trademark Stella 12-string guitar.

Unfortunately, Leadbelly wound up in prison again, this time in Louisiana, after nearly killing a man in 1930. Providentially, John Lomax came to the penitentiary in 1932 to collect folks songs. Impressed by Leadbelly's abilities, Lomax began pressing state authorities to release the singer. Finally, in 1934, Leadbelly won a good-conduct release, and headed to New York City, where Lomax was lining up concerts.

By 1935 Leadbelly was performing to great acclaim. He played at clubs such as the Village Vanguard in Greenwich Village and appeared on the Columbia Broadcasting System radio show *Back Where I Come From*. He also performed with other folk singers such as Woody Guthrie and country bluesmen Brownie McGhee and Sonny Terry, and Big Bill Broonzy. In 1936 the MacMillian company published a book of 48 of his songs in *Negro Folk Songs As Sung By Leadbelly*. Though he played a wide variety of instruments, he was most noted for his 12-string guitar work. He created rhythmic bass runs with his thumb that prefigured later developments in rhythm and blues music. His legacy includes dozens of compositions such as "Goodnight Irene," "Midnight Special," "Rock Island Line," and "Old Cottonfields At Home."

Big Bill Broonzy was another country blues artist who influenced the folk generation of the '30s, though widespread recognition eluded him until 1951. He was born William Lee Conley Broonzy in Scott, Mississippi, in 1898, to a family of 17 children who worked throughout the state as sharecroppers until Bill was 16. Broonzy was exposed to wandering blues and spiritual singers in the black churches. He learned fiddle from his Uncle Jerry and took up the guitar in his twenties. Through his life Broonzy was employed at numerous menial jobs, even as he played and recorded. He played with many southern artists of the time, such as Blind Lemon Jefferson, Blind Blake, and Sleepy John Estes. In the '30s he lived in Chicago and turned out dozens of recordings of commercial and country blues. He had an enormous influence on folk and blues performers, and was a link between the traditional delta blues and the electric Chicago blues of the post-war years.

By 1950 he had become part of a group formed by Chicago folk artist Win Stracke, called Come For To Sing, who played to large crowds on major college campuses across the United States. Following that exposure, Bill made a triumphal tour of Europe in 1951. The Europeans were shocked to learn that he was still largely unknown in the United States. By the end of the year, however, his stateside reputation had grown as he performed with Sonny Terry, Pete Seeger, and others. By the mid-'50s he had become an established artist on the burgeoning folk circuit. However, as with many other black artists in that era, it was only during these last years of his life that he was able to fully support himself through his music, and many of his best recordings were released only after his death in 1958.

Politics and folk music have always been natural bedfellows, in America and elsewhere. The strong role of political protest in '60s folk music had plenty of precedent, with roots going back to the nineteenth century. Traditional songs and ballads, often updated with new lyrics, were common at rallies in the early days of union organizing. Traditional black blues and spirituals sang a tale of despair about the implicit slavery of the Jim Crow era. Folk songs were an important tool for Appalachian coal miners, out-of-work longshoremen, and civil-rights activists throughout this century. Folk music became particularly political during the '30s and '40s, when it came to be identified in the public mind as a music of populism and political protest. And the most important force behind this development was the songs of Woodrow Wilson Guthrie.

Woody Guthrie was an unlikely hero, with few instrumental skills and a thin, nasal voice. But his songs showed a powerful, innate sense of social justice ("Pretty Boy Floyd"), that complemented his patriotic sentiments ("This Land Is Your Land") in depression-era America. Though he had contacts with many left-wing organizations Woody was a populist through and through. He wrote one or two songs a day, and like many folksingers, often put new words to old melodies. He believed that true folk songs evolved over many years from the efforts of many individuals, and often expressed opposition to

(Below) Woody Guthrie's songs of protest and patriotism made him perhaps the most famous of all American folksingers. (Bottom) Politics and music: The Rev. F.D. Kirkpatrick and Pete Seeger sing at a pro-busing rally in 1975.

copyright laws.

Woody worked in California in the early Depression years. Later in the decade, he moved to New York, where he met Pete Seeger, and many other folk artists. During these years he frequently donated his time to sing before union groups, migrant farm-workers, and anyone else who suffered economic hardship.

In 1941 Woody appeared briefly with the Almanac Singers. This group, originally composed of Seeger, Lee Hays, and Millard Lampell, would sing at rallies and "hootenannies," (a northwestern regional term popularized by Seeger, which translates roughly as "whatchamacallit" or "thingamajig"). Their first album, released in 1941, was called *Talking Union Now.* In 1942 they recorded *Dear Mr. President*, which urged full participation in the war effort. It included "Reuben James," written by Woody to the tune of "Wildwood Flower." An album of anti-war material, recorded prior to the album, was withdrawn after Hitler attacked Russia.

The Almanac Singers never regrouped after the war, but they did serve as the forerunners of the phenomenally successful Weavers. The Weavers were formed in 1948 by Pete Seeger, Lee Hays, Ronnie Gilbert, and Fred Hellerman. The hit songs "Goodnight Irene," "On Top Of Old Smokey," and "So Long, It's Been Good To Know You," made them a top draw at concert halls in the U.S. Their role in popularizing traditional folk music can hardly be overestimated. They performed music from many lands, and were able to maintain artistic integrity despite commercial success. The polish of their material, with Seeger's driving banjo and strong vocal harmonies, helped make the music attractive to an increasingly urbanized America.

In 1952 the group disbanded, for a variety of reasons, not the least of which was that they were subject to blacklisting and witch-hunts during the McCarthy era. But, the group reformed at their historic Christmas eve concert at Carnegie Hall in 1955. Pete Seeger left the group in 1957 and was replaced by a succession of banjoists, including Erik Darling, Frank Hamilton, and Bernie Krause. The group subsequently reunited at infrequent intervals, making its final appearance in 1980 at two concerts that were filmed for public television and theatrical release under the title *Wasn't That A Time.* Lee Hays died shortly thereafter, but today Ronnie Gilbert and Pete Seeger are still active, and appeared together most recently on a live album, *Harp*, with Arlo Guthrie and Holly Near.

Ask any young banjo players of the '50s and '60s what made them pick up the instrument in the first place, and the likely response is "Pete Seeger." Pete Seeger has been an inspiring songwriter, talented picker, and perhaps the most influential folk performer of our times. His trademark Vega longneck banjo became the most sought after instrument for young pickers. Through his records and books, urban kids got exposed to the banjo, later taking to the bluegrass styles of Earl Scruggs and Don Reno.

Another important influence on the folk boom of the '60s was the magazine *Sing Out!. Sing Out!* evolved from the original People's Songs, Inc., an organization formed in 1945 by Pete Seeger, Paul Robeson, Irwin Silber (who later was editor of *Sing Out!* and founder of Oak Publications), and others. They published the legendary *People's Songbook* as well as a regular *Bulletin* of topical songs, designed to promote progressive causes with music. People's Songs went bankrupt in 1949, but from its ashes rose People Artists, Inc., which presented concerts, provided booking services for folk artists and, in May of

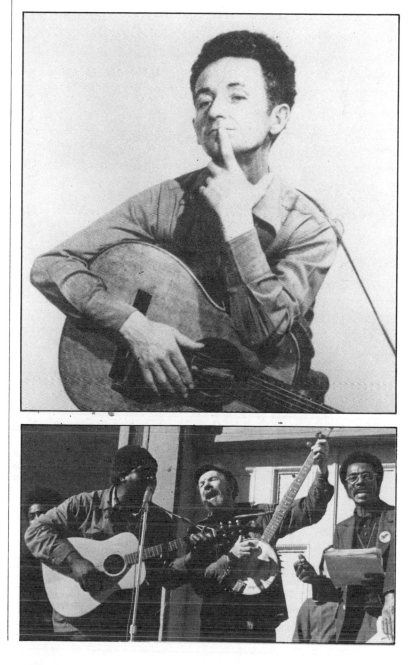

Mandolinist Bill Monroe singlehandedly invented bluegrass. (Below) Peter, Paul, and Mary became a highly popular act during the folk boom. Today, they have regrouped and are touring again.

Another big influence on urban folk activism was *Broadside*, started in 1962 by Pete Seeger, Agnes "Sis" Cunningham, Gordon Friesen, and Gil Turner. Its pages were the first to make available contemporary folk music by such talents as Eric Andersen, Richard Farina, Janis Ian, Phil Ochs, Tom Paxton, Buffy Sainte-Marie, Patrick Sky, Mark Spoelstra, and others, including Bob Dylan, whose "Talking John Birch" was featured in the first issue.

The Kingston Trio gets credit (and the blame) for launching the most commercial phase of the urban-folk boom. Their immense success with "Tom Dooley," made folk music a nationwide campus craze. Record companies rushed to fill the demand, and signed dozens of groups like The Wayfarers, The Tarriers, The Brothers Four, The Limeliters, and The Chad Mitchell Trio. Folk festivals also got underway, with the first Newport Folk Festival in 1959, drawing 15,000 fans.

Purists objected to the Kingstons from the first. Not only did the group have a sanitized sound, they also worked hard to banish all political content from their material, frequently changing the words of traditional tunes. But the Trio undeniably opened the door to hundreds of other artists, by proving there was a huge market for folk music.

During its heyday, commercial folk culture continued to be cross-fertilized by foreign influences. Harry Belafonte introduced his calypso music to the mainstream of American folk. Theodore Bikel, an Austrian by birth, performed folk songs from Russia, Eastern Europe, and Israel, recording many albums with Elektra, beginning in 1958.

By the early '60s there were coffeehouses on many college campuses and folk clubs in every major city—from the Ash Grove in Los Angeles to the Club 47 in Cambridge, Massachusetts. There were plenty of venues for young players, and the number of talented singers and songwriters who rose to prominence during the 1957-65 era is astonishing in retrospect. These included Phil Ochs, Bob Dylan, Tim Hardin, Tom Paxton, Patrick Sky, Eric Andersen, Judy Collins, John Stewart, Mark Spoelstra, Carolyn Hester, Ian & Sylvia, Joan Baez, and Dave Van Ronk, not to mention dozens of bluegrass and folk vocal groups.

The unofficial capitol of this music movement was Greenwich Village. Dozens of clubs featuring folk performers—Gerde's Folk City, The Gaslight, Cafe Wha?, and others—made the Village a mecca for aspiring songwriters and hot, young pickers. Every weekend, Washington Square Park became an outdoor festival of young guitarists, banjoists, and mandolinists such as Stefan Grossman, Eric Weissberg, Roger Sprung, Bob Yellin, David Grisman, and hundreds more gathered to jam and trade songs. The park became so crowded that on one occasion the city tried to ban music from it. In typical '60s fashion, a march was held and the ban was lifted.

Greenwich Village was easily the most exciting spot in the country during this period. Its streets and

1950, began publishing *Sing Out!* The first issue featured the Pete Seeger-Lee Hays composition "If I Had A Hammer" on the cover. That song became a hit, and a protest anthem, for Peter, Paul, and Mary twelve years later. Over the past three-and-one-half decades *Sing Out!* has continued to present traditional and contemporary folk music, with an emphasis on art as an instrument of social change. It has published music by hundreds of songwriters since then.

**Blues interpreter Dave Van Ronk was a tremendous influence on many young players in the '60s, including Bob Dylan (below with Joan Baez).**

clubs were home to a kaleidoscopic collection of folksingers, artists, poets, writers, political radicals, aging beatniks, and individualists of every stripe. The seeds of the countercultural revolution of the '60s—from free love to pop art—were being planted. In this creative and tolerant atmosphere, the music prospered. Young artists climbed the ladder of fame and older ones were rediscovered by the new generation. Ramblin' Jack Elliot, an old travelin' buddy of Woody Guthrie's (of whom Woody once said, "He sounds more like Woody Guthrie than I do."), was a star at Gerde's Folk City. Earl Scruggs appeared at the first Newport Festival in 1959, and soon it seemed as if every college kid in New York was learning his original style. Young blues interpreters such as Dave Van Ronk shared stages with the rediscovered southern blues artists of the previous generation.

Like any popular art, the folk boom was subject to the ups and downs of commerce, and its demise began with the Beatles-led "British Invasion" of 1964. The record companies began searching for new electric bands. Not only the folk artists, but also popular crooners of the late '50s, such as Paul Anka and Bobby Darin, were rapidly eclipsed. There were still folk hits, and sell-out concerts, but folk musicians were no longer the biggest idols of the young. By the end of the decade many of the major folk groups had disbanded, and some artists who had filled concert halls a few years earlier could no longer get a record contract.

However, the impact and legacy of that era are strong. The consistent themes of social protest in much early '60s music, were echoed in numerous compositions about the Vietnam war. Many musicians of the psychedelic rock-era, such as Country Joe MacDonald, Roger McGuinn of The Byrds, and Jerry Garcia of The Grateful Dead, got their start in folk and traditional music. The same could even be said of '80s star Bruce Springsteen, who sang Dylan-influenced folk songs at the Gaslight in the early '70s. And many of the blues artists rediscovered in the early '60s, furthered their careers during the blues revival later in the decade.

The greatest legacy of that era may be in the lyrics of popular music. Prior to the folk boom popular song lyrics, for the most part, were mired in the "june/moon/spoon" school of music. Folk music took popular song to a new level of personal and social expression. Artists such as Dylan introduced the idea that youth could use music to talk about the most important things in their lives—anger, sexuality, alienation, frustration, hope, politics, and protest.

Of all the folk forms, the blues had a particularly profound effect on vocal and instrumental styles in popular music. Artists such as Janis Joplin, and groups such as the Rolling Stones, began their careers by copying the great blues singers of earlier generations. The blues vocal style, with its emotional, unpolished delivery, was a perfect vehicle for a generation seeking relevancy in its art and music.

JIM MARSHALL

In some respects, folk is like jazz—it has continued to grow and evolve even though it has been displaced from the commercial limelight. Though it may be hard to find blues, folk, jazz, or bluegrass on television or commercial radio, there are dozens of specialized record companies, FM and college radio stations, and enthusiastic publications that continue to promote them. The diversity of the music has never been greater. Today, it's possible to hear everything from French sea chants, bluegrass, and Cajun fiddle tunes, to jazz, American Indian, and Celtic music at a "folk" festival. Many of the institutions that began years ago, including *Sing out!*, *Broadside*, and events such as the Philadelphia Folk Festival, continue today as healthy as ever. Each year, there are more than 1,000 folk, bluegrass, and traditional music festivals and camps nationwide.

Celtic music, and New Acoustic Music, are two forms that have gained fans in recent years. The Cel-

The mandolin remains a vital component of bluegrass today. (Left to right) A 1981 mandolin summit conference in Kentucky with David Grisman, Buck White, Mike Marshall, and Sam Bush in attendance.

tic invasion had its roots in the British folk revival of the '50s. By the '60s, several English bands, fusing traditional influences with rock instrumentation, became a hit with American audiences. These included Robin Williamson's Incredible String Band, the Richard Thompson-led Fairport Convention, and Steeleye Span. Before them, groups such as the Dubliners had been a hit with folk audiences. By the '70s, traditional Irish and Scottish bands such as Boys Of The Lough, Planxty, Battlefield Band, Silly Wizard, Clannad and DeDanann were appealing to North American audiences. Today, many of the Celtic music stars, such as Triona and Michael Ni Dnomnhail., Johnny Cunningham, and others, live in the U.S., and increasing numbers of U.S. and Canadian musicians now play Celtic music.

New Acoustic Music is a catchall term that describes a group of young, mainly ex-bluegrass players, who are exploring an instrumental fusion of jazz and traditional styles. Their respect for instrumental technique no doubt stems from their background in bluegrass, a form that puts a high premium on one's instrumental abilities. Players such as Tony Rice, David Grisman, Sam Bush and Bela Fleck of New Grass Revival, Tony Trischka, Andy Statman, and others have created a new brand of acoustic music, borrowing from players as diverse as Django Reinhardt and Bill Monroe.

Many other styles of folk have continued to thrive. A whole subculture of Women's music, with its own record companies and promotion agencies developed in the '70s. A generation of young guitarists and pianists, such as George Winston, Michael Hedges, William Ackerman, Alex De Grassi, Pierre Bensusan, and others, are attracting sizable audiences

with solo music that draws on folk, classical and improvisational styles. Some of these new folk styles are called "urban folk," "Windham Hill" (named for the record label that promoted some of these artists to prominence), and "progressive" music. Many of these musicians have folk backgrounds, cutting their teeth on such influential guitarists as Leo Kottke and John Fahey. Audiences also exist in varying degrees for traditional fingerstyle guitar, blues, ragtime, Zydeco bands, old-time string band music, "New Age" music, and of course, "traditional" bluegrass and string band music. Such musical variety is one of the enduring legacies of the urban folk boom.

This book is about a few of the musicians who have made a major contribution to American folk music. Some left their mark long ago, some are still highly active. All of these stories and interviews, with two exceptions, appeared originally in *Guitar Player* and *Frets* magazines over a period of 16 years, from 1970 to 1985. It is a diverse group, ranging from Pete Seeger and Woody Guthrie to more pop-oriented performers like Gordon Lightfoot and the Kingston Trio. These stories are not intended to provide a complete biography of these artists, or a comprehensive overview of the entire spectrum of American folk music. That would require an encyclopedia several volumes in length. These interviews attempt to document the instrumental craft of a group of musicians who have greatly influenced the folk music of their time. Their stories should be of great interest to fans of the music, and particularly to other musicians.

Phil Hood
Editor, Frets Magazine

# MAYBELLE CARTER
## AND THE CARTER FAMILY

**Maybelle, A.P., and Sara**

The first family of traditional music has had a lasting impact on the development of folk and country music. Though their music always stuck to the traditional themes of home and religion, Mother Maybelle was a distinctive guitarist, and one of the first musicians to feature the instrument in a lead role. The family's musical tradition continues today through June Carter Cash, Maybelle's daughter and wife of singer Johnny Cash, and Maybelle's granddaughter Rosanne Cash. Doug Green, at the time the chief executive of the Country Music Foundation, wrote this retrospective for *Guitar Player* in March 1979.

**By Doug Green**

MAYBELLE CARTER WAS a legend, and it seemed that she would go on forever, like the impassive Appalachia from which she came. But she had been in failing health for several years—especially since the death of her longtime husband, Ezra J. Carter, in 1975—and she died suddenly of natural causes on October 23, 1978, leaving country music—and indeed all of American music—without one of its most influential guitarists.

Mother Maybelle, as she came to be known, was the creator of the "Carter lick" on the guitar—the playing of the melody with the thumb while brushing the strings for rhythm. This style had a profound effect on guitarists of her own generation and those that followed. She also incorporated hammer-ons, pull-offs, slides and other folk-type embellishments into her style.

Less than three months after the death of Mother Maybelle, Sara Carter Bayes, the last surviving member of the original Carter Family, passed away in her home in Lodi, California. Born in Wise County, Virginia, on July 21, 1898, Sara, like her sister-in-law Maybelle, learned to play the guitar and autoharp at an early age, although she never attained the proficiency and creativity that made Maybelle's playing revolutionary.

(Below, left to right) Helen, Mother Maybelle, and Anita: the Carter Family in 1972.

Where Maybelle came up with her innovative lick is a matter of conjecture. The guitar was still a relatively new instrument to the Virginia mountains where she grew up, yet she played it as a teenager. Some have credited Leslie Riddles, a black guitarist and blues singer from nearby Kingsport, Tennessee, who did in fact subtly influence the Carter Family's music and performance in later years, but he was not there when Maybelle began playing the instrument.

The information provided in Maybelle's 1949 song folio is oblique: "She started playing the autoharp at the ripe old age of four. When the newness wore off four years later, she took to plunking the banjo and pretty soon the plunking changed into good banjo playing. About five years later she laid down the banjo in favor of a guitar." In 1961 she told historian Bill Malone that she "learned from her brothers;" although both brothers were musicians,

neither had Maybelle's talent.

However shrouded in mystery, the origin of her style may lie with the simplest of explanations: She was a young musician with an instrument that was relatively new to her area. She spent a great deal of time with it, and mainly for her own pleasure she developed an effective way to play melody on the guitar, probably adapting her technique from the banjo.

If the Carter lick does not seem terribly revolutionary today, one must place it in the context of the times: Maybelle was a competent guitarist who had already developed this style when she married Ezra on March 23, 1926, at age 16. Other than on Nick Lucas recordings, the guitar was not heard much in popular music, either onstage or on 78s. It would take country singer Jimmie Rodgers' supple bass runs and Maybelle's deceptively simple lead playing to expose the guitar via record.

In recorded country music, the guitar was usually used as a rhythm instrument; it was fuller—though often less expressive—than the banjo when used to accompany a fiddle, singer, or string band. Though Riley Puckett, an early country performer, demonstrated many flashes of brilliance in his bizarre, erratic guitar playing, it was the stylings of Jimmie Rodgers and Maybelle Carter that suggested the instrument's new potential in country music.

Mother Maybelle was born Maybelle Addington on May 10, 1909, in Nicklesville, a small town in the Poor Valley of mountainous southwest Virginia. She was courted and wed by Ezra Carter, and through him she was introduced to his older brother, A.P. Carter, a cheerful though somewhat haunted man who fiddled a bit and sang. He married Sara Dougherty on June 15, 1915. A distant cousin of Maybelle's, Sara possessed a stunning voice: deep and clear. She had learned to play banjo, guitar, and autoharp, and she frequently performed with A.P. A Carter family legend has it that when A.P. first saw Sara she was playing the autoharp and singing "Engine 143."

It seemed natural that A.P., Sara, and Maybelle would get together to play. A.P. sang bass, and he had a massive collection of traditional folk tunes he'd gathered in his years as a carpenter and tree salesman, and Sara and Maybelle harmonized well, though somewhat stiffly by contemporary standards. They began to harbor aspirations of a professional career, and in late July 1927, they drove 25 miles from their homes in Maces Spring, Virginia, to the town of Bristol, which was divided in half by the Virginia-Tennessee state line. The trip took them eight hours, but it was worth the hardship. There Ralph Peer, a talent scout, was auditioning for Victor Records. If he liked what he heard, he'd record a musician on the spot.

Peer heard many singers, musicians, and bands during the week he spent in Bristol, but he liked the tubercular railroader Jimmie Rodgers and the Carter

**The original Carter family lineup consisted of Maybelle on guitar, her sister-in-law Sara on autoharp, and Maybelle's brother A.P. Carter.**

Family best of all. On August 1, the Carters made their first recordings in the upper story of a house at 410 State Street. By August 4, they had completed six sides: "Bury Me Under A Weeping Willow," "The Poor Orphan Child," "The Storms Are On The Ocean," "Little Log Cabin By The Sea," "Single Girl, Married Girl," and "Wandering Boy." Maybelle used a Stella guitar for her earliest sessions, replacing it in 1929 with a Gibson L-5 that she was to use for the rest of her career.

Between 1927 and 1934 the Carter Family recorded most of their best-known songs for Victor, including "Foggy Mountain Top," "My Clinch Mountain Home," "Forsaken Lovers," "Thinking Of My Blue Eyes," "Lulu Walls," "Sweet Fern," and the song that was to become the anthem for country guitarists, "Wildwood Flower." When the songs were not in the proper key for singing, the solution was simple: Maybelle either capoed up to the proper fret, or, reversing direction, simply tuned the guitar down— at times as much as five frets, allowing her to finger in *C* while actually playing in *G*. Like her approach to music, her approach to innovation was direct, straightforward, and simple.

The distinctive characteristic of the Carter Family guitar sound involved Maybelle's right-hand picking technique: Melody executed with a thumb lead in the bass; rhythm filled in on the treble strings with brush strokes (the "Church Lick") executed by one or more fingers (usually the second, since it is the longest); and melody and rhythm enlivened with bass runs, hammer-ons, and pull-offs.

Besides using the capo, Maybelle often tuned her guitar down one to one-and-a-half steps, assumedly to retain the *C*-chord forms with which she felt most comfortable when changing keys to match A.P.'s bass and Sara's low-alto vocal ranges.

The piece most often associated with the Carter name is "Wildwood Flower," first recorded at Camden, New Jersey, May 9, 1928. This selection proved to be the group's biggest seller—over a million sales in 78 rpm's alone.

The Carter Family's career was spotty. Though they were known all over the United States by the late '20s, they did not travel much, and their influence was largely felt on record. In 1932 Ralph Peer united them with Jimmie Rodgers for a recording session in Louisville, Kentucky. Included among these sides are two duets by Jimmie and Sara, "The Wonderful City" and "Why There's A Tear In My Eye," the only sacred song Rodgers ever recorded. "We recorded with Jimmie Rodgers not more than a year before he died," Maybelle later recalled. "In fact, he wasn't able to play his guitar very much, he was that sick, so I played for him and he sang. I had to play like him, you know, so everybody would think it was him. But it was me."

Ever hardworking, the Carter Family recorded 20 new songs for Victor in December 1934, each of which was done in one take. In 1935 they moved to

the American Record Company (ARC). They recorded "Lonesome Valley," "Single Girl, Married Girl," "Sunnyside," and many of their earlier hits for ARC before moving on to the newly-formed, energetic Decca label in June 1936. Many Carter Family buffs consider the three years spent with Decca to be the family's finest period. They were writing as well as preserving genuine Appalachian ballads, and Maybelle's guitar playing was at its peak: In addition to her Carter lick, Maybelle had learned to fingerpick as well, and she had also learned to coax lead lines from an autoharp. The material they recorded ranged from spirituals ("Honey In The Rock") to blues ("Coal Miner's Blues") and railroading songs ("Reckless Motorman").

In 1938 the entire family moved to Del Rio, Texas, to play a twice-daily show over the powerful Mexican border radio stations, XEG, XENT, and XERA. At the same time it could be said that the Carters became less and more of a family. A.P. and Sara had divorced a few years earlier, though they still recorded together, and in 1939 Sara married Coy Bayes. A.P. and Sara's children, Joe and Janette, became a frequent part of radio and stage shows, as did Ezra and Maybelle's daughters, Helen, Anita, and June.

The Carter Family recorded a set of sessions for Columbia in 1940. On October 14, 1941, they journeyed to New York City to record for Victor; it was their final session. In 14 years of recording, they had produced nearly 300 sides.

The family finally disbanded in 1943 while they were working at the WBT radio station in Charlotte, North Carolina. Coy Bayes took Sara with him to California; she had been the least driven and least compelled performer of the trio, and left music without any apparent reservations. A.P. returned to Maces Spring to open a little country store—which still stands, although the area is now named Hiltons. He drifted in and out of music, often performing and occasionally recording with his son and daughter, until his death in 1960.

But Maybelle had more than her talent; she had an ambition the others had lacked. With her three daughters she formed an act called The Carter Sisters And Mother Maybelle, first joining *The Old Dominion Barn Dance* show on WRVA radio in Richmond, Virginia, and then later moving to the *Grand Ole Opry* show in 1949. The group recorded with Victor and Columbia.

Oddly enough, Maybelle's role was diminished in the new group she nominally headed. Helen's accordion playing, June's boisterous humor, and Anita's lovely solo voice were all main features of the act. Maybelle added a bit of harmony, a few measures of her once-unique guitar playing, a couple of solo "heart songs," and some autoharp flourishes. Mother Maybelle felt her guitar playing to be so out of step when they joined the Grand Ole Opry that she brought along a lead guitarist whose more modern style was, she felt, better suited to the times. His name was Chet Atkins.

The Carter Sisters And Mother Maybelle was a popular bread-and-butter country act for years. A number of widely-spaced events in the last 15 years of Maybelle's life helped rescue her contributions from the obscurity to which she had relegated herself. One was her appearance at the 1963 Newport Folk Festival, where her influence on the guitar playing of folksinger Woody Guthrie, and through him to

Bob Dylan, Jack Elliot, Joan Baez, and other folk singers and country artists was recognized and lauded. Here a new generation was introduced to her music.

In 1967 Maybelle and Sara were professionally reunited in an appearance at the Newport Folk Festival, after which they made *An Historic Reunion*, their first recording together in over 25 years.

June Carter married country singer Johnny Cash during the '60s, and the Carter Sisters And Mother Maybelle became a firm fixture on his touring show and TV series. Another major event in Maybelle's career was the election of the original Carter Family to the Country Music Hall Of Fame in 1970, an acknowledgement of her pioneering role from her peers. In 1973 she joined with the Nitty Gritty Dirt Band and a host of country stars for the recording of the LP *Will The Circle Be Unbroken*.

Joe and Janette, A.P. and Sara's children, began a series of Carter Family reunions in the mid-'70s. It was at these affairs that Sara made her last appearances. Though frail, she still played her O-28 Martin guitar simply and straightforwardly. The years did not seem to have affected the quality of her voice; even though it had grown deeper with time, it was still supple and strong—characteristics that Sara herself embodied. Her death, at the age of 80, came in the early morning hours of January 8, 1979.

During the mid-'70s, age began taking its toll on Maybelle; when arthritis stilled the magic of her fingers on her guitar, this quiet, unassuming, stoic woman continued on autoharp. After Ezra's death, however, she appeared less and less frequently with Cash and was in and out of the hospital. She had been off the road a year, in declining health, when she died at age 69.

Suddenly she was gone, and she was missed. Over 50 years before she had begun a revolution in guitar playing that is still being felt. Her recorded output is large, and much of her best work can still be heard. By today's standards her guitar work, though lovely, has none of the flash of recent players, but its clean, understated elegance tells volumes about the times and places that produced one of country music's most important pioneers, and about this shy, reserved woman, one of America's most influential guitarists.

## A Selected Carter Family Discography

**Solo albums:** *Carter Family Album*, Liberty (dist. by United Artists), 7230; *Happiest Days Of All*, Camden, ACL1-0501; *Lonesome Pine Special*, Camden, 2473; *Mid The Green Fields Of Virginia*, Victor, ANL1-1107; *More Golden Gems From The Original Carter Family*, Camden, 2554; *My Old Cottage Home*, Camden, ACL1-0047; *Original And Great Carter Family*, Camden, 586; *Precious Memories*, Camden, 9020; *Three Generations*, Columbia, KC-33084; (Sara and Maybelle only) *An Historic Reunion*, Columbia, CL 2561; (Maybelle only) *Mother Maybelle Carter*, Columbia, KG 32436. **With others:** Nitty Gritty Dirt Band, *Will The Circle Be Unbroken*, United Artists, 9801; *50 Years Of Country Music*, Camden, ADL2-0782; *Stars Of The Grand Ole Opry 1926-1974*, Victor, CPL2-0466; *World's Favorite Hymns*, Columbia, C-32246.

# WOODY GUTHRIE

No balladeer has ever captured dreams and aspirations of the American people as well as Woody Guthrie. His "This Land Is Your Land" became an unofficial national anthem, and his championing of populist causes helped make folk music a political weapon for the disadvantaged. As the major influence on artists such as Ramblin' Jack Elliot, Pete Seeger, and Bob Dylan, Woody was the spiritual father of the folk boom in the late '50s. He was profiled in the August 1971 issue of *Guitar Player*.

**By Michael Brooks**

IT BEGAN WITH CHARLES GUTHRIE, professional guitarist, prizefighter, and land-trader in Okemah, Oklahoma. On July 14, 1912, he became the proud father of Woodrow Wilson Guthrie, named after the 28th President of the United States. Woody was born to a musical family; his mother sang old folk songs and his father played and shouted the Indian square dances and black blues of the time. As a child, Woody was thrust into life with tragedy. Within a short period Charles' land trading company went bankrupt, two of his houses were burned to the ground and another was destroyed by a cyclone. Later, Woody's sister Clara was killed in an oil stove explosion; his mother developed Huntington's disease and died in a state asylum.

Woody recalls the environment in an interview with Alan Lomax *Woody Guthrie—Library of Congress Recording* [Elektra]. "My older sister caught

**Woody Guthrie's impact on the direction and style
of American folk music was enormous. He
was the biggest musical influence of
Pete Seeger, Bob Dylan, Ramblin' Jack Elliot,
Cisco Houston, and many others.**

afire while ironing on the kerosene stove. The next day she died. Then my mother died in an insane asylum in Norman, Oklahoma. And then my father caught afire—I chose to think it was on purpose."

Woody was first adopted by Sam White, but in 1927, at the age of 17, he was re-adopted by a wealthier family. Soon Woody ventured onto the highways and tracks of the central southwest. He explained to Lomax why he left his adopted home. "Well, they were a wealthier family and they had a bad hen and it was my job to take care of that hen. I hated it. So I thought why be a chamber maid to a hen, so I took off."

Woody met his first guitar while on his initial adventure. He had a job selling corn whiskey, disguised as root beer, and the owner of the stand had a guitar laying around. While Woody was "wheelin' and dealin,'" he started to teach himself a few chords. The first song he ever learned was "Greenback Dollar," a three-chord change, and it was from here that Woody grew to write over an estimated 1,000 songs between 1932 and 1952. He played "with reasonable talent" the guitar, mouth harp, mandolin, mountain fiddle, spoons, tin cans, and just about anything else he could get his hands on.

In his early twenties, Woody witnessed and documented the historic Oklahoma dust bowl storms of the mid-thirties. He wrote countless songs about the deprivation of the Okies and the dust bowl refugees, some of which may be heard on *Dust Bowl Ballads Sung by Woody* [Folkway Records]. One of the most popular of these songs was "Talkin' Dust Bowl Blues." Woody is often credited with having created the talking blues, which later became commercially popularized by artists like Bob Dylan and Ramblin' Jack Elliott. Woody had a good grasp of the blues and what it meant to him.

Woody, in the interview with Alan Lomax, said, "Well, the blues, Alan, is ah . . . I always called it just plain old being lonesome. Now a lot of people don't think that's a big enough word, but then you can get lonesome for a lot of things. People down where I come from are lonesome for a job, they're lonesome for some spending money, lonesome for some drinking whiskey, lonesome for good times, pretty gals, wine, women, and song like they see stuck up in front of their face by other people, thinkin' maybe that you're down and out and discussed, busted, and can't be trusted. Why it gives you a lonesome feeling that somehow the world's turned against you or there's something about it you don't understand. Being out of work, being lonesome. Or either being in jail. Now some of the best blues come from jail houses, where people are put for different reasons. Blues, awful popular in jails. Blues is sort of a complaint, er I mean a lament, er I mean sort of hellraising in your own system that you want to get out. You want to sing about. You know there is something wrong and you look around and you see a lot of things that you think are causing things to be hard

and just kinda gettin' ta singin' the blues."

With the dust bowl refugees, Woody migrated to California, then the land of false promise. Among his songs at that time was "Do Re Mi," whose lyrics tell the story: *California is a Garden of Eden, it's a paradise to live in or see, but believe it or not you won't find it so hot, if you ain't got the Do Re Mi.*

While in Los Angeles, Woody became interested in the union labor movement and happened to get a job on a Los Angeles daily radio show, WKVD, playing and singing for a dollar a show. It was in this city that Woody first met his long-time companion, Cisco Houston. Woody happened to meet Cisco in Los Angeles' "Skiddiest of all skid rows . . . he called his self the Cisco Kid," recalled Woody in his autobiography *Bound For Glory* [E.P. Dutton & Co., Inc., New York, 1968]. He was a good singer and yodeler. He banged on the guitar pretty good, and like me, come rain or sun, or cold or heat, he always walked along with his guitar slung over his shoulder from a leather strap."

When Cisco and Woody met, they started entertaining together in the local dives on skid row, lucky to make 40¢ a bar, hitting about five or six bars every night. They would start around eight o'clock at night and sing until the early morning hours, making as much as a buck to a buck-and-a-half per night.

Being void of pretense, and despising it wherever he found it, Woody did not like doing radio shows. He explained in *Bound For Glory* that "most radio stations, they won't let ya sing th' real songs. They want ya ta sing pure ol' bull manure an' nothin' else." It's ironic that Woody once did an audition at the Rainbow Room in New York's Rockefeller Center. While auditioning, "I took the tune (that he was playing) to church, took it holy roller, shot in a few splitnotes, oozed in a fake one, come down on barrelhouse, hit off a good old cross-country lonesome note or two, trying to get that old guitar to help me, to talk to me, talk for me, and say what I was thinking, just this one time." This kind of explanation, along with "I drug my thumb down acrost the strings of the guitar," is the sum total of Woody's comments about his playing technique.

It is well known that Woody's guitar playing comprised what today is commonly called basic folk and country. He used the church lick and had done some Carter-style picking, but for the most part, his guitar playing was basic, yet effective for what he was attempting to accomplish. His playing included many alternating bass notes, wtih quick up-down brushes across the treble strings. He often used bass melodies and runs through his songs. His most common rhythm style was:

(1) (and) (2) (and) (3) (and) boom, tap, boom, tap, boom, tap-tap-tap-tap-tap.

About Woody's guitar playing, his son Arlo recalls, "I don't remember it bein' that great, but that wasn't

the whole point of it, right? Most of what I remember is what Ramblin' Jack [Elliott] said about Woody's playing. What Jack said was that there were a few licks that Woody knew that were impossible to duplicate, because they weren't learned things, they were just the way he started playing. So there were a few licks that were really complicated when you tried to analyze them, and that took him years." In attempting to describe the full sound of Woody's style, Arlo commented, "He had his own little licks that were really weird, that whole kind of double-action scene, where you're playing the melody on the treble strings, and playing the bass, and then the

rhythm, all at the same time. You see, Woody was one of the first guys around playing it all at the same time; I don't remember anybody else playing that way, because there was nobody playing with Woody at first."

Woody was probably one of the first folk guitarists to play with an orchestra. In *Born To Win* [The Mac-Millan Co., New York, 1965], a collection of Woody's poems, stories, drawings, letters and lyrics, Woody wrote to Irving Lerner about Lerner's film "Banjo Pickin' Boy," "Peter Lyon and myself done a radio script for the DuPont Company, on their program 'Cavalcade of America,' which won the ribbon for being their 'Most American Cavalcade.' It was all built around a big long ballad I wrote about the 'Life Of Wild Bill Hickcock,' with a hundred-piece orchestra vamping an *E* chord in back of my guitar."

Woody has written countless songs of all brands and breeds. When Alan Lomax asked Woody where he got the material for his songs, Woody replied, "Everywhere you look. Out of books, magazines, daily papers, at the movies, along the streets, riding buses or trains, even flying along in an airplane, or in bed at night. Anywhere."

In 1941, Woody, Pete Seeger, Lee Hays, and Millard Lampell started one of the super folk groups of the century, the Almanacs. Based in Greenwich Village, the group would frequently tour cross-country. In 1944, Cisco, Woody, and a friend, Jimmy Longhi, joined the Merchant Marines together. They formed a trio, "sort of a Torpedoed Seaman's Outfit," of the National Maritime Union. But by this time, group singing was "old hat" with Woody, who had sung with Hally Wood Stevenson, Burl Ives, and Pete Seeger [The People's Song group]. He once spent a whole night singing protest songs with Pete Seeger at the meeting hall of the Tenant Farmer's Union in Oklahoma City, but in *Born To Win* Woody recalls, "The best and loudest singer that I ever run onto his name was Huddie Ledbetter and we all called him Leadbelly, his arms was like big stove pipes and his face was powerful and he picked the 12-string guitar."

Also in *Born To Win*, Woody described the way he formulated his tunes as, "I mix up old tunes, I wheel them and I deal them, and I shuffle them out across my barking board (Woody also refers to his 'Barquero guitar'), I use half of two tunes, one-third of three tunes and one-tenth of ten tunes."

When it looked as though Woody was going to land a career-oriented job, his feet got itchy and he hopped a train out of town. Woody lived his life "hoboin' and freight-trainin'," but this carefree life belies the concern and sensitivity he had for the welfare of others. He devoted much of his time attempting to organize the laboring classes and fighting any forms of oppression.

But Woody's life work in writing and singing is probably best summed up in his own words from *Bound For Glory*, "Sometimes I was lucky and found me a good job. I sung on the radio waves in Los Angeles, and I got a job from Uncle Samuel to come to the valley of the Columbia River [Bonneville Power Administration Ballads] and I made up and recorded 26 songs about the Grand Coulee Dam among them 'Roll On Columbia,' Grand Coulee Dam,' and 'Pastures of Plenty'). I made two albums of records called *Dust Bowl Ballads* for the Victor people. I hit the road again and crossed the continent twice by way of highway and freights. Folks heard me on the nationwide radio programs, CBS and NBC, and thought I was rich and famous, and I didn't have a nickel to my name, when I was hitting the hard way again."

The words in this story are sketchy and in odd combination to describe the elusive character of this man who shaped smiles and brought tears to the eyes of thousands upon thousands of people's faces. He brought out their feelings and emotions through the medium of song. The landmark, common-knowledge information about Woody Guthrie is fairly inconclusive within the story of this monumental man with bushy hair and slight build. But he was shy, inward, and sensitive to people's problems, and would probably blush if he read this account of his life. The man of "So Long, It's Been Good To Know You," "Hard Traveling," "Blowing Down This Old Dusty Road," "Union Maid," "Tom Joady," "This Land Is Your Land," "Pretty Boy Floyd," and "Pastures Of Plenty," really had one statement to make: "I ask you, Mister President, please let everybody, everywhere, sing all night long. . . . This will cure every soul in our jails, asylums, and sick in our hospitals, too. Try it and see. I know."

On October 4, 1967, the *New York Times* wrote, "Woodrow Wilson Guthrie, the American folk singer and composer, died yesterday at Creedmoor State Hospital, Queens, following a 13-year illness. He was 55 years old."

Civilization is spread more by singing than anything else because whole big bunches of people can sing a particular song where not every man can join in on the same conversation. A song ain't nothing but a conversation fixed up to where you can talk it over and over without getting tired of it. And it's this repeating the idea over and over that makes it take hold. If the conversation is about good crops or bad, good politics or bad, good news or bad, good anything else or bad, the best way to circulate it amongst the people is by way of singing it.

—Woody Guthrie, 1941

---

### A Selected Woody Guthrie Discography

*Dust Bowl Ballads*, Folkways, 5212; *Early Years*, Tradition, 2088; *Greatest Songs Of Woody Guthrie*, Vanguard, VSD-35-36; (On Folkways): *Woody Guthrie Sings Folk Songs*, 2483; *Lonesome Valley*, 2010; *This Land Is Your Land*, 31001; *Songs Of The Spanish Civil War*, 4327.

# THE LOMAX FAMILY

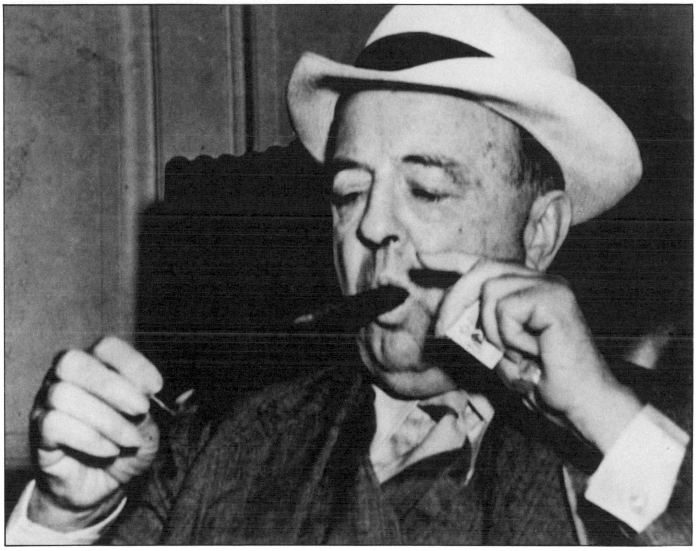

John Lomax

As early as the late nineteenth century, archivists were decrying the disappearance of real American folk culture. John Lomax, and later his son Alan, proved it was still there if you knew where to look. For more than fifty years they made field recordings and published books of songs that helped preserve our unique musical heritage. They were also instrumental in bringing to public attention dozens of folk artists. Their story appeared in the *Frets* April 1985 issue.

## By Jas Obrecht

SIGNIFICANT PORTIONS OF America's musical heritage would have been lost forever were it not for the pioneering work of musicologist John Lomax and his son Alan. For years, the men journeyed around the country to record folk songs on location in rural dwellings, lumber camps, cotton plantations, farms, penitentiaries, and other haunts of the common man. In the process, the Lomaxes discovered such talented artists as Leadbelly, Woody Guthrie, and Muddy Waters, and made the largest single con-

tribution to the Library of Congress' Archive of American Folk Song. Their books have served as starting points for countless performers and have set patterns for the scholarly study of folk song.

John Avery Lomax was born in Mississippi in 1875 and raised in the Southwest. From his earliest years, he demonstrated a perceptive ear for music, scribbling down lyrics he heard sung by farmhands and itinerant musicians. Near the turn of the century, he showed his collection to a professor at the Univer-

An after-hours jam session at the 1976 Annual Meeting of the American Folklore society brought together Saul Brody (harmonica), Bess Lomax Hawes, Alan Lomax, Mike Seeger (mandolin), Ralph Rinzler (guitar), and John Herald.

sity of Texas, who suggested they were of little value. Little use was made of his material until 1906, when, as part of his master's degree work at Harvard University, Lomax submitted examples of the lyrics to Barrett Wendell. The impressed professor introduced him to the nation's leading folklorist, George Lymann Kittredge, who encouraged him to continue his work.

John bought an Ediphone (a crude recording machine using wax cylinders) and returned to the Southwest for three years to make recordings on the range and around cowboy campfires. He published his findings in 1910's *Cowboy Songs And Other Frontier Ballads*, a landmark anthology that sparked a surge of interest in folk songs of all kinds. Subsequent material was issued in 1917 as *Songs Of The Cattle Trail And Cow Camp*.

Lomax continued to study folklore as an avocation while earning most of his living as an administrator at the University of Texas and as a banker. When the Depression caused his bank to fail, he planned another major collecting tour and signed a publishing contract with Macmillan to help defray expenses. Accompanying him in the summer of '33 was his 17-year-old son Alan, who helped him install a 315-pound recorder into the back of their Ford sedan. They collected hundreds of songs on this historic trip through the South, recording, among others, Huddie "Leadbelly" Ledbetter at the State Penitentiary in Angola, Louisiana (upon his release, the Lomaxes became the Texas songster's promoter).

After publishing his findings in *American Ballads And Folk Songs* and sending the discs to the Library of Congress, John was invited to Washington in 1934 to become the head archivist and curator of the infant Archive of American Folk Song. He continued to make field recordings—notably Booker White in 1939 and Blind Willie McTell the following year—and built the folk collection into one of the world's finest. He and Alan co-authored several books, including *Negro Folk Songs As Sung By Leadbelly, Our Singing Country*, and *Folk Song, U.S.A.*. By the time of his death in 1948, John Lomax had achieved worldwide recognition for his work.

The most widely recognized authority on folk music, Alan Lomax was born in Austin, Texas, in 1915. After studying at Harvard and earning a degree from the University of Texas at Austin, he made his first solo field trip in 1937, recording native songs and voodoo rituals in Haiti. From 1937 until '42, he served as assistant archivist under his father. Travelling extensively, he cut over 3,000 12″ records for the Archive of Folk Song during those years, including over 100 sides with jazz pianist Jelly Roll Morton. In 1939, Alan began broadcasting *Wellsprings Of America*, a radio show that demonstrated the panorama of America's music. The folk program is credited with having introduced Josh White and Woody Guthrie, among others, to the public at large. To this day, Lomax cites his work with Guthrie as his single most important accomplishment. Blues fans, though, equally appreciate his early '40s field recordings of Son House, Fred McDowell, and McKinley "Muddy Waters" Morganfield.

Following the War, Alan became director of folk music for Decca Records. During the '50s, he returned to the airwaves with Mutual Broadcasting's *Your Ballad Man Alan Lomax* and a series of folk music broadcasts for the BBC. He edited Columbia Records' 18-volume *World Library Of Folk And Primitive Music*, and cut albums as an artist himself, notably Tradition Records' *Texas Folk Songs* and Kapp Record's *Folk Song Saturday Night*. Alan's 1959 *Esquire* article, "Bluegrass Background: Folk Music With Overdrive" is credited with being the first widely read appeal for Americans to recognize bluegrass music. In addition to performing at festivals himself, Lomax co-founded the Newport Folk Foundation and served as an advisor to the Mountain Dance And Folk Festival in Asheville, North Carolina.

Alan's classic study, *The Folk Songs Of North America* [Doubleday], was published in 1960. Since then, he's taught at major universities and concentrated on developing cantometrics, an approach to the anthropology of music. In the late '70s, Alan Lomax journeyed back down the dusty Delta roads he had traveled in his youth to film the excellent PBS documentary, *Land Where The Blues Began*.

# BILL MONROE

Bill Monroe was and is the father of bluegrass music. Borrowing from the traditional musics of the South, and combining them with his own rhythmic style, he created bluegrass in the late '30s and remains its most influential proponent today. Now over 70 and recently remarried, Monroe and his band The Blue Grass Boys still keep a busy touring schedule. *Frets* interviewed "the Bossman" in May of 1979.

**By Dix Bruce**

**B**LUEGRASS MUSIC IS A recent arrival on the American scene. It was born at the turn of the fourth decade of this century, predating the advent of rock and roll by only 10 or 12 years. The face of bluegrass, unlike that of rock and roll, is the image of one man: bluegrass' progenitor and main influence, Bill Monroe. Certainly, bluegrass has its roots in the folk music of the southern Appalachian mountains,

and there have been bluegrass innovators since Monroe; but no one can deny that bluegrass music is Bill Monroe's own creation.

There are few non-classical mandolin players alive who do not owe the foundations of their styles to Monroe. While he has inspired the gamut of blue-grass, jazz, and even rock mandolin players, he himself has seldom strayed from tight stylistic parameters

of melodic, distinctively rhythmic playing.

The style, form, and themes of Monroe's music are strictly bounded. The basic band is always mandolin, guitar, banjo, string bass, and fiddle. The guitar and bass are rarely featured as lead instruments; with the chop chords of the mandolin, their function is to provide the punch rhythm of the band. The chord progressions are simple, usually limited to two or three changes per tune. The lead instruments—mandolin, fiddle, and banjo—generally trade solos with the vocalists. The beauty of the music lies in what is so elegantly stated within these limitations.

Monroe's instrumental compositions express a range of sound and emotion unequaled by any performer in his field. They have come to comprise a primer of songs that every mandolin player must address. "Rawhide," "Kentucky Mandolin," "Bluegrass Stomp," "Bluegrass Breakdown," and "Wheel Hoss" are all challenging bluegrass mandolin classics. Many echo the fiddle tunes Monroe heard as a child; others are intense, fast pieces that communicate his own energetic musical vision. The songs he writes convey a haunting reality, almost always concerning themselves with some aspect of love—love cherished, rejected, fulfilled, or lost. Some songs reflect Monroe's childhood and culture, "Uncle Pen"—an ode to the man who taught him music—probably being the most famous of these. Some songs deal

with the lonely existence of life on the road, others are honest expressions of Monroe's religious beliefs. All of Monroe's songs cut straight to the heart with a simple and beautiful poetic quality.

There is virtually no comic or novelty material, because Monroe is a very serious man who cares deeply about his music. For nearly 40 years, he has been striving to bring that music up from his heart and deliver it to his audience.

It all began on a farm in the hills near Rosine, Kentucky, in 1911, when Bill Monroe was born. He was the youngest of eight children. Throughout his childhood he was exposed to hoedown music and to the blues. He mentions a black guitarist and fiddler, Arnold Schultz, as being one of his main influences. Monroe's uncle Pen Vandiver, a fiddler, further sparked his interest in music, and the fiddle was Monroe's first choice as an instrument. Unfortunately, his brother Birch had already claimed the family's fiddle. Bill's second choice was the guitar, but his brother Charlie had claimed it. That left only the mandolin.

Monroe did get to play guitar somewhat, initially, and would regularly "second" on the guitar for his uncle Pen at local house parties and hoedowns. Monroe says that if things had turned out a little differently, he might have been a blues singer. It was the early cross-influence of the blues and hoedown music

Bill Monroe is famous for his Gibson F-5 mandolin. Once when he was upset with the Gibson company, he hacked the word "Gibson" out of the peghead logo. The instrument has since been repaired.

that led Monroe to his synthesis of the two styles into bluegrass.

Both of Monroe's parents died before he entered his teens and he went to live with his uncle Pen. At 17 he left Kentucky to follow Charlie and Birch north in search of work. Jobs were scarce, but eventually he found employment in the Chicago area, stacking barrels at the Sinclair oil refinery. At times, he was the only one of the three brothers working and he supported the other two on his small salary.

Bill, Charlie, and Birch had continued with their music after the move north and gradually they began to get scattered jobs as a trio. House party dates led to short road trips for WLS radio's *Barn Dance Tour*, with the brothers also doing some exhibition square dancing. For a while Bill continued at Sinclair, taking time off to do the WLS show, since all three brothers agreed that though music was a more enjoyable way of making a living than refinery work, it was nowhere near as steady. But finally the brothers were performing enough that Bill quit Sinclair altogether. It must certainly have been a difficult step. The country was in the depths of the Depression, and any job was a good job. Being employed was an incredibly lucky situation that one didn't walk away from. Quitting Sinclair was a gamble; but for Monroe, it paid off.

After some initial touring with the WLS *Barn Dance*, Birch settled into a steady refinery job and left the group. Charlie and Bill continued as a duo, the Monroe Brothers, and through a series of associations with radio stations they gained a following throughout the South and the rural Midwest. Their recordings sold well, but the brothers had difficulty getting along and after six years the act split up. The Monroe Brothers went in entirely different directions. It's generally accepted that Bill found his position as the younger brother to be unworkable; that he longed to prove himself with his own music, independent of Charlie.

Bill immediately set about putting together his special style of music, something through which he could express himself in an exciting and different way. It was 1939 when the first "Blue Grass Boys" appeared on radio station WSM's *Grand Ole Opry*, and they caused quite a stir. Their music was supercharged, even in its seminal form. Originally a quartet with mandolin, guitar, fiddle, and string bass, the Blue Grass Boys didn't add banjo for two years. That step would finally and completely define the classic bluegrass sound.

Dave "Stringbean" Akeman, who played in the frailing style of Uncle Dave Macon, was Monroe's first banjo player. Also joining the group was an accordionist, Sally Ann Forrester; Monroe later said that he chose to add the accordion because his mother had played the instrument. The accordion was gone from the group by autumn of 1946, however, as was Akeman's banjo when Monroe made his first recording with 22-year-old Earl Scruggs. Scruggs had joined Monroe in December of 1945, and his rapid-fire

three-finger banjo picking, unheard of at the time, was the final ingredient in the bluegrass sound. The Blue Grass Boys at that point became the classic Monroe band of Monroe, Lester Flatt on guitar, Scruggs on banjo, and Chubby Wise on fiddle, and Birch Monroe on bass.

The music was at an incredible peak, having jelled both stylistically and commercially. There was nothing else like it. Monroe and his Blue Grass Boys toured constantly, in many cases with their own tent show (featuring performers like Uncle Dave Macon) and an exhibition baseball team, returning to Nashville each week for the *Grand Ole Opry* broadcast. It was the beginning of a movement, and Monroe had no peer as a composer or as a performer. Others were to follow shortly, but Bill Monroe and the Blue Grass Boys, with their lightning playing and exciting singing, were on top.

Many classic bluegrass pieces came from this era. One of the Blue Grass Boys' early signature tunes was a reworking of Jimmy Rodgers' "Mule Skinner Blues" into Monroe's own style. Monroe's tenor voice was high and clear, and it seemed to express a feeling of deep lonesomeness. His mandolin playing had developed significantly by this time, emphasizing strong melody and a syncopated, driving rhythm that pushed the band. A hard worker, he expected his band members to be the same and he must have been a difficult man to work for at times. But always, his main concern was the music.

The late '40s were good for Monroe, but times were changing. Lester Flatt and Earl Scruggs left the Blue Grass Boys to form their own bluegrass-style band, and there began a succession of Monroe bands through which passed virtually every great figure in bluegrass music, save its mandolin players. Carter Stanley, Jimmy Martin, Don Reno, Mac Wiseman, and many others were once Blue Grass Boys.

The early '50s saw the start of a difficult period in Monroe's career. Country music in general was having an identity crisis in light of the rock and roll revolution. Though bluegrass had never, since its inception, been mass culture, Monroe had always made a good living, but with rock and roll sweeping the country, and with the advent of television, much of Monroe's economic base was eroded and jobs became harder to secure. Ironically, one of Elvis Presley's early recordings included Monroe's "Blue Moon Of Kentucky" on its B side.

It must have hurt Monroe deeply to see his expanding career suddenly and severely decline. What attention the world did give bluegrass went to Flatt and Scruggs, who had managed to make inroads into other entertainment circles. Monroe did his best to survive musically and financially, withdrawing to his Kentucky farm when jobs were scarce. He resisted all temptations to revamp his music along more popular lines. Through his intense pride, even his stubbornness, he weathered those lean times. The roots of his perseverance may have gone back to his

**"I wanted to use some kind of name so people would know where I was from," says Monroe. "So I took the name 'bluegrass.' There's not a prettier name in the whole world."**

childhood when, the youngest of the family and troubled by poor vision, he developed a need to excel, to be successful. Through that he forged a single-minded attitude about himself and his music; he drew upon all his experience and strength of will to achieve his goals, realizing that the music was the most important thing in his life. It has never been otherwise. He has always stayed on top of his music, never changing, never faltering.

The folk revival of the early '60s helped Monroe toward a comeback. It also brought him a new audience of northern college students. On the heels of this renewed interest came the popularization of bluegrass festivals, and Monroe was able to found his own at Bean Blossom, Indiana, in 1967. While Monroe had always been regarded as the father of bluegrass music, his achievements at last became more popularly recognized and he was elected to the Country Music Hall of Fame in 1970.

Today, Monroe continually tours the country and still performs regularly with the *Grand Ole Opry*. Any other artist who had made such a monumental contribution to his field might be content to rest on his laurels, but Monroe's drive is as strong as ever. He says simply, "The road life—I like it. I like to travel. I like to see the country."

Throughout the development of Monroe's music, from the '30s, on into the mid-'60s, there has always been a great deal of movement within its strict boundaries, especially in his mandolin playing.

Monroe has always tried, he says, to make the music he plays fit with the group he is in, though in his own style. Because of that, his playing has covered a great range; at times it has been subdued and at times it has been intense, but it has never been flippant or contrived.

To accent his backup playing, Monroe developed a powerful right-hand rhythm chop with an almost drum-like effect. Using a loose, limber wrist motion he gained incredible speed on his solos. Drawing on a great deal of blues phrasing and noting, he punctuated his leads with an outrageous syncopation of right-hand downstrokes. The result was one of the most distinctive and remarkable mandolin styles of our time.

. . . .

OVER THE YEARS, *in talking about how you began playing, you've mentioned a guitar player named Arnold Schultz as an early influence. Could you tell us a little about him?*

Arnold Schultz. He was a black man, you know, and he played guitar and was a wonderful guitar man. Played the blues, that was what he played. If he was following a fiddler or somebody with a guitar, he really played a different style. I never heard anybody could play anything the way that Arnold Schultz played it, behind fiddle numbers. He played a

wonderful rhythm. He could also play the fiddle, you know, a few fiddle numbers, and he played for some square dances.

*Did you learn songs from him?*

No, sir. I've always loved the blues played on the guitar, and when he would play them I loved the way he could do it. There's other people that could play blues too; there was people around where I was raised who could sing the blues like that.

*Were these black people?*

No, they were white people. They was very few colored people that would come around Rosine, Kentucky, where we lived; but Arnold was a fine man and I always loved to hear him play. There's really no man that you could pinpoint to say that his music is in my music, the way that my music is lined out. It's just like Jimmy Rodgers: I've sung some of his numbers, but they was done bluegrass style, which would override his style. If I was going to do Jimmy Rodgers alone, I would just use the guitar myself and do it the way that he did.

*But you never tried to do that, did you?*

Back in the early days I could have, you know, but mandolin's been my instrument ever since I was a young boy.

*I've never met a bluegrass mandolin player that didn't—at least at first—try to play like you. What is your reaction to everybody trying to copy Bill Monroe exactly?*

Well now, I feel good about it; every man has to start somewhere, and if my music helped him get started, why I'm one hundred percent for him to do that. I guess a lot of people learned from that and went on into other kinds of music, and a lot of people still play it the way they learned it.

*How did you react in the early '50s when Elvis Presley recorded your song "Blue Moon Of Kentucky"?*

I thought Elvis had a good voice. He apologized to me for the way that he changed "Blue Moon Of Kentucky," he did, there at the Grand Ole Opry, when he came there and sung it one Saturday night. The record company told him that he needed a style of his own, and so that's what he was searching for when he recorded "Blue Moon Of Kentucky," and I think he had it right for his new style. So, I told him if it would help him get that then I was one hundred percent for him.

*Something that's always been remarkable about your playing through the years is the many subtle changes it's undergone. For example, when you played with your brother Charlie you played in a different style. You've said that style was not yet bluegrass.*

That's right. It was a style to match his kind of singing and the kind of singing that we'd do in the early days.

*Were you concentrating less on the mandolin exclusively then and more on the entire sound?*

No, I was searching for things on the mandolin

then. But, to fit our kind of singing, what I was playing then was what we needed. The kind of style that I play now wouldn't have matched me and Charlie back in the early days.

*It seems that the one person other than Arnold Schultz whom you emphasize as an early influence is your uncle Pen Vandiver.*

Yes, sir, him being the first fiddler that I ever heard, naturally. He was a good fiddler too. He was hard to beat when it came to playing old-time square dance numbers. He had the most perfect time of any fiddler in the world, and he had a wonderful shuffle, you never see anybody today that can play that kind of shuffle.

*How old were you when you began listening to him and playing with him?*

I would say from around six years old, something like that, on up through to ten and twelve years old, I listened to him close. Then on up through my teens Uncle Pen and I would play for square dances

*With you on the guitar?*

Yes, sir, just where we could make a little extra money, you see. Back then, that was in the Depression when a dollar really meant something. We did a lot of house parties, and some of them had square dances there at the house. The people would all dance and they would donate 15 cents a set.

*Another early influence in your music was the church. What were your early church experiences?*

I guess, back in the early days, with the Methodist and the Baptist churches, everybody come there to hear the singing and the preaching. They had a Methodist church there at Rosine and a Baptist church.

They had a good choir singing there; a good lead singer, and back in them days they had tenor singers and bass singers and alto singers. That was way before baritone singing came around.

*Do songs like "Wicked Path Of Sin" come out of that tradition?*

I would say it might have touched it in some way, but through the way I was searching for the bluegrass style of singing gospel I wouldn't take a whole lot from Baptist or Methodist. It's a different gospel altogether from Methodist and Baptist. I don't believe I ever heard a quartet there in church. Bluegrass gospel, I think, is wonderful.

*When you were playing with your brothers, before you played with Charlie as a duo and while you were working for the Sinclair Oil Company, had you played professionally much?*

Well, just back to Uncle Pen and me playing for dances and house parties.

*Did you think much about future economic opportunities with the oil company when you decided to try being a musician?*

It wasn't that I decided to be one or the other. Times was rough back then and musicians didn't have the best chance in the world. Very few radio stations paid anything, you see. It was taking a big chance, leaving a good job and going into music.

*Through playing with Charlie and later, when did your music become bluegrass?*

When me and Charlie broke up, I went to building around myself to form the music that I wanted. Any man that I hired had to play my style or he didn't belong in my group. It went to building from that,

**"Bluegrass" says its father, Bill Monroe, "tells the truth. A lot of songs are true songs."**

doing the numbers that would help us get started in that kind of music.

*What made it "bluegrass"?*

The state of Kentucky gave it the name. That's the state I'm from, and I wanted to use some kind of a name from that state so the people would know it was where I was from. So, I took the name "bluegrass." There's not a prettier name in the world than that.

*As far as the music goes, though, what were the changes that you made? Is it true that in 1938 you got a band together to play your music and rehearsed for a month?*

Well, I went to working on it back in late '38 and on up into '39. You see, it gave whoever was going to play for me a chance to practice and get it right. Maybe if a man was holding down a job or something, he'd like to play and sing but he wasn't ready for a big

radio program like the *Grand Ole Opry*. So, I had to rehearse them and get them just the way I wanted them.

*There are many stories about your first appearance on the* Grand Ole Opry—*that people listening couldn't believe it. Did you expect that?*

I knew I was going to go in there and give them everything that I had. I had heard the *Grand Ole Opry* for a long time, and I didn't think that they had anything on me in the way of being better than what I was because I wasn't in their class. I wasn't doing old-time country music, singing, or playing old-time mountain fiddle numbers, whatever you want to call it.

*Did you have a feeling of bringing a new kind of music to these people?*

I had a feeling of bringing it to everybody that I played in front of, whether it was the *Grand Ole Opry* or otherwise. I was going to take that to 'em and they could accept it or not.

*Did it matter to you whether they accepted it?*

Well, I wanted them to accept it, 'cause I knew I had to have them on my side if I was to really put it over and make money at it.

*Over the years you've avoided changing your sound for commercial reasons or any other consideration. How have you been able to keep the Bill Monroe sound so pure?*

It's been hard at times. You might have a fiddle player or a banjo player that wants to put his stuff in it, you see. So, it comes right down to where he either had to play mine or he had to get him another job. And he couldn't win out, because if I didn't want his music, why, he'd have to play mine. I couldn't sell his style on the *Grand Ole Opry*—it had to be mine. So, I had to watch people like that and be sure that they played what I wanted. Record companies never gave me any trouble. I always done what song I wanted to do. They never told me I had to do anything. I think they knew to start with that I wouldn't do it. Now, if they gave me a song that I thought I could do, and it was a good song, why I would do it; but it would be in bluegrass style.

*If you could pick a band that was the greatest Bill Monroe band, who would you pick?*

Well, you know now, if I told you this—if I said I would take somebody by the name of George over somebody by the name of Frank, and they'd all been Blue Grass Boys, it would hurt 'em, you know. Say if you worked for me three years and it was a wonderful group, then you and the rest of the group left and I brought in a new bunch; well, your days would have been fine, but when they come along with theirs, their days would have been fine. So you couldn't say that any group could have beat different groups down through the years. I've tried to keep good clear singers that could sing with me—a lead singer who played a good guitar. I've tried to keep the right kind of banjo player and the right kind of fiddle player. And a good bass, to help me keep time straightened out. But, I think each man with me has had his chance; and when he was with me, he would have been hard to beat. They was all good in their day, and I give every man credit.

*Could you tell us about some of your experiences with your tent show back in the '40s, when you had people like Uncle Dave Macon and harmonica player DeFord Bailey on the bill with the Blue Grass Boys?*

You talk about the tent show—I had that for years, and that gave us five days of work, Monday through Friday; and then back to the *Grand Ole Opry*, so that made six days. If, say, I went on 15, 20 minutes with me and the Blue Grass Boys, then we'd have some comedy for about 15 minutes, then go back to the bluegrass quartet, then maybe have a good fiddle number, and then DeFord Bailey. So it gave you a fine lineup down through the show.

*Was DeFord Bailey a novelty act?*

No, sir, no. There was no comedy with DeFord. It was strictly the harmonica the way it should be played; "Pan American Blues," "Lost John," "The Evening Prayer Blues," numbers like that. You couldn't beat him. He was fine.

*How about Uncle Dave Macon?*

He was a fine showman. Had a good voice and played a good 5-string banjo in his style, and he done a little comedy down through his show. When he was going over fine, he went along just like a clock working. Everything was perfect.

*You had comedians with some of your early band, but you got away from that later. How did the change come about?*

Well, back in the early days the people was trained all over the whole world for so much comedy in a show, so that's why I carried one comedian. Later on, when Stringbean [Dave "Stringbean" Akeman] would work with me, that would give me two comedians. Two working together, they was really powerful, on stage, you know. They could really get the laughs. And that would break the monotony of going from one number to another. It would let the musicians have a little break. Later on there got to be so many numbers like "Blue Moon Of Kentucky," "Mule Skinner Blues," "Footprints In The Snow," and "Uncle Pen," that the people would pay their money and want to hear; and they would want to hear fiddle numbers, banjo numbers, the quartet. So, by the time you get to all that, you don't have much time for comedy. And I think comedy takes away from a good bluegrass show. Bluegrass is way further up in the world than a lot of people give it credit for being. It tells the truth. A lot of songs are true songs. It gives me a good feeling to hear good bluegrass. And I know that a man, if he's a hard worker in it, is doing his best because he wants to hear it that way and he hopes it'll touch you the same way. That's the way I am with my music; I like to play it for myself, and I hope that it's really getting next to the people who listen, too.

*A lot of the songs you've written are songs about being on the road. Is the road a difficult part of your life?*

Well, I raised two children James and Melissa, and they knew that if I went out and worked five days and made what money I could, that I was coming home to them. They knew that I'd be back there, and that I would want to see them just as much as they would want to see me. And they allowed for all that, you know, so that's the way it went for a long time. The road life, I like it. I like to travel, I like to see different country.

*How do you go about writing songs—say, "Kentucky Mandolin"?*

If I'm writing a number like "Kentucky Mandolin" and I've got it started to where I enjoy the first notes, I search for the notes to tie on to that, to keep it going on the way I want it to where it still sounds good to me. Of course, there's brakes in any number where you might not be crazy about where you're going to take it right then, say, whether you can get to another position in another key. "Kentucky Mandolin" was a number that I was writing when I was here in California years and years ago. Doc Watson was playing it with me and I didn't have a title, so he give it the title "Kentucky Mandolin."

*Do you change songs any after you get the basic form down?*

No, I stay as close as I can to the way that I write a song. That's the trouble with a lot of musicians; they want to do it their way, and their way ain't the right way. They ought to think about the man that writes the song and try to do it right, try to do it his way. It would be much better for them, because they don't know where they're going with it—a lot of them don't. They're jazzing a song up, putting a lot of wild notes in it to show off more that anything else.

*Is your mandolin the Bill Monroe mandolin [a Gibson Loar F-5]? Is that the one that matches your style?*

Yes, sir, it's been a good mandolin down through the years.

*Are you particular about the picks you use?*

I like a heavy pick. I don't like a real light, thin pick because I don't think you can get a tone out of the mandolin with a thin pick. I let the point wear off, because if it's too sharp, why, you don't get the tone. I've tried tortoise shell and it's pretty good. I use Gibson bronze strings.

*You sometimes use a different tuning—on "Get Up John," for instance. Are there others that you haven't recorded yet?*

Yes, but it's been so long [laughs] I can't remember how I tune them.

*How do you feel about amplifying the mandolin, either by using an electric instrument or by attaching a pickup to an acoustic one? You've never done that yourself.*

No, sir. I've played other people's mandolins a little bit that was electrified. I guess it's alright, according to what kind of music you're playing, what you're trying to do with it. I think it'd be good to play for dances like that, probably.

*Do you still practice a lot?*

We do. We sing and practice some. We play as we ride the bus, you know. If you're working every night, you get a lot of work right there, and a lot of times you can come up with something new right from the stage that will help your music.

*Does new material come to you when you're up on the stage?*

Sometimes it does, yes sir. I listen for music or where it could go to; where you could start from one note and go into something that would really help a number.

*Do you play set solos? In "Bluegrass Break-down," for example, you might play the melody in one solo. Are you trying to create new things in that way onstage?*

If it's the "Bluegrass Breakdown," I do the best that I can do with it. I try to play my break as good as I can do it. I don't think it should be changed. It should stay the way it was wrote. With numbers like "Arkansas Traveler," "Katy Hill," I don't think you need to make it do something and ruin the number; and that's what you would do if you tried to put other kinds of music in it. They're for square dancing. You know what time a number should be and if you get out there and make it to where it's a hundred miles an hour, you've lost your mind. It could never be right; no way in the world it could be right. It's just like a waltz number. If you go out there and play it so fast nobody could waltz—who wins there? And who loses? The musician does. The dancer, he can't do it, because you've ruined it. Any musician ought to learn timing. Now, that's the main thing in music—and there's a lot of different times. Any young musician ought to be sure to learn it the right way. There's numbers like the "Orange Blossom Special" where you know it's a show-off number, a selling number just like "Rawhide" or "Black Mountain Rag" or something like that. But you just got a few of them numbers, so get back to the real thing. If you're going to play the "Watson Blues," why, it's an old southern style of blues and you don't need to put hot notes in it. You need to learn where a hot note should go, and not let it override the number to where it's going to

hurt it. If you're going to play jazz or if you're going to play round dance music then you can throw every hot note in there that you want. Wouldn't hurt a thing.

*Is the same thing true of singing?*

Well, it works sort of the same way. If you've got a voice that can handle the song right, you stay on the note and follow your melody your voice will have a good chance and will help that song. The people out there will hear what you're doing. When you go to putting extra stuff in it, they know it don't go that way so you're only kidding yourself. If you're going to sing "Blue Moon Of Kentucky," you better hold close to the way it was wrote. Or "Kentucky Waltz," or "Uncle Pen"—that's a true song so you wouldn't want to make a show-off song out of it; you want to let the people hear the fiddle music and every word the way the story goes.

*Of all your songs, are there any you sing better than others?*

I wouldn't think so. On any song I would do my best. I don't ever go out onstage and piddle around with it. I give my throat and my voice a chance. By doing that, you've done your best right there and put some power behind it. That's all you need to do with it.

*Do you enjoy having the audience sing along with you?*

Oh, I love that. That's a great part of a lot of our shows today.

*You once said that you thought of bluegrass as a type of competition between band members. Is that the way you view it today?*

I think that's the way it is. You know you've got competition in bluegrass music. If you play a banjo number the best you can play it, the next man that's out there, he's going to play it hard. You've got people up there like Earl Scruggs and Don Reno to face, and you better come with the best that you've got or you're not going to sell. It's the same thing with the singer. He'd better do it good because there's another man they're going to introduce who's going to come out and sing his best. Same thing about the mandolin, or a quartet, or anything. It's a challenge. It's music that needs a lot of practice. You need to practice every time you get a chance.

## A Selected Bill Monroe Discography

**Solo albums** (on MCA): *Bean Blossom*, 2-8002; *Best Of Bill Monroe*, 4-2090; *Bluegrass Instrumentals*, 104; *Bluegrass Memories*, 2315; *Bluegrass Ramble*, 88; *Bluegrass Special*, 97; *Bluegrass Time*, 116; *High, Lonesome Sound of Bill Monroe*, 110; *I Saw The Light*, 527; *I'll Meet You In Church Sunday Morning*, 226; *Kentucky Blue Grass*, 136; *Mr. Bluegrass*, 82; *Bill Monroe, Country Music Hall Of Fame*, 140; *Bill Monroe's Greatest Hits*, 17; *Bill Monroe Sings Bluegrass, Body And Soul*, 2251; *Road Of Life*, 426; *Uncle Pen*, 500; *Voice From On High*, 131; *Weary Traveler*, 2173; *Lester Flatt Live Bluegrass Festival*, Victor Records, APLI-0588; *Stars Of The Grand Ole Opry*, 1926-1974, 2-0466; *Bill Monroe And His Blue Grass Boys*, Columbia, CS-1065; *Bluegrass Style*, Coral Records, 20077; *Bill Monroe Sings Country Songs*, Coral Records, 20099. **Singles:** *Footprints In The Snow*, MCA, 60074. **With James Monroe:** *Father And Son*, MCA, 310, *Together Again*, MCA, 2367. **With The Monroe Brothers** (On Camden Records): *50 Years Of Country Music*, ADL2-0782; *Smokey Mountain Ballads*, ACL-7022; *Sound Of Bluegrass*, ACLI-0535; *Feast Here Tonight*, Victor Records, AXM2-5510; *Bill And Charlie Monroe*, MCA, 124.

# PETE SEEGER

Pete Seeger helped to stamp modern American folk as a music of conscience, through songs like "Where Have All The Flowers Gone," "If I Had A Hammer," and "Turn, Turn, Turn," and a lifetime commitment to peace, justice, and environmental issues. His banjo-playing inspired an entire generation of young pickers to take up the instrument. Today, Pete continues to perform and publish. He was interviewed in *Frets* September 1979 issue.

**By Marty Gallanter**

L ANGUAGE, EVEN FOR THOSE of us who make our living working with it, can be a frustratingly inadequate means of expression. When we reach for words to convey deep appreciation or to bestow high praise, inevitably we find ourselves groping for something beyond the same old, tired superlatives; and inevitably we end up feeling cheated by the rigid limitations of the words available to us. How does one introduce an artist of the stature of Pete Seeger and give him all the honor that is his due, without sounding like a toastmaster at some sort of musicians' testimonial banquet? "Ladies and gentlemen, here is the most accomplished, the most respected, the most influential . . . ." I struggle for eloquence, and feel lost.

But I know I'm on solid ground when recalling the many people who play music for enjoyment, or who earn their living from music, or the great artists I have interviewed, who have all replied in some way to the question "What influenced you?" with the name "Pete Seeger." And I would guess that anyone who has been involved in traditional acoustic music for any length of time, and particularly anyone who has been involved in folk music, would know who he is and all that he represents. I can certainly guarantee that anyone just developing an interest in music will quickly learn that Pete is one of the strongest roots of the tree of modern American music.

The name of Pete Seeger is often linked with the name of Woody Guthrie, and no wonder; it's been nearly 40 years since the two folksingers began voicing the music of our land, singing the songs of the working man, carrying their message to gatherings in every corner of America. They came up hard against the Establishment of that era, earning admiration in some circles and notoriety in others. In 1942 Woody and Pete sang "The Sinking Of The Reuben James" on a CBS network radio program. The following day, one newspaper headline proclaimed, "Commie Folksingers Try To Infiltrate Radio."

For years Woody and Pete were banned from the air, never yielding to the powers who told them, "If you sign this loyalty oath, you can go on." Instead they searched out audiences who would hear them. They formed the Alamanac Singers with Mill Lampell, Bess Lomax Hawes, Arthur Stern, and Sis Cunningham, until Woody shipped out for a tour of duty with the Merchant Marine. Pete then became the focal point of the Weavers, along with Lee Hays, Ronnie Gilbert, and Fred Hellerman, carrying on through the blacklisting days of the McCarthy era. But Pete had to sing on his own; to keep delivering *his* message. His public life has been associated with many political causes; civil rights, peace, union rights, and environmental issues. But these issues are really inseparable from Pete's music. For the simple themes of truth and justice have long been at the heart of American folk music. The desire for an honest day's wage, to be free from hunger or oppression, or to partake of all the rights entitled one born in a democracy, are common to the poor or disenfranchised of any era. Pete's personification of these goals, through his music, made him the most influential folk musician for an entire generation of Americans.

．．．．

*Y*OU HAVE BEEN INVOLVED *in social causes throughout your career. Do you feel that a performing artist has a certain social responsibility?*

An artist, any kind of an artist, is also a citizen and has a citizen's responsibilities. This means voting, among other things. You can argue about that I suppose; but citizens' responsibilities go even further. We have a duty to inform ourselves, and when you inform yourself, you want to communicate what you learn. I think it is a mistake to think *any* music doesn't have a message of some sort. Some music has a message that says, "Eat, drink and be merry, for tomorrow we die"; and many musicians really, sincerely feel that is the sum of an intelligent response to life. I'll admit there's a big grain of truth in it. Some music has a message saying that there's hope to make things better here on earth; your only hope is that after death there will be eternal joy and pleasure, if you say the right words in the right places. I don't argue with people who feel that way. Music has, throughout history, played a very large part in preserving the status quo—good or bad. Plato, the Greek philosopher, was most emphatic. He said that for the good of the state, it was very important that the music which was heard by the people should be of the right kind, because the wrong kind of music could be very destructive. So, I take a very broad view of politics and causes. It is an oversimplification to say that a person like me is involved in causes, and other musicians are not. Just pick your cause.

*There was a time when causes and the stands you took on them affected your ability to work. What was life like in those days?*

For me, it was not hard at all. I had a small circle of friends who kept me singing. I'd sing for the students in some little college and they'd pass the hat. I'd make my fare and a little extra. The circle gradually grew wider. It's really as simple as that. Some people had their lives ruined by the McCarthy period—the "frightened Fifties," I call them. They had to change their location of residence, their jobs. I feel very grateful to my little home town here. My children were never injured in school, to my knowledge. The principal called in the teachers and said, "Now, you know Mr. Seeger is on trial for contempt of Congress. I just want you to let me know if anybody makes it hard on his children." She wasn't taking a stand as to whether I was guilty or not. She just wasn't going to let it affect some kids that she liked. So, I have nothing to complain about. Although it was a terrible period for many people, my wife and I survived. Occasionally, nasty things happened, but we could shrug them off and it was nowhere near as bad as situations many people face every day of their lives. I think of black people who have their homes burned because they simply bought a house in a neighborhood where it was unusual for black people to live. I think of people who have been denied jobs because of their religion or their national background. This business about freedom of speech or freedom of song is one that everybody faces. It's a worldwide problem. It must be ancient, ancient human tendency that when you meet people who have an opinion that you despise, you don't want them around. To learn to live with people that you don't like is one of the great arts of civilization, and we're slow to learn it. Now, this doesn't mean that I'm in favor of absolute freedom of speech myself. I'd agree you don't shout "Fire!" in a crowd. I also don't like to joke about things that are life-and-death issues to another person. Imagine if you had your shoulder rubbed and rubbed until it was raw, and I came along and just touched it. You would wince in pain and anger, and all I had done was touch you. But because you had already been rubbed raw, my slightest touch would cause that kind of pain. For example, I don't sing a song—a funny song, some say—that I used to sing. It goes, "It's a shame to beat your wife on Sunday, it's a shame to beat your wife on Sunday when you've got Monday, Tuesday, Wednesday, Thursday, Friday, Saturday, Oh, it's a shame." In this country there are a lot of women being battered by frustrated husbands and it's a big problem. I don't sing the song anymore. In a way, everybody has to be their own censor. I'm not against censorship. I'd just like everybody to be their own censor; and if they're not a good enough censor for themselves, then I think we have to help them. This isn't necessarily done best through a law, which is rather inflexible, and also very expensive to enforce. Justice, as you know, ain't free. The jails are full of people who would not be there if they could afford a good lawyer. But, I'm convinced that this problem of freedom of speech may be the most difficult one for the human race to solve. Sooner or later we will be able to share food, so there's not going to be anyone hungry in centuries to come. But, it is going to be much more difficult to share information. There is not a single nation in the world that has solved this problem. There is even some information that I wouldn't even want to see exist, much less be shared. I don't want to see people experimenting with nuclear reactors that could poison future generations. I don't want to see some curious scientist experimenting with what they call the "recombinant DNA molecule" and maybe inventing some bacteria that could wipe out the human race. Absolute freedom of speech and absolute freedom of information will simple lead to the end of the world within a few hundred years, if not sooner. I don't kid myself that I'm in favor of it.

*Recently, you said you'd made some changes in the way you approach your own music. What were those changes?*

An awful lot of the best musicians I've ever known didn't play a great many different kinds of music. But what they knew, they sure knew well. Take Sonny Terry, the blind harmonica player. He plays blues mostly. Boy, how he can play 'em. He can play them fast or slow, in one key or another. He just gets better and better. Lately, I seem to keep coming back to tunes that I learned to play years ago. Tom Benton [Thomas Hart Benton], the painter, taught me and my father the song "John Henry" in 1931. Only about five years ago did I realize that I had finally found the way I like to play it best. I kept experimenting. I cut out a lot of chords. I don't play as many chords now. I play a lot of single strings. Just sometimes, the right note, in the right place, is worth ten notes in the almost-right place. So, instead of concentrating on expanding my repertoire a whole lot more, I'm working hard on trying to do better what I've been doing for years.

*The Pete Seeger style of banjo picking has a distinctive sound. Can you describe your picking technique?*

I picked up a style of strumming, which I called a "basic strum," both from a man named Pete Steele, who still lives in Hamilton, Ohio; and from a guy named Bascom Lunsford, who's dead now, but who was a country lawyer in Nashville, North Carolina. Of course, it's not the only basic strum—there's a hundred of them. This one is basic for me. You pluck up on a melody string—it might be any one of the middle strings of the instrument—with your first finger. Half a beat later, you strum down across one, or two, or three, or four, or even five strings with the back of your fingernail. Now, that could be the back of your ring finger, or the back of your first finger. You get a slightly different effect depending on which finger you pluck up with and which finger you pluck down with. This coming up on the downbeat and brushing down on the offbeat is the essential part of this particular strum. Between these notes, you can get some notes with your left hand; I'm actually quite proud that I'm the one who named that technique: I call it "pulling off" on a string. Violinists call if "left-hand pizzicato"—Paganini did it—but I call it "pulling off." Your left hand pulls off the string with a plucking motion right after you've plucked the string with your right hand. Or, you can "hammer down" on a string. That's also a term I invented 30 or 40 years ago. That is, you've plucked up on the string and you immediately come down it with your left hand, fretting it in a new place. You get a new note with a special quality that is unique. You can't get that kind of note with your right hand. The left hand has to get it. Then, on a 5-string banjo, after you strum down with the back of your fingernail, just before you get your melody note, your thumb hits the short fifth string—what they call the thumb string—and that keeps digging away through the whole song, the same note. It's the "ring" in, "Ring, ring the banjo." What I've just described can add up to four notes, and if they're done right, it gives a lovely, rippling, bubbling tone. If you do it wrong, it sounds sloppy. Sometimes, it can take years until you get it to come out just right on some certain song. You can emphasize any one of those four notes, or you can de-emphasize any one of those four notes, depending on which string and which finger you use. It can sound very different, which is why I've found it to be a very flexible kind of strum. If I were writing my banjo book [*How To Play The Five-String Banjo*, self-published, 1962] over again, I would now call it simply, "a simple strum that can be used to accompany lots of songs." I will say this—I'm convinced now that my banjo book should not have started off with that strum. I should have started off with single strings, because the banjo is at its best playing single notes. Chords are all right, and when I get a crowd singing, I wham across all the strings and just strum a chord. But, it you want to really hear a banjo, you want to hear single strings. That's why I think Earl Scruggs and people who play bluegrass, and people who frail and play clawhammer banjo, are the best banjo pickers in the country. I really do. I think my favorite type is probably a good clawhammer the way my brother Mike plays it. He's very good, and I envy him.

*Tell us about your banjo, the one you always have with you.*

I've had it about 20 years. I made the neck myself out of lignum vitae. It's a South American hardwood

**Pete Seeger's feelings about music are advertised on the skin of his banjo. "This machine surrounds hate and forces it to surrender."**

so heavy it sinks in water. They make marine equipment out of it because it doesn't rot. The drum is from an old Vega banjo that I had around. I've taken to having a neck longer than on those other banjos because I like to play a few songs, in certain keys, that need a few low notes. All the long neck gives me is a few extra low notes. I don't use them except occasionally, but if I need them, I've got them. If you're playing with a guitar to accompany you, then you don't really need them. The guitar can play the low notes, or of course, so can any other bass instrument.

*What was the story behind Vega's "Pete Seeger Model" banjo?*

Oh that! It was years ago. I got a letter saying that Vega had received many requests for a long-neck banjo like mine and that they wanted to sell a "Pete Seeger" model. I said, "Sure, go ahead and use it." They asked me if I wanted a royalty and I said, "No, not thinking many people would want the instrument. A few years later, I found out they were selling hundreds, thousands, of them and I figured I should have asked for a royalty after all. Well, it didn't really matter. The Vega people gave me a nice long-neck banjo that I used to keep as a spare until I gave it away to a nice young newspaper reporter in Florida. We were raising money for *Sing Out! Magazine* and I said that I would give my spare banjo to anybody who would sell a hundred subscriptions for *Sing Out!*

*After all these years of performing, what is it you think about when you go out onstage alone?*

I think about a lot of people out in front who may disagree with each other about a lot of things, but I'm hoping that I can get them to agree, at least for a few minutes, on a few things. This gives me hope to keep on going. I don't think there's much hope for the human race unless we can learn to get together a little more than we have in the past. We have to agree to disagree. It's foolish to think that we are ever going to agree about everything—that's impossible. But you can hope that we'll agree to disagree long enough to get together on accomplishing a few things. Like the song says, "Inch by inch, row by row, gonna make this garden grow, gonna mulch it deep and low, gonna make it fertile ground." That song is by David Mallett—copyright 1937, I think.

*What are your techniques for warming up an audience?*

In the beginning, I often will do some song that people know already, and it will relax them to a certain extent. But it relaxes me too, so I can do a better job. It doesn't have to be something that they can sing along with, although quite often I like to start with the song "John Henry," because the last line in each verse is repeated and anyone who wants to can repeat it with me. Sometimes I'll start an evening with a song that has very few words, and the banjo says more clearly than any words who I am and what kind of music I like. Funny how a musical instrument like the banjo, or the guitar, or the mandolin, each says something slightly different, and can say some

things better than others. My 12-string guitar has some rumbly bass notes and can say somethings that the sparkling pinpricks of the banjo string cannot say—and vice-versa.

*Earlier in your career you played with a couple of groups: the Almanac Singers, the Weavers. What is your favorite group setting?*

I love a traditional American string band, which for me, in the old days, consisted of a guitar, mandolin, fiddle, and banjo. Now the people add bass, and I guess the bass is nice, but I don't think it is quite as important as the other four. I guess for a big dance you really need it. I'm not sure. Sometimes you can, of course, have a lot of fun with a completely different assortment of instruments. I've played with Latin American maracas and claves. Sometimes I'll find myself playing with accordions, and even with pianos or organs, but I keep coming back to those traditional four instruments. I really love 'em. They each add something special to a string band.

*Had you always planned to be a performer?*

No, I started out as a journalist and ran the school newspaper for three years. I had a lot of fun doing it. When I dropped out of college, I knocked on the doors of a lot of newspapers and failed to get a job. Even while I was starving to death, I was going to art school, because I thought I might like to be a painter. I spent one summer traveling around and swapping paintings for a night's lodging. Years later, I got letters from people around New York State and New England who were wondering if I was the Pete Seeger who painted the picture they had hanging on their wall. I still do a little sketching, but not much painting anymore.

*Who do you consider your strongest musical influence from the early days?*

I guess I could say Woody Guthrie; but my father, who was an old musicologist, a scholar, kept making suggestions throughout my life. I think his theories are more responsible for the revival of folk music in this country than most people realize. Back in the 1930s, my father and Alan Lomax, the Texas folklore collector, put their heads together and asked what needed to be done to let America know what wonderful songs existed in the country and had been handed down from generation to generation. They had the example of the mistakes made in Europe. Over there the folklorists picked out the most beautiful songs of the peasants and put them in books and said, "This is the best version of this song. Learn this version and don't change a note." They didn't leave anything for the young people to improvise on. Forty years ago, my father and Alan Lomax thought that was a mistake. Simply throw a lot of songs at young people and say, "You decide which are the best ones. You improvise. Carry on the spirit of improvisation. Don't think of folk music as a dead repertoire. Think of it as a living process." When people like me wanted to learn, they encouraged us not to learn out of books. Someone once told my father, "You must

get your son to study voice. He'll ruin his vocal cords." My father said, "If I catch him studying singing, I'll stop it immediately." Instead, he let me listen to recordings of people who were the real thing. The Library of Congress, even in those days, had thousands of recordings of people from back in the hills, out on the plains, up in the north woods. People who had learned their music by ear and were singing it and playing it by ear. I think that's still the best way to learn music. It's a handy thing to know how to read music, later on maybe, after you know how to *make* music. Once you know what kind of music you want to make, then it could be handy to know how to read it. But, it could be a real mistake to learn how to read

didn't have portable recording machines in those days—we wouldn't have most of these songs.

*What about Woody? What was Woody Guthrie's magic?*

He was always searching, never satisfied. He always had a sense of humor, and at the same time, he wasn't scared to be serious. Sometimes he would get deadly serious. He also kept his eye on the long, long-range view. He said, 'We've got to get together all the hard-working people of this world, and when we do, it's going to be a much better world."

*You do a lot of concerts with Woody's son today. Do you have special feelings about working with Arlo Guthrie?*

Arlo is his own man. He has some of Woody's qualities and a lot of brand new ones. He's one of the most conscientious musicians that I know. He thinks long and hard about the kind of music he wants to make. Then he gets onstage, and by gosh, he does his level best. I'm very proud that he likes to work with me, and I know that I love to perform with him. So every summer we go out and do some concerts, usually in these great big open sheds, which frankly I think are too big. From the back, I don't know how they can see us without a telescope. You can hear because they have good-quality sound systems now, but you sure can't see from the back. Otherwise, it's always a lot of fun playing with Arlo and [his band] Shenandoah.

*Do you ever play all by yourself, without an audience?*

Oh yes, quite often, especially early in the morning or late at night. I take a guitar or a banjo off the wall and play a tune or so for myself. I usually keep the instruments hung on the wall without a case so they're easy to take down. Sometimes I try to work out a new tune, but more often I'll just play an old one I've played a thousand times before. There's an interesting thing about music and there's a contradiction that I haven't been able to figure out. Music can be a very private thing at times. I know when I was a kid, I was very shy. When the rest of my classmates were starting to shave and go around with girls, I was still very immature. So, I would go off by myself and play a little music and it was a private thing. It didn't bother me that nobody was listening. I just wanted to have fun. Now, here's the contradiction: Music helped put me in touch with other people. The kids would say, "Hey, bring your ukulele into the party." I used to play the ukulele when I was age eight. When I was 13, I changed to the 4-string banjo, and changed again to the 5-string banjo when I was 19. Bringing the uke or banjo along to a party would have people asking me to sing some song that they all knew, and I'd comply. I'd always figure that I would compromise, and if people wanted me to sing some songs, I'd satisfy their request. Then, I'd sing some songs that I wanted to sing, some that might even surprise them. I still do that. When I give a concert, I want to make sure I meet them halfway. I sing

too soon. Can you imagine what it would be like to teach a baby how to read before it learned how to talk? There's a wonderful tradition throughout the world that you learn by watching, listening, trying, and feeling your way. So, I guess my influences, the strongest ones, came from my father, Woody Guthrie, and Alan Lomax. You know, it was out of Alan's collection that songs came that we just take for granted now. "House Of The Rising Sun," "Hush Little Baby," "Streets Of Laredo"—they all came from Alax Lomax. If it hadn't been for him—and his father John, who went around to the cowboy camps at the turn of the century and wrote down the words because they some songs they would like to hear, and I'll sing some songs that may surprise them, some that they might not even want to hear. It doesn't bother me if there is a dead silence after some of my songs. I'm glad that some of my songs give people pause for thought.

*What happened to your television show,* Rainbow Quest?

Way back, 10 or 15 years ago, my wife and I put all the family savings into it, and if just 20 local stations would have carried it, we could have broken even and kept it going. Only 13 stations took it, and finally, we couldn't afford doing it. Toshi kept an eye on things like that. She's the brains in the family. I get some wild ideas, but she stomps down the ones that are too hard to handle. She points out what has to be done to see the worthwhile ones through. The sloop *Clearwater* wouldn't be sailing today if it hadn't been for her tremendous hard work and thinking.

*Do you have any special plans for the future?*

I wish I could learn how to retire gracefully, but I don't know how. Every day a bushel of mail comes in and somebody says, "We are trying to raise some money here and it would help us so much if you came and performed." The next thing I know, I'm going through my calendar with my wife trying to find out if I can spare a few hours. I don't do as much traveling across the country or around the world as I used to, although I get invitations from many places. I really feel that I'd like to concentrate on the Hudson River and trying to bring the people of the Hudson Valley together. It's not easy, but I'd like to work on this. I'd like to live a long time, because it is going to take more than a few years to bring the hard-pressed people of New York City together with the hard-pressed people upstate. There are some who try to split us apart, you know. They say to the people upstate, "Don't have anything to do with those chiselers down in the city, those loafers. They don't care about this river. They just get it dirty." Down in the city they tell them, "Don't trust those people upstate. They're all a bunch of rich people. They don't want to see a dam built in their pretty little valley. They just don't want any powerlines to mar the view from their suburban estates. "I suppose there is just enough truth in both those charges that they keep coming back. The real truth of it is that there's a lot of hard-working people upstate and downstate, and until we get together, this river is not going to be cleaned up. And the same thing goes for the whole doggone world.

*What advice would you offer someone about to enter a career as a performing artist?*

I'd urge them to take the long view. Sometimes, one of the worst things that can happen is to suddenly make a lot of money when you're quite young. It can lead to being very disillusioned with the world, very cynical. It can really ruin your life. But, if you take the long view and stick to playing the kind of music you like, and get better and better at it, you are going to end up much happier. You may not make as much money; but also you just might. You know, Doc Watson was once asked about trying to make a living as a musician and he said, 'Well, it's OK as long as you've tried every other way first. Do it only as a last resort." Actually, I'd like to urge any person who likes music not to give up, even if you can't make a living at it. As you get better and better at music, as the years and the decades go by, if you love the music you make, other people are going to love it also. You can meet people and add an extra dimension to your life that is very rewarding, not only for you, but for your community; perhaps even for your family,—but beware, it could also be bad for your family. I think every professional musician has found that traveling is a heck of a lot harder on the family than they first realized. Whatever kind of music you like to make, slow or fast, loud or soft, polite or impolite, keep in mind that while money is necessary for all of us it's like air and water; you need a certain amount of it, but once you get enough—well, who wants to be a dog in the manger? There is a big, beautiful world that could be destroyed by selfishness and foolishness. We musicians have it within our power to help save it. In a small way, every single one of us counts.

## A Selected Pete Seeger Discography

**Solo albums** (On Folkways): *Abiyoyo* (*& Other Songs For Children*), 31500; *American Favorite Ballads*, 2320-23; *American Folk Songs*, 2005; *American Folk Songs For Children*, 7601; *Banks Of Marble*, 31040; *Birds, Beasts, Bugs & Little Fishes*, 7610; *Broadside Ballads*, 2456; *Camp Songs*, 7628; *Frontier Ballads, Vol. 1 & 2*, 2175/2176; *Goofing-Off Suite*, 2045; *How To Play The 5-String Banjo*, 8303; *Indian Summer*, 3851; *Love Song For Friends And Foes*, 2453; *Nativity*, 35001; *Newport Folk Festival*, 2431; *Pete Seeger Sings Leadbelly*, 31022; *Pete Seeger Sings Woody Guthrie*, 31002; *Songs Of Struggle & Protest*, 5233; *Pete Seeger Sings Folk Music Of The World*, Tradition Records, TRD 2107; *12-String Guitar*, Folkways, 8371; *Where Have All The Flowers Gone*, Folkways, 31026; *Wimoweh*, Folkways, 31018. **With others** (On Folkways): *Champlain Valley Songs*, 5210; *Hootenanny At Carnegie Hall*, 2512; *Lonesome Valley*, 2010; *Old Time Fiddle Tunes*, 3531; *Pete Seeger & Sonny Terry*, 2412; *Pete Seeger At Village Gate*, 2451; *Songs Of The Spanish Civil War: Songs Of Lincoln Battalion*, 5436. *America's Balladeer*, Olympic Records, 7102; *Anthology Of Folk Music*, Sine Qua Non Records, 270; *Essential*, Vanguard, VSD-97/98; *God Bless The Grass*, Columbia Special Productions, ACS-9232; *Golden Slumbers*, Caedmon Records; *Greatest Folksingers Of The Sixties*, Vanguard, VSD 17/18; *Pete Seeger*, Everest Records, 201; *Pete Seeger Sings Folk Music Of The World*, Tradition Records, 2107; *Songs Of The Lincoln & Int'l. Brigade*, Stinson Records, 52; *Together In Concert (Pete Seeger & Arlo Guthrie)*, Reprise, 2R-2214; *Tribute To Woody Guthrie*, Warner Brothers, 2W-3007; *Tribute To Leadbelly*, Tomato Records, 2-7003; *We Shall Overcome*, Columbia, CS-8901; *Harp* (w/Holly Near, Ronnie Gilbert, Arlo Guthrie), Redwood Records, RR409.

# EARL SCRUGGS

Earl's unique three-finger banjo-picking technique changed the entire direction of banjo playing. He was the major stylistic influence on the young banjoists of the '50s and '60s. Though he has slowed down in recent years, Earl still finds time to record, often working with his son, Randy. His latest album is "American Made, World Played," on Columbia Records. Earl was interviewed for the July 1980 issue of *Frets*.

**By Roger Siminoff**

**M**ANY ARTISTS STAND OUT in the history of music as important innovators in technique, or in style, or in instrument design. But few musicians have so wholly established the foundation of a musical idiom as Earl Scruggs, who almost single-handedly created and shaped a kind of music that has at its heart the magical, tantalizing, twangy, syncopated voice of his 5-string banjo.

Although the 5-string banjo had been popular in the nineteenth century as a fixture in minstrel shows and as a parlor instrument, and although it had come back into the limelight during the '20s and '30s in the hands of frailing-style entertainer Uncle Dave Macon, it wasn't until the '40s that it found its greatest advocate: Earl Scruggs. Scruggs turned it into a major lead instrument, thrilling the ears of thousands of listeners, and started a stampede of 5-string banjo en-

thusiasts that carried to every corner of the world. Almost without exception, the great banjoists that developed during the '50s and '60s credit Earl Scruggs, along with Pete Seeger, as the source of their musical inspiration.

I remember meeting a Czechoslovakian band at the Grand Ole Opry several years ago. Onstage they could mimic the lyrics of any bluegrass tune, but offstage they had to communicate through an interpreter. The banjo player knew only one English word, but it spoke volumes: "Scruggs."

*Scruggs*. The word conjures up sounds, techniques, and images of a special type of banjo, a picture so complete in the minds of most string musicians that any definition would be redundant. And non-musicians know the word too, whether they associate it with *Bonnie And Clyde*, *The Beverly Hill-*

*billies,* or Flatt And Scruggs. The banjo man from North Carolina's western hills has become more than a part of American music; he has become an integral part of American life.

Earl Eugene Scruggs was born on Jan. 6, 1924, in Shelby, North Carolina, in an area known as the Flint Hill community. His father, George Elam Scruggs, was said to have played some banjo and fiddle; but Earl's memories of his dad are vague. George died when Earl was only four years old. Earl's mother, Lula Ruppe Scruggs, was an important factor in his musical development. Her encouragement allowed him the freedom to leave home and pursue a life in music.

Earl's brothers, Junie and Horace, and his older sisters, Eula Mae and Ruby, all played banjo and guitar. By the time Earl was six years old Junie had done enough experimenting with the banjo to spark Earl's interest. However, the major influence, as Earl remembers, came from a relative named Smith Hammett. Hammett played banjo with a form of three-finger picking, and he had a small banjo— which he generously gave to his young admirer. Earl began to emulate Hammett in a childhood game that acquired more importance when he learned that "local folks really loved it, they'd just stand around and listen."

Before long, the child prodigy had become a local star. By the time Scruggs entered his teens, he was playing at some nearby square dances. His desire to increase the exposure of his new-found musical gifts was curtailed by his obligation, as he says, "to be the breadwinner" after his brothers and sisters married and left home. The responsibility of providing for his mother, and their household, was his.

The music business was an unknown quantity for him then, and looking into it was like "looking into a dark room," remembers Earl. He played with a few local bands, and was "forced to weigh carefully whether it would be stable or not." At the age of 15, Earl got a job playing with Wiley and Zeke Morris, who billed themselves as the Morris Brothers. Zeke played mandolin, and Wiley played the guitar. At that time, their style came under the heading of "country" music.

Earl's distinctive three-finger picking technique was beginning to take shape. Still, he felt it needed refinement—but wasn't quite sure what that would take. "I wasn't happy about what I was doing, but I didn't know what to do about it," he says. Since he was breaking new ground, there were no other musicians with whom he could trade licks and ideas.

At the end of World War II, Earl's mother encouraged him to pursue music as a career. In 1945, at age 21, Earl had the opportunity to meet Bill Monroe, and it wasn't long before Scruggs was invited to come aboard Monroe's band, the Blue Grass Boys. In addition to Earl on banjo, the band consisted of Cedric Rainwater on bass, Chubby Wise on fiddle, Monroe on mandolin—and a guitarist named Lester Flatt. That group played together for three seminal years, firmly establishing the foundation of the music style that was to become recognized as "bluegrass," a term coined from the band's name.

In early 1948, discouraged with the music business, Scruggs left Monroe to move back to North Carolina. A few weeks later, Lester Flatt also resigned. Scruggs and Flatt then decided to organize a band to work in the Carolinas/Virginia area. The new group featured Howard Watts on bass, Jim Schumate on fiddle, Lester Flatt on lead guitar, Mac Wiseman on rhythm guitar, and Earl on banjo.

The band's theme song was a Carter Family tune called "Foggy Mountain Top," and from that song the band derived its name, the Foggy Mountain Boys. In the summer of 1948, about six months after the band was formed, it recorded its first series of songs: "God Loves His Children," "I'm Going To Make Heaven My Home," "We'll Meet Again Sweetheart," and "Cabin In Caroline." During the following two years the band recorded 29 78 rpm sides for the Mercury label. In the fall of 1950, the group signed for its first recording session with Columbia; and Earl has been with the label ever since.

The band was very active during the early '50s, playing show dates in most of the southeastern states. On one trip, Scruggs was approached by a salesman from the Martha White Mills flour company and was asked if the band would be interested in working on the company's radio shows. The program aired six days a week on WSM, out of Nashville. The musicians agreed, and made their first appearance for Martha White Mills in June 1953.

By 1955, the Martha White radio promotions had developed so much interest that the company increased Flatt And Scruggs' exposure to a series of 30-minute TV shows, aired in six different cities. In additon, the band was put on the *Grand Ole Opry*, with Martha White as the sponsor. The band taped the morning radio shows and then traveled 2,500 miles each week by car to Columbus, Georgia, on Monday; Atlanta on Tuesday; Florence, South Carolina, on Wednesday; Huntington, West Virginia, on Thursday; Jackson, Tennessee, on Friday; and back to Nashville for WSM-TV on Saturday. In 1960, the Foggy Mountain Boys appeared on a national TV show entitled "Folk Sound USA." Soon afterward, the band was invited to perform at the Newport Folk Festival. The Foggy Mountain Boys had a sound that was enjoyed by folk musicians, bluegrass devotees, and general audiences alike.

The Sixties saw the music of Earl's banjo carry onto virtually every airwave in the nation. The band's "The Ballad Of Jed Clampett," the theme song of the TV show *The Beverly Hillbillies*, became a No. 1 single in late 1962. Later in the decade, Earl's classic "Foggy Mountain Breakdown" topped the charts as the hit theme of the film *Bonnie And Clyde*. The Sixties also saw Earl's three sons enter musical maturity, and family jam sessions were common in the Scruggs household. Earl soon realized that the three

**Earl Scruggs' unique three-finger banjo picking brought the instrument to a new level of popularity in the '50s and '60s. Along with Pete Seeger, he attracted a new generation of players to the instrument.**

young gentlemen, who had become part of his musical tradition, might very well be destined to play an active part in his musical future. The home jams took on more intensity, and after 40 years of banjo playing, Earl discovered a new and even more exciting challenge.

In 1969, Earl was ready to make the most dramatic change in his entire career: the formation of a

"Earl's Breakdown" in another time and place, yet still coming from the hands of their creator, Earl Scruggs.

The gifts Scruggs has given to the world of 5-string banjo are priceless, and the future holds even more in store. Scruggs is one of a kind. Although many banjoists have emulated his style, none have surpassed his solid, syncopated licks. While some

band featuring Gary, Randy, and Steve Scruggs, performing with Earl under the banner of the Earl Scruggs Revue. In the heat of much controversy sparked by bluegrass die-hards, Earl moved to another plateau, creating new sounds with his 5-string banjo. Many of the tunes he plays today have the same titles as those originated and performed with strictly acoustic musicians. Now the backup is a combination of acoustic and electric—and the sound is eclectic. It's "Foggy Mountain Breakdown" and

banjoists have run chromatic circles around "Shucking The Corn," none have ever laid it down like Earl.

. . . .

*After your 40 years of banjo playing, did you go through a relearning process when you got into the music of the Revue?*

Quite a bit. Like, many chords I already knew—but had never exercised or activated. The rhythm patterns for much of the Revue material were different from what I had done for so long. But Gary and Randy had been playing a lot of the current material at home, and I was sitting in on a lot of jam sessions with them, and friends would drop by; so really it didn't jump out at me all that much. But it has been a refreshing, happy, and rewarding challenge.

*Have you found situations with the Revue where you can't get what you want from the banjo?*

There are definitely tunes that I don't think the banjo should be part of. I've found that true in all forms of music.

*Do you have trouble maintaining your volume level with the other members of the band? Do you find that you have to play harder, or that they have to hold themselves down?*

No. I use an amp on stage strictly as a monitor. If somebody's too loud, the engineer on the board will cut him back. We only run into amp volume level problems when we are in a small auditorium, and find that the acoustics are extremely good. Our main mix always comes from the board.

*Do you bring along your own sound equipment?*

We use primarily rental equipment, and the only things we take along are our instruments and amps. I have a bus, and we carry our own stage equipment with us.

*Are there any new mechanical developments for the banjo, like the Scruggs tuners [pegs that allow controlled detuning of a string], that you see in the offing for your current style of music?*

I would like to add one more bass string—a fifth/fourth string [laughs], if you know what I mean—to get a low note for some tunes. I've tried a de-tuner [a single peg with controlled stops] on the fourth string, but the problem is that the winding doesn't let the string slide all the way on the nut accurately enough. I've got an idea I'm working on that should give me a way around the problem. If it works, it should be much more accurate.

*Do you use the Scruggs tuners much today?*

Yes, I still do "Earl's Breakdown" and "Flint Hill Special" using the tuners. Those still go over well onstage; they are good picking tunes for me and they come off well. I've played some of those tunes so much that I wouldn't sit down and play them for my own amusement. But I'm out there to entertain, and I like to see a good smile from the audience and watch them get into the rhythm.

*What was the first banjo that you used professionally?*

I had a Gibson, but it wasn't a Mastertone and it didn't have a metal tone-ring in it. It was real shiny and it was blue. They called it a model RB-II, and the one I had was an original 5 string. The fretboard was made to look like pearl and the back of the resonator had a large, colorful design on it.

*Don Reno once told me that he traded banjos with you. Can you tell us what happened?*

Well, Don traded me his banjo and a guitar for my banjo. I liked the sound of his banjo, and he liked mine. I didn't do it to get the guitar; I just liked the tone of his banjo.

*Have you tried other banjos that are available today?*

I'm trying the OME banjo out on the road now, just to see what they can build. I find it to be pretty good.

*What are your feelings regarding flat-top tone chambers versus arch-top tone chambers?*

I prefer the flat-top. The main thing I have noticed in the sound of the flat-top, as opposed to the arch-top, is that it has more depth in most banjos. You might say it's like a 10-inch speaker compared to a 12-inch one. I prefer a deep, mellow tone; however, you will notice variations in either type of tone chamber.

*Do you find that one records better than the other?*

I wouldn't say one records *better* than the other, but I've been able to get a more mellow result from the flat-head.

*Do you look for a different quality of banjo sound in the studio than you do onstage?*

No. I try to get the same sound in the studio as I get any place else. It takes a little time to EQ the board and find a mike that will do the job. I've searched very hard to get exactly the sound that I like when I get onstage. Your engineer helps too. Most of the time, I work very closely with him to get what I want whether I'm on the stage, in the auditorium, or in the studio.

*You are using a pickup now, aren't you?*

Yes, I'm using a Barcus-Berry. I have the pickup positioned underneath the head, about an inch back from the bridge. I've found that if you get too close to the bridge, you're going to start muting the tone of the banjo. The position I use seems to eliminate losing any volume or quality; and if I want to go acoustic I can just leave the pickup in there. It doesn't affect any type of work I want to do.

*Do you run the banjo through an equalizer?*

I do use an equalizer most of the time, and on concerts I just go straight through the board.

*Do you also work into a microphone?*

Well, I used to work just into the mike on our concerts. I get basically the same tone with the pickup—not *quite* the same, but it gives me the freedom to maneuver around onstage.

*When you were working into the mike, where did you position it in relation to the banjo head?*

On our last recording session, I noticed that just in front of my hand, in the lower section of the head, worked out okay.

*Have you experienced any right-hand technique problems since you began using a pickup?*

No. I get most of my tone variation with my right hand. I don't get quite as much depth with the Barcus-Berry as I do with the mike; I lose a little bit there. But I still move away from the bridge when I play backup to mellow the tone as much as possible.

*Do you have a favorite recording studio in Nashville?*

There are a number of good studios. Randy and Steve, my two younger sons, have put in a studio [Scruggs Sound Studio] and I don't want to plug something because it's my boys'; but of course, I'm more at ease there and the sound is great.

*Is there anything you do in the studio to improve or enhance the recording characteristics of the banjo?*

I like the sound of the banjo, as I hear it, to come through as much as possible. Sometimes we will switch around with mikes to get what I want. In the last two or three studio sessions we have done, I used the mikes and no pickups.

*Have you tried many different kinds of heads?*

With my banjo I have to use the heaviest of everything, both bridge and head. Otherwise my banjo seems to be tinnier. I've tried to thin the bridge down and stuff like that. I've tried the 5-Star [Stewart MacDonald] head and found that it is the best-constructed head that I have run into; but it seems to be just a little bit thinner than the Remo Weather King, so I do use a Weather King head on my banjo.

*Do you prefer plastic heads over the skin ones?*

Well, if the humidity was very low, and everything was right for the skin head, a head like the Roger's Three-Star [a famous brand of skin heads, no longer available] was superior to anything that I have used since. But 85 percent of my working time, the humidity was at a point where the tone would be dull—just not there. The only way to compensate for that was to tighten the head, or dry it out, and fool with it every day. And, if you forgot to loosen it, and the humidity went down, you'd burst the head. So, I never knew when I got to a performance whether I had a head on my banjo or not. The plastic head solved that problem, but I think I lost a little bit of tone quality there. If I look back over the years on a day by day basis of reliability, I've gained a lot. What I've lost is tone, but I've gained in reliability.

*How about strings? What kind are you using?*

I've been trying several different brands. I use a medium-gauge. I've tried Stelling, Vega, and so on. Actually, I like a .010″ high *D*, a .012″ *B*, a .014″ *G*, a .016″ low *D*, and a .010″ fifth string.

*Do you recommend a particular tailpiece height?*

I just bring it down enough to have the proper amount of tension so that the bridge won't slide. I have also found that if the tailpiece is too long, and gets too close to the bridge, it will start muting the tone.

*Do you try to play everything open, or do you use a capo?*

I use a capo a lot. I don't use a sliding capo for the fifth string, I use the little L-head spikes [in the fretboard] instead.

*Have you developed any new tunings for the Revue music?*

I've just been using the standard *C* and *G* tunings, and going to *D* tuning for songs like "Reuben's Train."

*Who do you use for repair work?*

I've been using Henry Buck in Hampton, Georgia. He's the best that I've found. He does necks, inlays and all kinds of building. I've had him do some refinishing work and refretting, and he really does some fine work.

*Do you have any thoughts for up-and-coming banjoists?*

Speed is one thing that I never put emphasis on. You must keep the syncopation and tempo so you can handle the tune. Try to play as clean as you can. Years ago, I was picking a boogie thing, just playing it by myself. I was going over and over it. It had no special tune to it, just a boogie style. My mother heard it, and she said "Earl, if you're going to play, play something that has a tune to it!" And the reason she said that was because there wasn't a guitar player with me to follow the chords. I figured that if she couldn't figure out what I was playing, certainly somebody that didn't hear me every day couldn't tell what I was playing either. That's when I became a firm believer that you should stick to the tune as much as possible. The other thing is that I *was* trying for speed, and found that it was better to slow down and be clear. What I concentrate on is playing the tune. In that I include pick-up notes—that is, going into a line. And when you get through with a line, finish it clean. Play as much of the tune itself as possible, and let the other things like rolls [right-hand fill patterns] be just icings and goodies; because they will only work if the tune is being played clear. Also, concentrate on learning good backup if you're picking with others, and on *when* to do fill-ins—not just *how* to do them. Your rolls and other goodies should be secondary. But intros to a tune, and coming out of a line, are so important. In other words, phrase what you're trying to say. That's my theory.

## A Selected Earl Scruggs Discography

**With The Earl Scruggs Revue** (on Columbia): *Bold & New*, JC-35319; *Country Chart Busters Vol. 1*, C-32718; *Country Chart Busters, Vol. 2*, C-32720; *Dueling Banjos*, C-32268; *Family Portrait*, PC-34336; *I Saw The Light*, C-31354; *Live At Kansas State*, KC-31758; *Nashville's Rock*, CS-1007; *Earl Scruggs—His Family & Friends*, CS-30584; *Earl Scruggs Revue*, KC-32426; *Earl Scruggs Revue, Live From Austin City Limits*, PC-34464; *American Made, World Played*, FC-39586; *Storyteller And The Banjo Man*, FC-37953; *Top Of The World*, FC-38295. **With Lester Flatt:** (on Mercury/Phonogram): *Country Music*, MG-020358; *Flatt And Scruggs With Foggy Mt. Boys*, MG-020542; *The Original Sound Of Lester Flatt*, SR-060773.

# ELIZABETH COTTEN

"Libba" Cotten was discovered while working as a domestic for the Charles Seeger family. Her "Cotten-picking" guitar style, including moving bass runs and basic right-hand picking patterns, have had an enormous influence on folk and blues guitarists. Elizabeth, now 93, recently celebrated her birthday by performing with Taj Mahal. This interview first appeared in the January 1980 issue of *Frets*.

**By Alice Gerrard**

ELIZABETH "LIBBA" COTTEN has had a profound influence on the lives and music of many people. Probably nobody else plays quite like her; and yet her guitar style has had a major impact on the two- and three-finger picking, rhythmic sense, solid timing, and melodic and chordal feeling of both well- and lesser-known guitarists. During the early Fifties, when she worked for Charles and Ruth Crawford Seeger, the Seegers' daughter Peggy picked up and adapted Elizabeth's guitar style to her own playing. Peggy became a successful performer, and the style thus spread to many folksingers of the early Sixties, who in turn influenced others. Elizabeth's songs have been performed and recorded by musicians around the world—particularly her classic, "Freight Train," which she composed as a young girl.

She is an artist with a gift for personalizing her performances, no matter whether she's in front of 50 people or 5,000 people—telling stories, singing songs, playing tunes, and letting everyone know about her life. It's always a great joy to watch and listen to her, and see the interaction that goes on between the audiences, who love her, and Libba, who knows she is loved and who loves them in return.

A strong and determined person, Libba Cotten is proud of herself and her accomplishments. She was born in Chapel Hill, North Carolina, black, female, and poor—which, as things went, didn't present many possibilities in terms of opportunities and free choices in life. As a child, she worked hard to save money to buy a guitar. Passionately determined to learn how to play, she persisted and she succeeded, creating a unique style in the process. This same strength and determination carried her through many hard years.

Libba has been an active performer since 1959. She plays in basically five styles, playing left-handed on instruments that have conventional right-hand stringing. Of first importance is her ragtime or two-finger style, for which she is best known. She plays the three bass strings with her first finger and the three treble melody strings with her thumb, picking one string at a time, alternating between treble and bass (although in her church songs she often plays treble and bass simultaneously). Her unique sound quality comes in part from the reversal of conventional thumb and finger roles. This two-finger style can be heard in her Folkways LP recordings of "Freight Train," on her 1957 album *Negro Folk Songs And Tunes* and on her more recent *When I'm Gone*.

Second is her banjo style, which she sometimes plays on 5-string banjo and sometimes on guitar. "Rattler" and "Georgia Buck," on *Negro Folk Songs And Tunes*, illustrate the style on banjo; on guitar, the style is well illustrated in her recording of "Ruben" on her 1965 album *Shake Sugaree*. In transferring the style to the guitar, she picks melody with her first finger, strums with her second finger, and uses the first string as the thumb string.

In a third style, she utilizes clusters of notes, playing them with her thumb and two or three fingers, often in arpeggios. "Buck Dance" and "Washington Blues," on *Shake Sugaree*, offer good examples of this style.

Fourth, she sometimes plays with a banjo-like roll, as in "Fox Chase" on *Shake Sugaree*. This roll is similar to the pre-Scruggs-style banjo roll.

She uses a fifth style for backing songs that don't particularly lend themselves to melody picking, such as "Time To Stop Your Idling," sung by her granddaughter Johnine Rankin on *When I'm Gone*, and such as the title cut on *Shake Sugaree*. In this style, she picks the bass with her first finger, strums upwards with her other fingers, and sometimes plays the first string with her thumb.

She often mixes these styles within a given song, hardly ever plays her tunes the same way twice, and is constantly improvising. She consciously works with her tunes—adding to them, changing licks, sometimes making almost new tunes out of them.

Today, Libba Cotten plays an OOO-18 Martin from the late 1940s, although in her earlier recordings she used a variety of other guitars—primarily dreadnought Martins. She uses extra-light or silk-and-steel strings, sometimes tuned down a whole step or two.

She uses three tunings: the standard *E-A-D-G-B-E*, bottom to top; another tuning two whole-steps lower, *D-A-D-F♯-A-D*, which she calls her "Vastopol" tuning; and *D-G-D-G-B-D*, which she calls her "Flang Dang" tuning.

In general, her guitar style is a synthesis of turn-of-the-century parlor music, blues, church songs, and a little ragtime, and is heavily influenced by the piano. Her choice of material comes from many sources—songs and tunes she heard growing up, songs and tunes that she composed or helped compose, and the songs and styles of other musicians, that she heard as she began touring more in the mid-'60s.

She has always been open and receptive to different sounds, ever aware of how she might translate or absorb them into her own musical scheme of things. On many different levels, it is an inspiration to know her; and to see how, as she gets older, she becomes more determined than ever to do and be what she wants, and to experience the enjoyment she is getting out of life.

Here now, in her own words, are Libba Cotten's recollections of her upbringing, and her thoughts on her career and her music.

·  ·  ·  ·

**M**AMA CALLED ME "Babe." My daddy called me "Shoat." His name was George Nevills. I don't remember him too much. Sometimes I see pictures on television and it reminds me what I think he should look like. He must've come from around Chatham County, I reckon—I'm just guessing now—but not from Chapel Hill. My mama used to tell me how my daddy's mother was a slave. Her boss was a Nevills or something. That's how they got the name of Nevills, I think I heard Mama say.

In Chapel Hill my daddy worked in a mine. It must've been an iron mine. It was right off the railroad track that I've talked about so much. He was the dynamite setter.

He made liquor when Mama and him used to live in the country. There wasn't much money in the country and he'd make liquor, I guess to sell, and he kept it in jugs just settin' around.

I was small, and after he passed away we would wash for the doctor to pay off Daddy's doctor bills. There wasn't much money in circulation then, and not much for the colored people anyway. We washed for that man, and they'd have the biggest old nasty wash. We'd just hate to see that wash come in.

Louisa Price Nevills. My mama was a second child. I think there was three girls and seven boys. She lived in Siler City, North Carolina. I don't know whether she was born there or not. My mother's father was a hard worker; he worked the children very hard—he

Elizabeth Cotten bought her first guitar for $3.75 when she was 12 years old. She learned to play with treble strings on top and has played that way ever since.

just about made a boy out of her. He was a man who loved to have plenty of everything. They were farmers. That's about the only thing there was at the time for colored people to do. They didn't live close nowhere that they could work for nobody.

Mama was a midwife. She delivered many a child in Chapel Hill and all through the country.

She told me—let me see if I can remember it— maybe it was just told to her—somewhere down in the South, down in Georgia, there was a man burnin' on a log. "That man is burning/Way down in the land of Georgia/That man is burning/He's burning on a log." Where Mama got that song I don't know. It sounds like way down in slavery times didn't it? She used to sing that song to us and she'd tell us about when the Yankees freed the Negroes. She said she was ten years old then. Not too far from where she lived, they had a plank thing that went across the water. She said it was the old plank road. She said when the Yankees freed the Negroes, you could hear the paddle of the horses' feet comin' across the bridge —you could hear it for so long, there'd be so many of them, you'd listen to 'em for a long time. And I think she said that they'd go around to white people's houses and tell the Negroes they was free. And some of 'em would leave and some wouldn't. Some was scared to go and others would take the people at their word and feel they was free.

I can imagine I see her sometime—doing something, you know, and just singing. All them songs. "Hallelujah 'Tis Done"—that's old, old. Mama'd give out her songs and sing 'em. She'd sing the chorus, then she'd stop and give out the verse, and she'd sing the verse, then she'd sing the chorus. Sometimes when I wake up in the night, sometimes a song like that comes to me. Looks like I can just imagine I see her sometime.

It like to killed me when she died. I felt like sayin', "Put me under that thing and cover me up too." I just didn't want to stay without her, you know. But I had to get over that. I just did all I could do, and workin' too.

"I remember, I remember/The house where I was born." That's somethin' we used to say in school. The first record player I ever heard in my life—I was going to school, and the teacher said that this man was coming. And he said, "Now, I want you all to be nice, don't be noisy," and the man brought this great big thing and he set it on top of the table, and this thing had a great big horn. And I remember the teacher telling us, "Now, if you don't behave yourself all he's got to do is to turn that horn. Something will come out of that horn to make you behave yourself." And the records the man put on was round and looked like a rolling pin.

We had a man teacher, and then I remember we had a woman teacher. They didn't want you to talk. They'd have these old long switches. Somethin' would hit your seat. She wouldn't hit you, she'd just hit on the seat. I loved school and sister hated school.

I went about as far as the fourth grade. I don't remember never goin' back to study no more. I started making a little money—my 75 cents a month to buy my guitar.

I'll never forget. There was a man who lived about a block from us, and he let the children come when he'd have this music, and dance in his yard. If any of the children could play any kind of horn, or any kind of music, he'd let 'em come in and join the music, and we'd have a nice time. When we'd hear that bugle, whatever it was he'd blow, we'd begin to worry our parents to let us go. Then when they'd say "Yes—come back here at a certain time," we'd always come back because we wanted to go back the next time. That's where I learned how to dance, waltz, and two-step, do the cake walk, Frisco, buck dance. And I just danced my little head off. My brothers were there and we'd all dance together. In the band they had some kind of horns, the drum, and this big, old guitar—double bass thing. That was years ago.

I was raised up goin' to Sunday school and singing. Everybody'd get a book and sit up there and sing the songs. If there was notes, there was somebody always who would know the notes. And he'd sing it for you and then you'd follow him. We didn't know no notes. He'd know when to tell you to sing or what. "Now, if I'm an alto and you're a soprano, here's the lead. All right, you sing your part, now you sing your part, you sing yours." Well, if you weren't singin' it right, he'd say, "You don't go up on that, you do down," or something for you to know what you were doing.

**Elizabeth gave up the guitar for nearly 40 years until she went to work for the Seeger family. Her career didn't really begin until she was well into her fifties.**

All my mother's brothers played music, every one of them—fiddle and a banjo. I don't remember myself ever trying to pick up a fiddle to play it. The thing I wanted was an organ or piano. My mother wasn't able to get it. I was so full of music, if somebody had just took a little time to find out how full of music I was, give me a few lessons or kind of help me or show me, I'd have been good. I know I would, 'cause I know from where I come from what I learned myself, just me. I think I was so full of it, looked like I could just feel music in myself. My brother had a banjo, and when he left home I didn't have nothin' to play, so I just decided I wanted the guitar.

I wasn't 12 years old and I went to work for this lady, Miss Ada Copeland. She paid me 75 cents a month. I was a lot of help to her. So she said to my mother, "We're going to raise little Sissie's wages." So they gave me a dollar a month. And if you think about it, it sounds like little enough money; but in them days for a child it might've been a good price. My mother was one of the top cooks in Chapel Hill, and she didn't make but only $5.00 a month. But anyway, I saved my money and bought me a guitar. There was only one place in Chapel Hill at that time that you could buy a guitar; that was Mr. Gene Kates's place. He said, "Aunt Lou, I'll tell you the truth. As long as you and your little girl wants a guitar so bad, you can have it for $3.75." And the name of that guitar was Stella. And I liked my guitar so very, very much, and that's when I began to learn how to play.

I had two brothers [then at home]; they played, and my sister, she chorded, but nobody had no music. They didn't know nothin' about no music. They just played, like all country people get together and play songs. I learn yours and you learn mine and just keep on like that. But I didn't even have that much chance when I was learning. Nobody to help me to play. I wanted music so bad I could just feel it.

I had learned a banjo upside down and I couldn't change [the strings] because it belonged to my brother. Then when I bought the guitar, so much was said like, "You better change the strings, you can't play it left-handed," that they was changed as much as two or three times. And I could *not* play it. I couldn't play it, I couldn't tune it, I couldn't do anything with it. So I just sat down and took all the strings off, then I put 'em back on the old way and I stopped askin'. I started playing, learning different little tunes on it. I'd get one little string and then add another little string to it and get a little sound, then start playing.

The first thing I did, I laid the guitar flat in my lap and I worked my left hand until I could play the strings backwards and forwards. And then after I got so I could do that, then I started to chord it and get the sound of a song—a song that I'd know, and if it weren't but one string I'd get that. Then finally, I'd add another string to that, and I kept on until I could work my fingers pretty good. And that's how I started playing with two fingers. And after I played with two fingers for a while, I started using three. And then I remember I'd start with my little finger, but I can't do it now. I guess all that was learning how, then. I was just trying to see what I could do.

My sister used to sing. We'd sing songs—like if I was singing a song and if I didn't know it right good, she'd jump in and help me. We'd sing songs, sitting by the lamplight singing and playing. I just loved to play. When I learned one little tune, I'd be so proud of that, that I'd want to learn another. Then I'd just keep sitting up, trying. You know a tune and you just learn it. Just keep the tune in your mind and just keep on workin' with it until you get something. The way I do, I play it to my own sound, the way I think it sounds.

You just put the sounds together, and what sounds all right you just go on with it. And all of them little things I play, that's the way I got it. I don't know nothing about no notes; I can't read music. You just get a song and know it and just keep fooling around with it till you get it to sound like you want it to sound.

Music is a funny thing. It's something you love. I don't know, it's just something comes in you, comes from inside of you. Comes out. And you can shut your eyes and go with it and repeat it. I'd pretend I was pickin' up my guitar and keep right up with the tune I was playing and never hadn't heard it before, wouldn't know what it would be until I had it in my mind to hum it. I can't do it now. That's how I got all of that when I was growin' up.

When I was in my teens, I got religion on that song "Holy Ghost Unchain My Name." After I was baptized, the deacons told me, "You cannot live for God and live for the devil. If you're going to play them old worldly songs, them old-time things, you can't serve God that way. You've either got to do one or the other. "Well, I got to thinking about it. I just gradually stopped playing. I didn't stop all at once 'cause I couldn't, I loved my guitar too good. And then it weren't too long until I got married, and that helped me to stop because then I started housekeeping.

I think the first time [my husband] Frank asked me to go with him to church, we'd just been playing ball together, just schoolchildren. And I went with him to church and that was it. We run away, then we got married [February 1910]. Then we went home the next day. We stayed at Mama's house, then finally we rented a house. We bought a stove and a little chair; we bought a bed and a dresser. And his sisters went downtown, and they bought me some very pretty curtains and I put them up. And I was keepin' house. My own boss. Nobody to say, "Go in the kitchen and wash the dishes, make up your bed, straighten up that floor, pick up." Did it if I wanted to and if I didn't, I didn't do it. Nobody tell me to. And I was so proud of that place.

It liked to have killed my mama. She said, "Why did you marry like that?" He say, "Get married," I say "Sure." You think you love one another, I reckon. I married at the age of 15. Birthed my baby when I was 16. And I didn't never have no more.

*Elizabeth and Frank Cotten, and their daughter Lillie, variously moved back and forth between Washington, D.C.; Chapel Hill; and New York City. Then Frank moved to New York, where he had a job as a chauffeur and later became the first black mechanic to operate his own business on South Broadway. At first, Elizabeth and Lillie remained in Chapel Hill, where Elizabeth was working. Eventually, both she and her daughter moved to New York to be with Frank and to get better wages. Lillie went to school in Yonkers and Elizabeth did day-work— cleaning, cooking, and working in a furniture store. The family lived in New York until Lillie got married; then Elizabeth and Frank were divorced. Ultimately, as children and grandchildren gradually moved to Washington, D.C., Elizabeth settled there, living with Lillie. She spent much of her time doing day-work for white families, and helped to raise her grandchildren and great-grandchildren.*

I'd never get up in time to have breakfast 'cause you'd have to go so far for your work. Usually they'd offer you a cup of coffee or say, "Would you like a slice of toast?" Well, if you have that you can go a long time on it, you know. You can go from then to lunch, anyway. But some of them didn't offer you anything. I'd go there in the rain, go there in the cold, be wet, and when I'd get there I'd say, "Ooh, bad rain this mornin', certainly is rainin'." They'd be upstairs eating and I'd think sure they'd call me after a while and give me a cup of coffee or a slice of toast or bread—anything. Nothin'.

I applied at Lansburgh's Department Store for work before the holidays; that must have been '47 or '48, somewhere along there. They hired me and they gave me a job up on the fifth floor with dolls. Mrs. Seeger [composer Ruth Crawford Seeger] came in the store. She bought two dolls from me and a little lamb. She brought her two girls with her. While the dolls were getting wrapped, Peggy wandered off. I found Peggy. When I brought her back to her mother, her mother says to me, "Have you worked here long?" and I told her, "No." And she says, "If you ever decide to stop working here, here's my telephone number. Give me a ring sometime." So when I stopped working for Lansburgh's I did call her, and I took the job to give them lunch on Saturdays and dinner, plus the other work I was doing.

That was nice times. Just work, and nobody standin' over you with a stick sayin', "You're gonna do this and then the other." I know what I have to do when I go there. No, "Do you think you'll get a chance to rub the silver today?" Nothin' like that.

*At about the time Libba Cotten went to work for the Seegers, Peggy Seeger was learning how to play guitar, Ruth Seeger gave piano lessons, and the whole family often sang on Saturday nights with Charles or Peggy playing guitar and Mike playing autoharp. Ruth Seeger was also in the process of compiling a collection of folk songs for children and she collected a few songs from Libba.*

I had forgot I could play guitar. Then when I went to work for them I heard all that music. I said, "I used to could play the guitar," and I decided to play it. I got [Peggy's] guitar and started playing. I was just playing what I had learned how to play down in Chapel Hill, and the more I could play it the better I could play it. When I first started playing it was kind of hard. I couldn't make it sound like I used to. But by playing it a little bit every morning—see Mrs. Seeger would go in there and start her music, I'd go in the other room and start mine, and I'd feel so good after I'd do that.

You don't mind doin' somethin' if it's somethin' you like. Just like playin'. I don't mind pickin', playing a few songs, get some money for it. 'Cause I know what I'm doin' it for.

I get to travel and get to go places. There ain't no other way in the world I'd ever get to go to the places I've been since I've been doing this kind of work. No way, no way. 'Cause I'd never have the money to do that, and I wouldn't know where to go. See, they send me places and tell me where I'm goin'.

Motels, hotels, and homes. A motel, it's so comfortable. You can play there, get undressed and just walk around, get your bath. You do what you want to do, just lay on the bed and study your music if you've got any you want to study; tune the guitar two, three ways, see if you can tune it in a chord that you can sing songs.

I'm trying to do what people want to hear. Lord knows I hate to sometimes set up there and tell the same story. So many times I don't want to talk. And sometimes I don't do much talking. And I look at people when the concert's over and I feel like I haven't done my part of what they would like to hear. So each time I just try to do a whole lot of singin' and a whole lot of talking. If you was to just give a concert, just sing, tell the name of the song if you want to—now that would please me to death. But I try to do it all to suit them. That's what keeps me goin' now. Look like I been tellin' it 20 years. They ought to know everything about me—ain't no more about me to know. I done told them everything from childhood up, from 11 years to 87. Now what can I tell?

So that's like it is.

But it's a little easier than workin', sure enough.

---

**A Selected Elizabeth Cotten Discography**
(On Folkways): *Negro Folk Songs And Tunes*, FG 3526; *Shake Sugaree*, FT 10003; *When I'm Gone*, FS 3537.

# PEGGY SEEGER

Peggy is an outstanding instrumentalist on banjo, autoharp, and guitar, whose appreciation and performances of British Isles folk music helped widen its popularity. A member of America's first family of folk, the sister of Mike Seeger, and half-sister of Pete, Peggy's interest in folk music was sparked at a young age. She married Scottish songwriter Ewan MacColl in 1958 and has spent the greater part of her career in the British Isles, where she is even more well known than she is in America.

## By Mark Greenberg

THIRTY YEARS AGO banjo playing was mainly a masculine preoccupation. But Peggy Seeger never let that stop her. "I was always told the banjo was a boy's instrument," she says, recalling the beginnings of a three-decades-long love affair with the 5-string. "I didn't have any feminist leanings then. I just loved hanging around in jeans, letting my hair hang loose, looking natural. And the banjo was a way of being different."

Today she remains one of the most influential folk banjo players, still following an approach that built a personal style out of traditional elements. In the process, she also brought a rare understanding and sensitivity to the much overlooked art of folk-style accompaniment.

That art is demonstrated by Peggy on guitar, dulcimer, autoharp, and concertina, as well as on banjo. On all of these she has sought to maintain a creed she stated 20 years ago, in the notes to her album *American Folk Songs For Banjo:* "The one and only reason for an accompaniment is to enhance the song, to allow it to flow in complementary surroundings. Accompaniment should be built from the simplest form up to whatever the player will finally use."

Strong as they are, however, Peggy Seeger's instrumental abilities represent only part of her accomplishments. As a singer and songwriter she has worked to broaden people's awareness of traditional songs and of contemporary issues, while also growing as an artist in both subtlety and sureness. Alone, and in her partnership with her husband, Scottish singer/writer/actor Ewan MacColl, Peggy has written some of the most widely-known topical folksongs, ranging from the early "Springhill Mine Disaster" to the women's Declaration of Independence, "I'm Gonna Be An Engineer."

For Peggy Seeger, born in 1935, folk music was simply part of what must have been a quite extraordinary childhood. Her parents, musicologist Charles Seeger and composer Ruth Crawford Seeger, had moved to Washington D.C. to work with the Resettlement Administration. Later her mother worked as music editor of *Our Singing Country* with Alan and John Lomax. The latter was curator of the newly-created Archive of American Folksong. As a result, "The old greats were always drifting in and out—the Leadbellys, Woody Guthries, Pete Seegers," she recalls.

Pete, Peggy's older half brother, was already out on his own, sowing the seeds of the Folk Revival. Closer to her own age was her brother Mike; together they shared a passion for America's traditional music and often gained a direct exposure to the people who were making it. It was while working for the Seeger family that Elizabeth Cotten revealed her remarkable left-handed guitar style and introduced the folk music world to her composition, "Freight Train."

"The kind of thing that took place in our house for the first 10 or 15 years of my life has never really left me," Peggy recalls. "From as far back as I can remember we sang, and I was always associated with an instrument of some sort. I didn't learn so much as absorb, as osmose."

Peggy's first official instrument, at age seven, was the piano, which she approached as though it were a folk instrument. "When I first learned to play the piano," she notes, "I would try to copy what I heard on the folk records—music which was usually played on guitar and banjo." Her mother used the same technique to compose piano settings for the folksong collections she had begun to publish. Peggy describes the method as "almost Bartokian—she would create as the folk create. She would listen to what the banjo player did and not copy it exactly on piano, but make

something that sounded like it."

That attitude, however, did not sit well with Peggy's first guitar teacher. "When I was 10," she says, "I took up the guitar, but not seriously. I was asked if I wanted to study with Sophocles Papas, who was one of Segovia's teachers. I went for one lesson and just memorized the music by ear. He said, 'No, no, you look at the music and play it exactly as it is there. Or you have no lessons with me.' So I had no lessons with him—because I couldn't grasp that idea of music."

Her own ideas seemed to work well enough, and Peggy eventually acquired a reputation for her guitar fingerpicking and banjo frailing. "I was a compulsive player," Peggy says of the banjo. "I just couldn't lay it down. I learned every possible thing, including Scruggs. And when I discovered frailing, Scruggs' style just became meaningless to me."

Peggy credits Pete Seeger with helping to start her frailing. "Pete taught me an awful lot of banjo. I used to spend the summers up at his house. I don't know where he found the time, but if I'd say, 'Pete, show me that,' he'd show me. He's a very patient man."

One of the ideas that Peggy gleaned from her half-brother was that of playing a long-necked banjo. Her first banjo had been an old S.S. Stewart that she shared with Mike. Later, however, she switched and acquired the first long-necked Vega Pete Seeger model.

Her guitar at the time was a Tatay. In 1970, Mike brought her a Martin New Yorker [*that is, a C.F. Martin guitar dating from before 1898*], which languished on the shelf while Peggy continued to play a Mogford nylon-string guitar. "I had this thing about playing ethnic," Peggy says, laughing. "For goodness sake, *steel* strings are ethnic. Where'd I ever get the idea that nylon strings are the only way to play?" Finally, one day, Peggy picked up the old Martin. "I fell in love with it. It was a total takeover. I was playing for two or three hours a day, the guitar was so beautiful." She's been playing it ever since, except for a period when Peter Abnett, an instrument maker from Rochester, Kent, in England, was restoring it after it suffered major damage. "It fell off the mantlepiece onto the stone fireplace," says Peggy with a wince. "It was in about 20 pieces."

By the late 1950s, Peggy Seeger enjoyed the admiration of growing numbers of folk music revivalists, through her concerts and recordings. In particular, the Folkways release *American Folk Songs For Banjo*, spotlighted her instrumental originality and versatility. Many songs featured rippling accompaniments, some in 3/8 or 6/8 time, based on guitar arpeggios.

Rather more spectacular was her note-for-note rendering of a group of fiddle tunes, including "Devil's Dream," in a three-finger style that foreshadowed Bill Keith's "melodic" arrangement of a few years later. The basic principle of both the Seeger and Keith versions was that no two successive notes be played on the same string. Peggy's explanation is disarmingly simple: "You cast around on the frets to see where you can pick up the notes you want. It was the easiest way to play fiddle tunes with any speed."

Interestingly, Seeger used her right-hand thumb, first, and *third* fingers for this type of picking. Her second finger was reserved for frailing, which she did with a fingerpick worn backwards. Today, she frails without the pick and uses her second finger mostly for the "brushing down" frailing stroke (the first half of the second beat).

Peggy also dismisses much of her early work today, calling it "soulless" and lacking in "pulse." "The rhythm is there," she says, trying to pinpoint the element of pulse. "But there's something missing. I feel a lot of my earlier records were very immature. I don't like to listen to them. It's really only the records in the last four or five years that are enjoyable for me. A lot of my early records were just too fast.

"This is one of the problems with getting good on an instrument," she continues. "You want to show how good you are; and the best way of showing how good you are is to show how fast you can play without making a mistake. Of course, some people do get both speed and pulse. [Virginia banjo player] Hobart Smith got it. He was one of the best banjo players I think I've ever heard—even when he was playing slow, which wasn't very often." Other old-timers whose playing Peggy admires include Buell Kazee and Clarence Ashley.

Many of Peggy's attitudes toward music and playing jelled after she moved to England, where she met and married Ewan MacColl in 1958. She also became heavily involved in British traditional music and in the developing folk movement there. As in America, her skill with fashioning accompaniments proved useful and influential. "I was the only banjo player on the scene—and guitar player too—who really understood what to do with the Scots and English songs. What I was trying to do was to accompany songs that had not been accompanied for two hundred years."

Everybody else, Peggy points out, was trying to fit this essentially modal music into a three-chord, diatonic format. "But I understood the modes," she adds, "because my mother had made me understand them. So I would not play a tune in a mixolydian mode (*G-A-B-C-D-E-F-G*) by putting a chord which had the raised seventh (*F#*) in it. Every song is different. You have to find something that will fit it."

Seeger's interest in accompaniments and her respect for the primacy of the song led her, along with MacColl, to investigate the music of a wide range of related cultures. That led to her discovering a number of musical constants—constants she found could be applied to a variety of traditional accompaniment styles.

"First of all, the drone principle is used over and over," Peggy asserts. "This is a principle that classical music doesn't particularly like. I began to think that a lot of the principles of classical music were developed purely and simply so they wouldn't be like the rude sorts who were doing this naturally. Another thing that they always teach you in classical music is that your accompaniment should never be parallel to the song. And yet this is universal in folk music—the instrument follows the tune all the way through, which necessitates the accompanist's knowing every word and the way the person who's singing is going to do it.

"Another principle was that of having a textured accompaniment, which we know in our simplest form as just um-chunk-chunk, um-chunk-chunk." Instruments, Seeger points out, are capable of producing different textures based on the duration for which notes can be sustained—short (banjo), medium (violin), or long (bagpipe).

By employing these principles, particularly when accompanying British songs, Peggy attempts to preserve the integrity of the song itself and to retain its connection with tradition. "We found that a singer would sing a song differently when it was unaccompanied than when they accompanied it. It would mean speeding up, singing in a different key, even pronouncing the words differently. One thing we've always said is that if the singer has to change the song at all, then something is wrong with the accompaniment."

Although she recognizes the skill of many of the more recent crop of British folk-based guitarists, Peggy finds that their virtuosity often overpowers the songs. "I suppose," she says, "that it's hard for somebody who is very good at an instrument to withdraw to the background. My response to that was to not be so good at the instrument. I have a number of styles that I can play very efficiently. And I can create a nice bed of sound for the song to be sung over.

"But," she adds with the firm determination that has marked her career since her decision to take up the banjo, "people darned well better know what the song is about when I finish."

---

## A Selected Peggy Seeger Discography

*American Folk Songs*, Folkways, FLW 2005; *Animal Folk Songs For Children*, Folkways, FLW 7551; *At The Present Moment*, Rounder, 4003; *Folksongs And Ballads Of Courting And Complaint*, Folkways, FLW 2049; *Manchester Angel*, Tradition Records, TRD 2059; *New Briton Gazette*, Folkways, FLW 8734; *Now Is The Time For Fishing*, Folkways, FLW 3507; *Other Songs Of The Whaling Era*, Rounder, 4011; *Traditional Songs And Ballads Of Scotland*, Folkways, FLW 8760; *Two-Way Trip*, Folkways, FLW 8755; *Whaler Out Of New Bedford*, Folkways, FLW 3850; *Freeborn Man*, Rounder, 3080.

# NEW LOST CITY RAMBLERS

During the late '50s when folk music began to become commercially popular, the New Lost City Ramblers established themselves as the foremost representatives of authentic American string band traditions. Though they no longer perform together regularly, John Cohen, Tracy Schwarz, and Mike Seeger still regroup occasionally for concerts at East Coast folk festivals. The group was profiled in *Frets* October 1979 issue.

**By Mark Greenberg**

AMERICA WAS EAGERLY awaiting the next hearty pop-folk song from the neatly-packaged Kingston Trio back in 1958 when three rather mismatched young men—Mike Seeger, John Cohen, and Tom Paley—decided to pool their musical talents, instruments, records, and tapes and become the New Lost City Ramblers.

The success of the Kingston Trio's "Tom Dooley," a song taken from North Carolina fretless banjo maker/player Frank Proffitt, was spawning a rash of short-sleeved urban folk groups, each armed with well-scrubbed versions of songs from rural sources.

What was unusual about the Ramblers, aside from their name and perhaps the length of their shirt sleeves, was that they were moving in an entirely different direction.

The Ramblers were attracted to the soulful sound and free-swinging vitality of the southern string band music recorded in the '20s by commercial record companies and the Library of Congress. They decided to stay as close to their sources as possible. Others had collected this music and a few had studied it; but virtually no one had performed it—in its own style—until Mike, John, and Tom rambled along.

Twenty-one years, 15 albums, and one personnel change—Tracy Schwarz replaced Paley in 1962—later, the evidence of the Ramblers influence is everywhere: from the numerous old-time bands, both amateur and professional, scattered across the country, to the recognition received by such traditional artists as Elizabeth Cotten, Dock Boggs, and Roscoe Holcomb, to widespread interest in many kinds of ethnic music and the growth of independent folk music record companies. The terms "old-time music" and "traditional music" may not be household words, but they are now commonplace in a musical world that can credit the New Lost City Ramblers for much of the expansion that it has undergone in the past couple of decades.

It was not always so. "Playing traditional music in a traditional way was a very innovative thing to do," banjo and guitar player John Cohen recently recalled. Cohen now divides most of his time between teaching art at the Purchase campus of New York State University and working on films concerned with traditional music and culture.

Mike Seeger, whose instrumental talents include fiddle, autoharp, mandolin, jews-harp, and mouth-harp, along with banjo and guitar, agrees. The first Rambler to actively pursue a solo career, Seeger now lives outside of Washington, D.C., the city in which he spent his formative years and which helped to make him, in his own words, a "border rider."

"We wanted to present the music in an honest fashion, which—as far as we were concerned—was not being done then," stated Seeger. "We were fighting the rube-hillbilly image, playing with it occasionally. We were pushing the audience. Usually we'd put in a few things that were hard for them, trying to reach them, but trying to challenge them as well."

Conceived more or less by accident, on June 1, 1958, the Ramblers have been, from the very start, a loose collection of strong individuals, sharing a vision yet never quite able to behave like a group. Cohen and Paley had met at Yale, where John was a fine arts student and Tom was a mathematics instructor. They had begun getting together to play the old-time music that they had both listened to in their native New York City on odd radio programs and on such early anthologies as Alan Lomax's *Mountain Frolic*. Paley, already something of a legendary character among budding revivalists for his stunning command of old-time guitar and banjo styles, moved on to the University of Maryland. When Cohen, now a freelance photographer living among the poets and artists of Greenwich Village, came down for a visit they accepted an invitation to play on John Dildine's Washington, D.C., folk music radio program. Joined by Seeger, who knew Paley from Washington-area parties and who had begun documenting traditional and bluegrass music for Folkways Records, they hastily ran through pieces of a few tunes in a back room at the station, then went on the air.

They all agree that it was the fiddle, at that time rarely found in folk music circles, that brought things together, the keystone for realizing an authentic rural sound. The resulting music was "pretty sloppy," according to Paley, who has been living in Europe since leaving the Ramblers, occasionally returning to the U.S. for some appearances. "But it was kind of alive at the same time," he says. "It was a promising sound. There really was something there, and we decided that we ought to do something about it." What they did was to find a name, for which Cohen receives the honors; arrange a debut concert at Carnegie Recital Hall; and make a record for Folkways—all within a few months.

Though they hardly met with mass success ("long-playing, short-selling" for many years has been Seeger's epithet for their albums) the Ramblers delighted the critics. In a thoroughly laudatory review of their appearance at New York's swank Blue Angel Supper Club, *New York Times* critic Robert Shelton found their "undiluted blend" of traditional music to be "as acerbic as apple cider," while blues and jazz collector/writer Pete Welding, writing in *Sing Out!*, labeled them "insidious crusaders for old-time music."

"Part of our function—a large part—was to get the word out," says Cohen, who is no longer entirely comfortable with the Ramblers-as-educators image. "We were acknowledging our sources—that was the least we could do. But we weren't up there giving an illustrated lecture. The idea was to help people get into it, as well as to convey the way we felt about the music—that this was something older than us, something that we valued, and that we respected the artists who gave it to us and the people who collected the artists. Those things were interesting and fun."

Fun, perhaps even more than their instrumental virtuosity, was the key to the eye- and ear-opening effect that the Ramblers had on their early coffee-house and campus audiences. Dressed in their un-identical grey uniforms of shirt-tie-vest, they would come briskly out on the stage, deposit an assortment of cases, extract some instruments, plunk some, tune some, adjust the few microphones, tune some more, maybe talk some, then launch into a loose-jointed, knock-down string band instrumental. It was like watching a Depression-era photograph spring to life. Between tunes, amidst the constant switching of instruments necessitated by the variety of styles they presented, and the endless bouts of tuning (for which the group, especially the irrepressible Paley, was becoming infamous), the Ramblers practiced "creative folklore," sniped at each other in stage-whispers, and provoked delighted hisses and groans from the audience with their barrages of puns and comical song titles: "I'm So Miserable Without You, It's Almost Like Having You Here," or "It's So Lonesome In The Saddle Since My Horse Died." On their most recent album, *Twenty Years Of Live Performance*, "Browns Ferry Blues" and "Foggy Mountain

**The latter-day Ramblers (Left to right) Mike Seeger, Tracy Schwarz, John Cohen.**

Top" capture the infectious irreverence of the group's first years.

"Those were high times," says Seeger of 1960 and 1961. During those years the Ramblers had gathered a zealous underground following and seemed on the threshold of a wider popularity that never, however, materialized.

Cohen, too, remembers those times fondly, also forgetting for a moment the continual hassles of trying to keep the show on the road and the instruments in tune. One occasion especially stands out, an early New York concert during which Cohen planned to surprise Paley with a guitar rigged to break when tuned. But Paley caught on, forcing Cohen to salvage his joke by wrecking the guitar himself. "I took the guitar and hurled it down on the stage and jumped on it—pre Who," says Cohen. "Tom look at the guitar and said, 'That guitar's flat, John!'"

Yet, even as they were making "old-timey" a favored campus adjective and inspiring growing numbers of young fiddle, banjo, and guitar players across the country (many of whom, such as mandolinist David Grisman and ragtime guitarist Eric Schoenberg, well-known acoustic musicians today), the Ramblers were finding their personal differences to be too much in the way. Paley left in 1962 and was replaced by Tracy Schwarz, whose childhood radio listening to cowboy music and to country and western music led to a growing involvement with old-time music and bluegrass.

With Paley gone, the Ramblers lost much of their on-stage craziness as well as a major old-time instrumental side of their sound. What they gained was a blossoming bluegrass fiddler as well as an all-around instrumentalist, and a strong singer with real country feeling.

Schwarz's singing and fiddling allowed the Ramblers to broaden their already expressive repertoire. Where their earlier music had centered on recordings made in the '20s and '30s, their interests now shifted forwards, towards the '40s, with an occassional nod to later music as well. Both Schwarz

and Seeger had earlier involvements with bluegrass, and it was only natural that songs in the early bluegrass styles of the Mainers and the Stanley Brothers should begin to appear in Ramblers' performances. Cajun music, a developing interest of Seeger's, became Schwarz's passion as Tracy came under the influence of Louisiana's Balfa Brothers. His Cajun-style fiddling, singing, and later, button-accordian playing, added a whole new sound to the repertoire. In additon, Schwarz began singing unaccompanied ballads, often the most moving part of a Ramblers concert, carrying the music back further in time.

"There were no rules in old-time music," according to Mike Seeger. In the days before the onslaught of the phonograph record and the radio, "everybody had their own style pretty much. People would talk differently. The musicians before media were extremely unique, because they framed their styles of playing very much on their own."

It was largely that great variety of sounds and styles that attracted the Ramblers to old-time music. Unlike some of the newer old-time bands that have focused on one style, the Ramblers have remained what Seeger calls a "repertory" band, drawing on many varieties of the music, at times recombining them to make new ones. Though they have always paid close attention to their recorded sources, which "sometimes meant learning something note-for-note to get its flavor," according to Schwarz, the Ramblers have generally avoided strict limitations. "The Ramblers have always had their own way of doing things, their signature," Tracy said. Cohen elaborated the same theme, "We used those old records as a basis for our own musical liberation. We did get ideas off the records, but we certainly didn't go out of our way to get the exact sound. We got *towards* the sound. We had to be true to ourselves and also true to this music that was setting us loose."

Both Seeger and Cohen had done important field work that resulted in the discovery and recording of such people as North Carolina ballad singer Dillard Chandler; and banjo player Dock Boggs, whose unique, haunting white blues had first been recorded in the '20s. In 1966 a tour of Europe was arranged with the Ramblers presiding over an assortment of musicians that included Roscoe Holcomb, Cousin Emmy, the Stanley Brothers, and the Cajun band of Adam and Cyp Landreneau.

In their dedication to getting back to the real thing and to the freedom and experimentalism of old-time music, the Ramblers were, if not a cause, at least a harbinger of the musical awakening of the '60s. Still traveling mostly from campus to campus, the ever-acoustic Ramblers began crossing paths with old fans who were now notable figures in the counter culture. Among them were the Grateful Dead's Jerry Garcia, Canned Heat's Al Wilson, and the Byrds' Roger McGuinn, Chris Hillman, and Clarence White.

As the Ramblers rubbed off on the '60s, so did the '60s rub off on the Ramblers. At one end of the spectrum there was a rally in North Carolina in support of striking textile workers. Seeger recollects: "I sang 'Cotton Hill Colic' and it was as if the song had been written for them." At the opposite end was the 1968 Sky River Rock Festival, near Seattle, with thousands of stoned revelers wildly greeting the clear-eyed Ramblers' weird and funky music.

This socialization of the Ramblers and their music, begun in the '60s, continued as the group moved into its second decade. Fostered by such groups as the Greengrass Cloggers and the recently-defunct Highwood String Band, a renewed interest in country dancing began emerging in the '70s. The Ramblers welcomed this development and acknowledged their debt to these younger pickers and dancers by having them participate, along with Elizabeth Cotten and Pete Seeger, in their Twentieth Anniversary concert, held in 1978 at Carnegie Hall.

So things are pretty quiet today in New Lost City, but the Ramblers will continue to get together a few times a year for special events. Mike, always the most musically active Rambler, now tours both as a soloist and with his wife, Alice Gerrard. His emphasis has fallen more and more on home-style music, the way it was made before the media came to the mountains. Tracy went back to school for an education degree, then began devoting himself more to his farm. Together with Mike he formed the now-disbanded Strange Creek Singers, which leaned more towards bluegrass and modern country music, and which also included Alice Gerrard, Hazel Dickens, and Lamar Grier. More recently, he has been performing with his wife, Eloise, and his 11-year old son, Peter. In addition to his continuing involvement with Cajun music, Tracy has recently begun to attack the complexities of the pedal steel guitar. Partly as a response to the 1968 Democratic Convention in Chicago, which left him feeling that "politics on a national scale looked like a disaster," John turned his attention, both politically and musically, to more local matters. He formed the Putnam String County Band, which combined old-time style with contemporary social concerns. The band, which also included Jay Ungar, Lyn Ungar, Abby Newton, and local Hudson Valley fiddler Bud Snow, broke up when Jay joined David Bromberg. But it still regroups for a yearly command performance at the Town Crier in Beekman, New York, close to home. Today, John often plays late into the night on a fretless banjo and tries, with his family's sufferance, to learn the fiddle.

Coming on stage with lots of stringed instruments was a staple for any Rambler's show. Here's what Mike Seeger, John Cohen, and Tracy Schwarz have to say about the variety of instruments they use on stage.

· · · ·

**W**HAT HAVE THE *Ramblers' concert instruments usually been?*

**Mike:** A Martin dreadnought, a pearl Martin, my [Gibson] Mastertone flat-head [banjo], John's [Vega] Whyte Layde [banjo], an F-5 [Gibson mandolin] post-Loar, a junky fiddle that I had, and a good fiddle that Tracy had. In the early years I used an Oscar Schmidt Autoharp. Now I use a hand-built Tom Morgan autoharp with a carved top. In the early days, people always looked over our instruments, and I still have a coule of odd ones. I have a plastic resonator guitar that we had fun with. I used a flour sack for a case, and we played the guitar with the flour sack around it so that we kept our chords secret. We've used banjo-guitar and banjo-mandolin sometimes, just to get a funky sound.

[Gibson] Mastertone flat-head [banjo], John's [Vega] Whyte Layde [banjo], an F-5 [Gibson mandolin] post-Loar, a junky fiddle that I had, and a good fiddle that Tracy had. In the early years I used an Oscar Schmidt Autoharp. Now I use a hand-built Tom Morgan autoharp with a carved top. In the early days, people always looked over our instruments, and I still have a coule of odd ones. I have a plastic resonator guitar that we had fund with. I used a flour sack for a case, and we played the guitar with the flour sack around it so that we kept our chords secret. We've used banjo-guitar and banjo-mandolin sometimes, just to get a funky sound.

*What is it like switching instruments on virtually every song?*

**John:** To even consider bringing that many instruments onto a stage is silly, and to consider tuning them is even sillier. I interpret it as our desire to get the sound right.

**Mike:** It's necessary for the repertory aspect of the group, though it's difficult. It makes it not as good musically sometimes, because you have to make the mental adjustment from one instrument to another.

*What instruments do you have in your personal collections?*

**Tracy:** I've got a few good instruments. There's a nice 1929 Martin OOO-28 guitar that a guy brought down to my house. I hate to have a real good instrument. You get in the ridiculous position where the instrument gets so valuable that you don't take it on the road with you anymore. So I just take a Japanese guitar. We call them "airline guitars"—plywood things. I've got a nice old Dobro, only it's not got as good a tone as some. One of the Dopera brothers said it was one of the first ten. I've nothing special in the way of banjos, except that Eloise has a nice old banjeaurine. I've got just a standard old Fender Artist's Model. In the early days of the Ramblers, I found a Joseph Schweitzer fiddle in a pawnshop. A lot of people like that fiddle. I was looking for a brassy one you can hear above a band. I've got my grandfather's fiddle. It's got real good tone for Cajun music. I'd like to get a nice Steiner some day just for playing around home. You have to be right on the microphone with them. That's what [old-time Texas fiddler] Eck Robertson had.

**John:** I finally had to sell my favorite guitar. It was a converted Martin OO-42-H, "H" meaning Hawaiian. It was on a lot of our records. The top started to become an arch-top instead of a flat-top. I traded it at [New York dealer] Matt Umanov's for another pretty good [Martin] guitar, an OOO-something-or-other. I've got an old D-28, a 1936 herringbone. I can't play it professionally. The insurance rates would be too high. For banjos, I have an old Vega-Fairbanks Whyte Laydie. I think the rim is Vega and the neck is Fairbanks. But they're both very old. Roscoe (Holcomb) used it on his early recordings, also.

*How do you feel about the proliferation of method books and records that claim to teach traditional music techniques and styles?*

**Tracy:** It would be hard for me to criticize the whole idea, because I produced a fiddle instruction record [*Learn To Fiddle Country Style*, Folkways]. I think it's good because it gets people started. They're good as long as you don't consider them the last word—even my own. Books are much harder to learn from than records.

**Mike:** I think that tablature can be very unfortunate, because some people don't listen to the music enough. You've got to listen to the music in order to make it.

*Any preferences as to strings, picks, other paraphernalia?*

**Mike:** I've always considered paraphernalia as a means to an end: I've begun playing more without picks and with lighter strings, because they used lighter strings before 1930. Most Martin guitars, for instance, weren't braced for steel strings until then, so you played with gut strings. And banjos had gut strings too. So I'm getting more with smaller guitars, and skin—not plastic—banjo hides, and both gut and light-steel strings.

**Tracy:** To me, the important thing is the way the instrument's played. You could pick up a matchbook and play if you put feeling into it.

---

## A Selected New Lost City Ramblers Discography
**Solo albums** (on Folkways) *Earth Is Earth*, FF-869; *Gone To The Country*, FA-2491; *Instrumental*, FA-2492; *Modern Times*, FTS-31027; *New Lost City Ramblers, Vol. 1, 2, 3, 4, 5*, FA-2396, 7, 8, 9, 5; *Old Timey Songs For Children*, FC-7064; *On The Great Divide*, FTS-31041; *Remembrance Of Things To Come*, FTS-31035; *Sing Songs Of The New Lost City Ramblers*, FA-2494; *Songs From The Depression*, FH-5264; *Songs Of Moonshine And Prohibition*, FH-5263; *The "New" New Lost City Ramblers*, FA-2491; *20 Years Of Concert Performances*, Flying Fish, FLF 102; **With Others:** *Folk Festival At Newport, Vol. 2*, Vanguard, VRS-9063; *Newport Folk Festival 1959-60*, Folkways, FA-2432; *Songs Of The Civil War*, Folkways, FH-5719; *The Folk Box*, Elektra; *The Newport Folk Festival*, Vanguard, VRS-9083-4.

# ODETTA

One of the most versatile voices in folk music, Odetta's style is a mixture of blues, jazz, gospel, and folk influences. This singer-guitarist-actress (she has also worked in opera) has been immensely popular with audiences of all ages for more than three decades. Her career was profiled in *Frets* April 1981 issue.

**By Robert Yelin**

ODETTA'S TALENT, IT has been said, doesn't plead for acceptance. It demands it. That majestic ability, which established her as the queen of folk music even before the folk boom of the '60s swept so many other artists to prominence, has made her one of the most important and respected performers in the American music scene.

Bob Dylan, the late Janis Joplin, and a host of other singers have traced their inspiration to folk music that Odetta recorded and performed. She has sung with symphony orchestras, headlined at major festivals, and won resounding ovations from audiences at clubs, concert halls, coffeehouses, and college campuses throughout the country—as well as in Europe, Japan, Scandinavia, Australia, Canada, the Middle East, Africa, and the Soviet Union. Since she made her first LP in 1956, she has recorded more

than 15 albums, in association with seven record companies. And she also has won critical acclaim for her acting in films and stage plays, and earned an award for a special television performance with singer Harry Belafonte.

Born in Birmingham, Alabama, on New Year's Eve in 1930, Odetta began her musical training in Los Angeles, where her family moved when she was six. Her first lessons were on piano, but as a teenager she changed her emphasis to classical singing. She wasn't exposed to folk music until she was 19, while acting in a San Francisco production of the musical *Finian's Rainbow*. She was deeply affected by the new experience and by the atmosphere of social reform in which she discovered it.

Her career as a folk artist was launched at one of San Francisco's most influential clubs, the hungry i.

From there she moved to a year's engagement at the Tin Angel, elsewhere in the city, and then went east to make her New York debut at the prestigious Blue Angel. Since then she has performed in venues as diverse as New York's Carnegie Hall and Nashville's Grand Ole Opry. Her achievements have been recognized by such institutions as Yale University, which made her a recipient of its Duke Ellington Fellowship Award.

In 1965, her hometown of Birmingham presented her with the key to the city. But for over 30 years, it has been Odetta's music that has opened the doors of the world for her.

. . . .

*Y*OU'VE BEEN BEST KNOWN *as a gifted, commanding singer; but your guitar playing has always been an integral part of your performance. When did you take up the guitar?*

Before I left San Francisco, I met a woman who had a guitar she wasn't using because she was too busy with her family life. She loaned it to me, and showed me *C, G,* and an easy *F* chord.

*How did you feel when you picked up that guitar and tried to play it for the first time?*

It was a plain old struggle. But I knew that was something I had to overcome. As time went on, I found that there is nothing like the guitar to soothe you and keep you company. Sometimes I just find myself lying flat on my back, in bed, just strumming chords. I love to feel the guitar vibrate next to my body. I find those vibrations to be healing to me.

*What part do you see the guitar taking in your role as a folk artist?*

I don't really consider myself a guitarist, but I'm good with what I do. I do not have the kind of drive, in the technical area, to become a guitarist. My area is singing, and the guitar flows with my voice.

*How did you develop your accompaniment style?*

People have shown me chords; but my style is self-defense. By that I mean I try to make the little I know on the instrument sound fuller. I'll play the same few chords, but by varying my strumming, by hammering notes within a chord and picking some other notes—that way I'll achieve the sounds of fullness. I love the opposite forces I can create by singing a smooth melody line and hearing my rhythm playing churning away beneath it. I love those dramatics in music.

*Often people comment on the very large guitar that you play. How did you come by that instrument?*

Up until the time I was hired to sing at the Tin Angel in San Francisco, I had been borrowing guitars from other people. But once I was working with a guitar, I needed to have one of my own. I went to a pawn shop and found the one you mean. I call her Baby. Baby is a wood-bodied National guitar. I'm told

that the last ones they made came out in 1903. It took me some time to pay her off, but I eventually spent my rent money and bought her.

*What did Baby look like when the two of you first met?*

She was one of those ghastly looking dark sunburst guitars. When I was in Chicago once, I took her to a repairman to have her adjusted and fixed. Because my strumming kept on scratching the soundboard, I kept on having bigger and bigger tortoiseshell pickguards put on her. But no matter how large the pickguards were, I still hit the wood. I can't explain why. Maybe it's because I'm an "earth" person, and tend to gravitate toward what is natural instead of toward what is synthetic. Anyway, while the repairman was putting the new pickguard on I asked him if he could change the color of the guitar. He asked me what color I'd like, and I told him Danish Modern [*laughs*]. Danish Modern furniture was very popular at the time. I find that natural-wood look soothing.

*Did you have any other alterations done to Baby?*

Yes, I had to. I understand that those old Nationals were made with Gibson bodies, and National put gears at the bottom of the neck so that you could raise the action and play the instrument like a dobro. The gears kept on slipping, so I had to have them removed, and have that area glued up.

*Did you ever consider getting a standby guitar, just in case something happened to Baby?*

Years ago my manager, who at that time was Albert Grossman, recommended that idea to me. He owned the Gate Of Horn club in Chicago. He went to New York to buy a restaurant, and when he came back he had a very big guitar for me. I thanked him for it, brought it home, and slid it under my bed. I did that so Baby wouldn't get jealous. I can laugh about that now, but I was really serious about it then. You can tell I was the older child in my family.

*But isn't it true that you have a second guitar today? Where did it come from?*

A few years later, I heard of a woman whose husband, a jazz musician, had just died and left her with many beautiful instruments. His last name was McGowan. She was looking for homes for the instruments, and she would interview prospective buyers. If she had a good feeling about you, she would sell you the instrument you wanted. I bought a guitar from her and named it McGowan. I didn't know how to handle putting Baby and McGowan together. Remember—I still had that other guitar under the bed. So I leaned the Baby on her butt against the couch and leaned McGowan next to her. They were touching shoulders. I told them, "Look, you two have to work it out together because I don't know how to deal with this." As it turned out, the Baby taught McGowan everything she ever knew. Everything I had ever arranged had been on the Baby, but I went out with McGowan and found she knew it all. Now there

Odetta's wide-ranging vocal abilities, in many different styles, have made her popular with a broad segment of the musical audience.

are times when I feel that the Baby plays better than I know how. I truly feel that there are personalities in these instruments. I see people who go around trading one guitar for another, and I just can't understand that. Sometime later, McGowan was ripped off from me between Miami and Kennedy airports. It really hurt! I miss McGowan.

*Did you try to replace McGowan?*

Yes. Later I was looking around for another wood-bodied National guitar, and I called Matt Umanov [Umanov Guitars] in New York City, to see if he had one in his store. He told me he did, but that it was in the window of his shop with a plant growing out of it. I said, "You really know how to hurt someone!" But I went to see him anyway, and I bought the Martin D-28 that I have now. I call her Baby II. She's a beauty. I put her next to the Baby and they had the same learning process. She's a splendid guitar.

*Whatever happened to the guitar you put under your bed back in Chicago?*

I still have her. I don't know the make. When friends of mine drop by, they pick her up and play her. She's a gorgeous-sounding instrument. Her sound is like butter melting. But I prefer the bright, brilliant sound that the Baby has.

*What precautions do you take to protect your guitar when you travel by air? Do you buy an extra seat?*

No, I check her as baggage. She is firmly packed with sponge, all around. I also tune her strings down to an open *D* tuning. I've been told that the regular *E* tuning can create too much pressure on the guitar during travel, and damage it.

*Speaking of strings, which kind do you prefer?*

At one time I was using Carboni strings. Piedro Carboni was a New York instrument repairman who used to own the Village String Shop in Greenwich Village, but he recently closed up his shop. It was one of those delicious places that was about two inches wide with three banks of instruments on each side of the store. I couldn't go there and just get strings; I would always spend a couple of hours browsing and playing. Since I can't get Carboni strings anymore, I've experimented with other brands and found that the Baby responds best to La Bella light-gauge silk-and-steel.

*You used to perform with bass and guitar backing you. Why do you now perform solo?*

I originally started in folk music as a solo performer. Then, for some time, I used bassist Bill Lee. I then toured for nine years with bassist Leslie Grinage; and for seven years, guitarist Bruce Langhorne joined us. But at one point I found I needed to be by myself and perform alone. Being alone gave me time to weave a tapestry of songs together, which later grew into a suite. I couldn't have come up with that suite if I was working with others. I also found that I needed to work alone because I didn't want to be a boss anymore and get involved in my group's personal problems. And because we didn't work from pre-

singing what I feel like singing, as opposed to what I rehearsed with other musicians. There had been times when I was working with the group that I didn't feel comfortable singing what we had planned. Now that I have the freedom to change my set, I find that my program flows easier.

*You mentioned that you "make-up" new chords. How do you go about finding them?*

I'll usually take the first-position open chords that I know, like *E*, *A*, or *B7*, and slide them up the neck. By playing them that way, I am harmonizing fretted strings with open strings. That is how I create my new chords and harmonies. I have been told that my playing of chords that way has made my guitar sound like a 12-string guitar. I also adore playing in open *D* tuning [*D-A-D-F#-A-D*].

*Do you have other techniques for giving a fuller sound to your accompaniment?*

I find that I can get a fuller sound by playing a small barre chord with three fingers, then using my fourth finger to play a note not found in that chord. For instance, if I want to play a small barred *A* chord on the 5th fret, my first finger would barre the first and second strings, my second finger would play the third string, and my third finger would play the fourth string. I would then be playing *A*, *E*, *C#*, and *A* with three fingers. I would strum that chord for two beats. Then I would hold that fingering and place my pinky on *F#*, on the second string, and strum that chord—*A6*—for two beats.

*Have the limitations of your guitar technique ever stopped you from performing a certain song?*

Yes, that certainly has happened. But if the song is important enough for me to sing, I'll find a way to accompany myself on the guitar. I would make up chords to fit the singing—I'm not a purist in any way, shape, or form. If I felt I needed to sing a song so badly, and couldn't play accompaniment for it, I would sing it *a capella*.

*What kind of feeling do you get from performing?*

I've always been interested in teaching, and passing on information that has been passed on to me. Performing satisfies me by allowing me to do that. I am also enthralled by the healing power of music. I have gone out on stage, sick as a dog, and at the end of the concert had to stop and think to remember that I was ill or in pain. Music heals me as well as people who listen to it. The best I could hope to be for an audience is a mirror, in front of each individual, where they look into it and see some part of their reflection that they like. The more individuals can see themselves and like what they see, the stronger they will become.

arranged charts, my group couldn't always match my feeling and the way I delivered a particular song.

*Do you feel you have a greater impact on the audience when you perform solo?*

I'm not sure; but I find I have greater freedom in

---

### A Selected Odetta Discography

*Best Of Odetta*, Tradition, 2052; *Essential Odetta*, Vanguard, VSD-4344; *Odetta*, Fantasy, 8345; *At Carnegie Hall*, Vanguard, 73003; *At The Gate Of Horn*, Tradition, 1025; *At Town Hall*, Vanguard, 2109; *One Grain Of Sand*, Vanguard, 2153.

# KINGSTON TRIO

While some purists derided their commercial sound, the Trio inspired hundreds of thousands to discover folk music in the '50s. Dave Guard's deft instrumental style, combined with the group's perfect three-part harmony, dominated the record charts in the late '50s and early '60s. The group's 27-year history was featured in the June 1984 issue of *Frets*.

**By William J. Bush**

THE STORY OF THE Kingston Trio is really the story of seven men—Bob Shane, Nick Reynolds, Dave Guard, John Stewart, Frank Werber, George Grove and Roger Gambill—who have guided and evolved the Trio since its formation in 1957. *Evolution* is an important concept to keep in mind when studying the Trio, for there have been three Trios, each with its own sound and viewpoint though retaining some faithfulness to the founding spirit of the group.

The original Kingston Trio was formed in and around Palo Alto, California, by Dave Guard, a Stanford University graduate student; and his two friends, Bob Shane and Nick Reynolds, from nearby Menlo

College. Guard and Shane both were born in Hawaii, and had been singing and playing together since their high school days at the Punahou School in Honolulu. Reynolds, from Coronado, California, was the son of a Navy career officer and had attended San Diego State and the University of Arizona.

"I showed up at Menlo not knowing a soul," recalls Reynolds, "and the first day I walk into this accounting class and here's this guy sleeping in the back of the room, during the lecture. So I said to myself, anybody that's got the guts to do that I've got to get to know. It turned out to be Bobby Shane, and we immediately went out and became really tight pals; I don't think we showed up for school for about two weeks afterward."

This mutual attraction of kindred spirits was further strengthened by an interest in singing, more as a way of improving their social life than furthering any professional aspirations. "Bobby had this tenor guitar and I had some bongos," Reynolds recalls. "We'd show up at these local spots and fraternity parties and get right in there. I was sort of his driver, you know, just hanging out, fascinated by this magnetic person. Bobby's a charmer; he could play three chords on a tenor guitar and attract more people than the London Symphony. Later on, he said 'I've got to introduce you to this guy I know over at Stanford,' which was Dave, and we just sorta fell together. I kinda mooched my way into that thing. Bobby and Dave had been playing together a long time in Hawaii, and people would want to hire us to play Hawaiian music at their luaus. They taught me some real Hawaiian songs, the third part, which was real easy considering I'd never been to Hawaii. After a while, we started working like two nights a week at these little beer gardens, one of which had hired me as a bartender."

While this grouping of Guard, Shane, and Reynolds was indeed to become the Kingston Trio, the group went through several personnel and name changes in the process. Shortly after introducing Reynolds to Guard, Bob Shane returned to Hawaii to work in his father's wholesale sporting goods and toy firm while pursuing a solo singing career as "Hawaii's Elvis Presley." Reynolds and Guard kept at it, adding Joe Gannon (on bass) and Barbara Bogue, billing themselves as "Dave Guard And The Calypsonians."

Reynolds, too, was to leave after graduation, to be replaced by Don McArthur in a group that became known as the Kingston Quartet. Nick's return was sparked, in part, by the mild encouragement of Frank Werber, a young publicist who had caught a couple of "Dave Guard And The Calypsonians" auditions at the Purple Onion and the Italian Village in San Francisco. "Frank was *sort of* interested in helping us," says Reynolds, "but he told us we'd have to get rid of the bass player. Joe wasn't really a bass player, he was just standing there faking it like a gut bucket. So Barbara says, 'If Joe goes, *I* go.' Well, I'd kept in touch with Bobby and I told him there was a chance of getting a gig if we really worked at it. So he came back and the three of us got involved with Frank."

Werber was in an excellent position to help the group. As the publicist for both the Purple Onion and the hungry i nightclubs, he had the connections. Even more important, he had a critical and astute eye for talent. Although not a musician, he knew well what it took to build and sustain a successful club act. He was tough and disciplined, and he demanded an absolute and total commitment from Guard, Shane, and Reynolds. He got it.

"We were interested in singing for the fun of it, to begin with," says Reynolds, "but if we were going to do this thing professionally—and Dave not continue his education, and me not go into business, and Bobby come back from Hawaii—we knew we were going to have to get *real* serious. And we did." Using Werber's office loft above the Purple Onion to rehearse, the group worked at putting together a 25-minute show for a week's fill-in gig for Phyliis Diller at the Purple Onion, arranged by Werber. It was no more than an extended audition.

Guard, the most promotionally minded of the three, sent 500 postcards to everyone the group knew at Stanford and Menlo, inviting them up for the week-long "party" at the Purple Onion. The ploy worked, with the Trio playing to sold-out audiences every night. What was to be a one-week engagement was extended to two, with the Trio eventually headlining at the Purple Onion from June to December of 1957.

The group now had a small but solid economic base, and with Weber as their mentor and critic, they began an intensive program of polishing, refining and expanding their act.

Repertoire was a key consideration. From the outset, the group had been doing primarily calypso (which Harry Belafonte was making enormously popular), Hawaiian and Tahitian tunes (from Bobby and Dave's background), risque college songs, and anything else that seemed to fit their vocal and instrumental abilities.

Shane, Reynolds, and Guard *never* considered themselves folksingers, going more for the spirit of the genre than for the authenticity of it. As Dave Guard once told interviewer Bruce Pollock, "We were sort of trying to sound like the Weavers. It was really the Weavers energy. We liked the authentic-sounding stuff." The group also was heavily influenced by the folk-based repertoire of the Gateway Singers, another San Francisco trio that the group watched and associated with on a nightly basis, especially member Lou Gottlieb. Sam Wilson, Theodore Bikel, Odetta, Burl Ives, Pete Seeger, even the Broadway show tunes of Lerner And Lowe, were just some of the many sources of material for the early Trio.

Despite their appreciation of such groups as the Weavers and Gateway Singers, the Trio avoided (for the time) any of the political or racial controversy surrounding these groups, carefully "sanitizing" all lyrics. Although Nick Reynolds had come from a family with relatively liberal politics, where tape recordings of the early New York union rallys (with their "thousands strong" singalongs) were played and appreciated, neither he nor any of the Trio members were even remotely radicalized.

"I remember sitting around Frank's office discussing the right moves to make," says Reynolds, "talking about the political trouble that the Weavers had gotten into, and deciding not to stir up any waves, to just take a middle-of-the-road approach to any material we'd do. By writing new bridges and changing these things around from what they originally used to be, a union song became a drinking song. At the time, it

**John Stewart proved a worthy addition to the Trio
when he replaced Dave Guard. (Left to right)
Nick Reynolds, John Stewart, Bob Shane.**

was a good idea professionally. We didn't *want* to preach, we wanted to be in show business. We were honest about *that*; we never tried to kid anyone, like some people who made it a *business* to protest. Later, when we did do some songs that addressed social issues, we did them sincerely, because we believed in them."

At Weber's insistence, the Trio began taking vocal lessons from teacher Judy Davis, not so much to change their voices as to preserve them. By July 1957, the Trio was doing three shows a night at the Purple Onion as well as rehearsing all afternoon. None had ever really learned how to sing properly, and they were, literally, shouting themselves hoarse.

With the exception of Guard, who took a few banjo lessons from Billy Faier, the Trio was almost entirely self-taught instrumentally. Reynolds had played ukulele since childhood, so the transition to playing tenor guitar in the Trio was a natural and easy move. While Reynolds says that inclusion of the tenor was initially to provide him with a prop, "something to put between me and the audience," the higher voicing of the tenor (it was usually capoed at the 5th, 7th, or 9th fret) added "bite" to Shane's open-chord rhythm playing, greatly filling out the overall sound.

It is interesting to note that the instrumental sound of the Kingston Trio, which today is identified as being so American in origin, really owes much of its rhythmic content to Shane and Guard's exposure to Gabby Pahinui, the legendary Hawaiian "slack-key" guitarist.

"Gabby is kind of a link between the Hawaiian past and the modern day, westernized stuff," says Dave Guard. "It's kind of a thumb, up-down-up with the index finger, strum—a hula beat with an Oceanic feel." Shane readily acknowledges the Pahinui influence, but adds that it wasn't a studied thing.

"I was just applying ukulele strokes to a guitar," says Shane. "When I started out, I was strumming with my fingers. Then I changed to a flatpick. But, yeah—our music definitely had Hawaiian overtones to it, even on the things that weren't Hawaiian at all."

Though the Trio was enormously successful at the Purple Onion, Weber decided that the boys needed the experience of performing before different—and tougher—club audiences. He booked them into the Holiday Hotel in Reno, Chicago's Mr. Kelly's, and the Village Vanguard and Blue Angel in New York.

"That's when the reality set in," laughs Nick Reynolds, "going to New York and seeing *gangsters*, with these people telling you to shut up and not sing that song, or 'Don't look funny at my girlfriend.' We were just *punks*, man, and here we were playing in these far-out clubs with some really heavyweight jazz people like Stan Getz, Mose Allison, and Thelonius Monk. For some reason, we always got along very well with jazz people; I remember one time Gerry Mulligan came on stage and jammed with us, and later we even closed the Newport Jazz Festival. But that first time out was *weird*."

In February 1958, between the Reno and Chicago club dates, the group recorded its first album for Capitol Records. It was entitled simply, *The Kingston Trio*. The boys had been spotted the previous summer at the Purple Onion by Jimmy Saphier, Bob Hope's agent, who took demo tapes to both Dot and Capitol Records. Dot said no; Capitol sent Voyle Gilmore up to San Francisco for a closer look. He liked what he saw and heard and signed the Trio to a seven-year contract.

Folk music was something totally new to Voyle Gilmore, who had previously produced Frank Sinatra dates for Capitol. His primary concern at this first Trio session was how he and engineer Curly Walters should mike acoustic instruments. Recorded in just three days at Capitol's Studio B in Hollywood, the album was little more than a studio version of the songs they were doing in their live act—which accounts for its fresh, spontaneous feel. Buzz Wheeler, the resident bass player at the Purple Onion, was enlisted for the session, giving some polish to the group's somewhat rough, "homegrown" accompaniment.

Many Kingston Trio aficionados consider this first album to be the group's best. It yielded such Trio classics as "Three Jolly Coachmen," "Scotch And Soda," "Hard, Ain't It Hard," and, of course, "Tom Dooley." According to Reynolds, "Tom Dooley" was learned one afternoon from an unknown singer auditioning for a job at the Purple Onion. Both the Trio and the Gateway Singers included it as just another ballad in their sets. It was not until Bill Terry and Paul Colburn of KLUB radio in Salt Lake City "broke out" the song from the album in July 1958 that "Tom

**Dave Guard, Nick Reynolds, and Bob Shane
infuriated the purists with their homogenized
folk sound, but they created a vast
new audience for folk music.**

Dooley" was considered anything special, prompting
Capitol to release it as a single. By October of that
year it had entered the *Billboard* Top 10 Singles
Chart—where it stayed until January of 1959, eventually selling more than 3,000,000 copies.

Guard, Shane, and Reynolds recorded their
second album for Capitol at about the same time as
their first was being released. It's a testament to the
vitality of *From The hungry i* that the disc remains in
print today. While musically indistinguishable from
their debut LP, the live recording does showcase the
group's tremendous rapport with its audience. The
between-songs banter, although carefully rehearsed,
is delivered with relish and spontaneity to an
audience that loves every minute of it. The album
literally crackles with personality, which was always a
critical element of the Trio's appeal.

(A sidenote to the hungry i album: It is not an
entirely "live" recording. "Gue, Gue," the French
lullaby on side one, is actually a studio-recorded version of the song—dubbed in to replace the live performance, which the Trio felt was poorly done.)

It was not until the release of the Trio's third LP,
*At Large*, that the group displayed the highly polished
vocal and instrumental sound that would characterize
all future Trio albums. Recorded in New York City
between shows at the Blue Angel in early 1959, *At
Large* is a watershed album, marking a dramatic
improvement over the rough harmonies and loose
accompaniment of the previous two albums. There
are several reasons for this.

First, the Trio constantly rehearsed. When the
group wasn't onstage performing, it was working on
arrangements and searching for new material. "We
were also in *real* good shape," adds Reynolds. "Our
chops were up, we had a lot of self-confidence from
the performing—we had it *down*, man. We were
constantly making lists of songs, listening to new
stuff. We had people bringing us songs, giving us
songs, it was a never-ending search."

Bob Shane points out, too, that recording techniques got better at the time of the *At Large* album,
and that the Trio became, out of necessity, "recording conscious." *At Large* was the first Kingston Trio

album recorded in stereo, and brought to bear Voyle Gilmore's full producing talents. Both in New York and at Capitol's Studio B in Hollywood, Gilmore recorded the early Trio on 3-track, half-inch machines, using three hanging mikes for the voices, and three standing mikes for the instruments. The bass, now played by David "Buckwheat" Wheat, was miked separately.

The unmixed working tape would contain one voice and one instrument per track, with bass being added to Reynolds' tenor guitar track for greater flexibility in equalization. If, for example, more bass was needed in the mixdown, it could be added more easily to Reynolds' higher-pitched tenor guitar track with less risk of obscuring the overall guitar sound. Because stereo recording was new, with no limiters or other means of controlling and directing sound, the quality of the recording was almost entirely a function of mike placement, baffling, and Gilmore's own critical sense of balance—of "what sounded just right."

Gilmore's and engineer Peter Abbot's contribution to The Kingston Trio sound cannot be over-emphasized. Even today, fans and audiophiles are amazed at the richness of the Trio's voices on the Capitol sessions, the result of Gilmore's "double-voicing" recording technique. Every Kingston Trio album after *At Large* was double-voiced in the following manner: On the first take, the voices were recorded softer than the guitars and banjo. Then the boys would put earphones on and rerecord the identical singing parts (with the exception of the solos) over the softer voice track, giving each song a 6-voice choral effect. The process was not easy. "Sometimes we'd get it real fast, other times some songs would take 50 to 100 takes before we were satisfied," says Bob Shane. Gilmore once estimated that it took twice as long to *mix* a Kingston Trio album as it did to record it.

Because *At Large* was recorded before double-voicing, it is perhaps a clearer document of their growing musical maturity, with stereo separation allowing the listener to judge the individual vocal and instrumental abilities. The instrumental format of Shane and Reynolds playing consonant, yet differently voiced, rhythm to Guard's guitar/banjo fingerpicking up and down the neck remained the same, but got much, much tighter.

Although Guard never considered his banjo picking as more than just adequate during his Trio days, he was a most inventive and versatile player. Like his mentor Pete Seeger, Guard employed a more melodic approach to banjo, almost as an extension of his guitar playing, although he was well versed in three-finger Earl Scruggs and traditional frailing styles. "Corey, Corey" from the *At Large* album displays some fine frailing work, while "Remember The Alamo" demonstrates his melodic use of the instrument. Guard also was a fine steel-string and classical guitarist; but it is difficult to categorize his guitar

work, because he was a student of many genres and styles of playing, borrowing freely from any and all to fit the instrumental needs of the Trio.

What also surfaces from both *At Large* and *Here We Go Again*, the Trio's follow-up album, is the unwavering accuracy and feeling of Bob Shane's rhythm playing. Unlike Guard, Shane had an unstudied approach to playing, viewing his guitar work as simply a support to his major role as a singer and entertainer. "People are always concerned so much with who plays the best licks," he says. "I was raised learning to play the guitar as backup to my voice. I was *singing* the lead, I didn't need to play it. Just give me three or four chords and a capo and I'm happier than hell; I can learn the more difficult things if I need to, but playing difficult things just because they're difficult is really something that doesn't jazz me.

"I would tell people that you should use an instrument for whatever it is that you *want* to use it for, and don't be embarrassed by it. I was embarrassed for years because I didn't feel I played a lot of guitar, but now I realize I do play a lot of guitar with my right hand, rhythm-wise." Shane also played banjo in the Trio, his technique limited mostly to strumming with a flatpick ("When The Saints Go Marching In") and single-note picking (the intro to "Worried Man").

Of the three Trio members, Nick Reynolds perhaps displayed the greatest individual growth during this period. From the outset, it was Reynolds' harmonization that made the Trio *work*; Shane and Guard were polar opposites, both vocally and personality-wise, and without Reynolds as the musical and emotional "middleman" the Trio simply couldn't function. It's often been said that it is Bob Shane's distinct baritone that defines the classic Kingston Trio vocal sound. In truth, it is Shane and Reynolds *together* that defines it, a combination that allowed the Trio to continue after Guard's departure in 1961.

Beginning with "MTA" on the *At Large* album, Reynolds began to make his own mark as a soloist within the Trio, and every album thereafter contained at least one Nick Reynolds showcase cut. Many Kingston Trio buffs consider "Hobo's Lullaby" from the 1964 album *Time To Think* to be the finest Kingston Trio performance ever recorded, based largely on Reynolds' highly-moving solo vocal. He also was responsible for the vocal "turnarounds" (or "inversions," as he calls them) that became a Trio trademark on the endings of their faster songs—a technique Reynolds applied to the Trio's arrangements after years of listening to the work of jazz bandleader Stan Kenton.

Instrumentally, Reynolds' 4-string (and later, 8-string) tenor guitar continued to fill out the basic rhythm of Shane's D-28. It was his conga and bongo drum playing, however, that really came to the fore at this time. No longer were the percussion instruments simply used as stage props; Reynolds was playing in earnest, and such songs as "I Bawled," "Bimini," and "Tanga Tika/Toerau" (from *Sold Out*) demonstrate just how skillful a player he had become. Reynolds says he learned to play congas by "hanging out in bars in Tijuana," but he was also professionally exposed to some of the top conga players of the time as well. "Coo Coo U," one of the least-known and most bizarre Trio tunes recorded, featured the playing of jazzmen Mongo Santamaria and Willie Bobo. Above it all, Reynolds established himself as the Trio's brightest star, the voice and personality that *everybody* dug; "clearly the best entertainer in the Trio and one of the best natural musicians I have ever worked with," as John Stewart described him years later.

From a commercial standpoint, the Kingston Trio successfully exploited virtually all segments of the record-buying market. With each new Trio album entering *Billboard's* Top 10 Chart, a Trio 45 single was receiving heavy airplay on pop, country, and, in the case of "Tom Dooley," even R & B stations. Their appeal seemed universal, prompting *Life Magazine* to feature the Trio on their Aug. 3, 1959, cover. In both the *Billboard* and *Cash Box* trade-magazine polls, they were voted "The Best Group Of The Year For 1959" by the nation's disc jockeys. The Ballroom Operators Of America awarded them their "Best Show Attraction Of The Year" award as well. They also picked up two Grammy awards: one for "Tom Dooley," and one for being voted "Country Western Vocal Group of 1958."

Of all the audiences the Trio performed for during their many cross-country tours, none was more enthusiastic and loyal than the college market. The Kingston Trio was *theirs*; the embodiment of the collegiate good-time ethic. Dave Guard explains the attraction: "The freshmen think that the seniors are hot stuff, but who do the seniors look up to? We were one of the first groups to come out of college and do our own thing. When we graduated, we couldn't face the prospect of putting on suits, so out of sheer panic we clung together and invented something to do out in the cold world. To tell you the truth, we were getting as much out of them as they were getting out of us. We were always in contact with college kids, going out to these parties after the shows. It kept us in touch."

Because of the large number of one-night stands they were working, the Trio often would charter a small plane to get to gigs—which on one occasion nearly cost them their lives. Following an appearance at Vanderbilt University in Nashville in March 1959, they boarded a six-passenger Beechcraft for a flight to South Bend, Indiana, where they were scheduled to appear at Notre Dame University. Midway through the flight, they ran into a blizzard. Then the plane's electrical system failed. Almost simultaneously, a fire extinguisher exploded under Dave Guard's seat, adding to the already high anxiety. With no radio, pilot John Rich brought the aircraft down to barn-top

level, looking for road sings and a place to land. Spotting an open field, Rich set the plane down, skidding past frozen dressed turkey carcasses left in the open cold. He stopped within feet of a fence that would have torn the Beechcraft apart.

"This happened just a few weeks after Buddy Holly and those guys got killed in a plane crash," recalls Guard, "and I remember going in for the landing saying, 'This one's for the Big Bopper.'" It was Friday, March 13, 1959, but luck was definitely with them. Collecting their instruments and baggage, they headed for the nearest grocery store, guzzled down two six-packs of beer each and drove on to Notre Dame—which turned out to be *the* highlight concert of their career. "It was great to be alive," says Guard. "Here we'd gone from nearly being killed to getting the greatest audience reception we'd ever experienced. We walked out onstage and the cheering was just deafening. We announced to the crowd that the only reason we were alive was because we were playing Notre Dame on a Friday. It was like going from the darkest to the brightest moment in your life in the same day."

Playing for such big crowds did more than just build their egos. According to Guard, it had a tremendous impact on their musical delivery. "What really changed our style was playing for 7,000 people in the fieldhouse at the University of Oregon. It was so big, with so many people, nobody could hear us. On the early albums, there was a lot of accelerando and nervous energy. That's fine if you're sitting in a small club where you're close to the stage. But if you're out in a big audience, the sound just blends together and nothing is clear. We had to take it from the way we were hearing it onstage and put it in a form that could be heard by everybody. To do this, we had to slow down the tempo of everything—the songs, the jokes, the introductions. That went a long way toward making things more *musical*; we extended it to big, round movements, making it easy for the fat lady to dance to, rather than the mosquito."

To the outside observer, it seems remarkable that the quality of the Trio's recordings continued to rise. For Guard, Shane, and Reynolds, it was getting tougher and tougher. After the *Here We Go Again* album, the Trio began to run dry on the supply of quality material that had characterized their previous albums. "We got our craft sky high, if not our inspiration," says Guard, "a lot of the later stuff just didn't grab our hearts. Capitol kept pushing for more albums, and it kind of got reduced to picking songs on the basis of whether they *sounded* like a Kingston Trio song. Nick was always making lists of songs we might sing, we were going into sheet music stores looking for things; I started putting songs together—take a verse from here, a chorus from there—creating new stuff."

"We had gotten it down to a formula," adds Reynolds. "Every Kingston Trio album would need an opener or a blaster; we'd need a closer; a Bobby

Shane tune; a Dave Guard original—we pretty much had it all laid out before we went into the studio. They were mostly head arrangements. Sometimes David would write out the parts for Bobby and I and put them on tape, and I'd listen to them while I was in the darkroom or doing something else at home. When we got into the studio, Bobby and I had our parts down. See, I could harmonize with Bobby, we were *together*, and sometimes we wouldn't even know what David was going to sing until we got in there. Dave would say, 'I'm working on my instrumental now; you guys get your parts down and do the song, and I'll just do my part when it's time; I know where my verse comes in.' And when he'd do the song, his harmonies were just *killers*. If I sat down and listened to the things I haven't listened to in 25 years, I would say *God*, it's David, his killer harmonies, he had a great ear."

Perhaps the most musically ambitious album recorded by the Trio is the one least known, *Last Month Of The Year*, their only Christmas album— withdrawn by Capitol after disappointing sales. Recorded in 1960 between shows at the Ambassador Hotel in Los Angeles, the album represented an attempt by the Trio to get back the quality of material and arrangements that each member found personally satisfying.

Although filled with traditional carols and adaptations of Christmas legends from Europe, England, and America's deep south, *Last Month* is not a traditional Christmas album in the popular sense. There are no Rudolphs or Frostys, which may explain why it never caught on. It was okay for the Trio to expose America to exotic music, but just don't mess with Christmas.

"It wasn't your standard Christmas album," Reynolds says, "that's why we called it 'Last Month Of The Year.' It was a pretty complicated little album, some very intricate stuff. David brought in a lot of the arrangements with stuff like bouzouki instrumentation; Buckwheat [David Wheat, the Trio's bassist] played some wonderful gut-string guitar. We really worked hard on that one, laying down a lot of the instrumental tracks before we did the vocals, working on the harmonies over and over. David was responsible for a lot of that album, but we all brought things in. My son had just been born, and I did a few songs that were aimed at that very personal thing. Musically, it came off very well; it just didn't sell."

Considering the profitability of the Trio's concerts, endorsements, records, and publishing interests, one less-than-successful album hardly made a dent in their finances. However, it was the issue of publishing money, combined with personal differences, that eventually led to the dissolution of the original Kingston Trio.

In October 1960, the Trio discovered a sizable discrepancy in its publishing account. Shane and Reynolds, while not liking the situation, were hardly alarmed. "The publishing money was like a bonus to us," says Reynolds. "What was missing was like a drop in the bucket compared to what we were earning. All of the funds were accounted for, incidentally— interest included." Guard, however, was furious. It was just one more irritant in his growing discontent over the financial and musical direction of the Trio. At the heart of it was a basic difference in personalities and viewpoint, primarily between Guard and Shane.

Although Dave and Bob had grown up together in Hawaii, and had been friends since high school, they were—and are—vastly different people. Guard is a brilliant man, intellectually curious and studied in his approach to everything; an experimenter who wanted to push the Trio to new heights of instrumental and vocal achievement. Bob Shane is naturally gifted, born with a voice and personal magnetism that cannot be studied and learned. ("On the natch," as Reynolds puts it). Shane is equally brilliant and sensitive to his own talents. He saw no need to disturb what he considered to be the already perfect formula for success. Reynolds stood squarely in the middle in terms of ability to view the situation objectively; but he sided with Shane emotionally. Today, he is the most objective of the three in his assessment of the situation.

"I'm probably in the best position to comment on it, 'cause I've got no axes to grind," he says. "I'm not professionally involved in the music like Bobby is, or emotionally involved like Dave might be. Basically, David wanted to take it on to another level. Bobby and I were just hangin' out, having a good time. We were happy with the format and working *way* too hard to consider sitting down and learning how to read music. So much of what made us successful was that it was a *natural* thing, a natural kind of energy, and it wouldn't have worked if it were studied or experimented with. It was spiritual, not scientific.

"We were killing ourselves as it was with the work, and David was insisting that we take lessons. He was also upset about the publishing thing, and didn't think people were taking care of business, and he became dissatisfied with everything—from the photography to the management. It might have been an overreaction on Dave's part, but I believe that he honestly wanted to take it to a higher plane; he was studying more and getting into the mathematics of musicology."

"I just felt we should keep on pushing to learn all kinds of instrumental techniques and to keep getting better every week," Guard told interviewer Bruce Pollock. "I told them we had a responsibility to the fans to be good musicians and that we should all take lessons to improve our stuff."

Of the split, Shane says only this: "Dave was right sometimes, wrong at others. The Trio to me has always been three people doing things together. Without that constant friendship and trust—that constant thing together—there was no sense going on working together."

So ended the first Kingston Trio. After the release of a final album, *Goin' Places*, and the meeting of several tour obligations, Shane and Reynolds set about forming a second—and totally different—Kingston Trio with John Stewart.

Only 21 years old when asked to join the Trio, Stewart had been an ardent fan and student of their music since his senior year at Pomona Catholic High School. "I was playing in a rock and roll band called The Furies," recalls Stewart, "And some friends of mine who'd graduated and were going to college in Santa Clara said, 'You're not going to believe this group that came through, the Kingston Trio—they're *phenomenal*.' Somebody had their album, and when I heard the banjo on 'Saro Jane' I said, '*Wait a minute!*' I'd never heard anything like it before. Dave Guard is one of my heroes; one of the guys who changed my musical direction. Just spun me around and showed me something I'd never seen before."

When the Trio appeared in Pomona a year later, Stewart made it a point to introduce himself.

"I had them sign an album, and then any time they'd come to town I'd hang around backstage, and they'd say, 'Hi, how're you doing,' just being polite; I was operating under that illusion that kids have that once you meet somebody, *they know you*. I was on Arwin Records as a single, just getting ready to switch from rock and roll to folk, and I was supposed to do a folk album, but instead the publisher sent my songs to the Trio. So now they knew me as a songwriter. I went down to see them at the Shrine Auditorium in Los Angeles and they said, 'John, these songs are so close, but write some more and we'll listen again.' When they played at the Coconut Grove, I hopped down there and played them 'Molly Dee' and 'Green Grasses.' Ten months later I got a check for $10,000, and I said 'Hey, why am I going to college? *This* is the promised land!' And that started our professional friendship."

With that friendship came Trio manager Frank Werber's connections and a recording contract with Roulette Records. Every label in the country wanted its own version of the Kingston Trio, and Werber was more than happy to oblige with a reasonable facsimile consisting of Stewart, Gil Robbins and John Montgomery. Billing themselves as "The Cumberland Three," the group did three excellent folk albums, for Roulette and toured extensively with comedian Shelley Berman. When Guard's departure from the Trio became imminent, Stewart was called and told to keep in close touch.

"We really didn't start auditioning people right away," says Nick Reynolds. "Bobby and I just sort of took a vacation and talked it over. We had the record contract, so we decided we wanted to go ahead with a new Trio, to give it a shot. We auditioned a number of different people—one of the guys from the Modern Folk Quartet, and a few others,—but John was the ideal one. He was *perfect* for us; we'd known him, he'd written songs for us, there was no hostility.

and he was bringing material, enthusiasm and new blood to jaded old Bobby and I, plus being in awe of what he was stepping into. John was just enough of a madman to fit in, fortunately, although he didn't realize it at the time and we didn't either. But you know, there are no accidents. We just followed our instincts with John, and it worked right from the start."

Musically, Stewart had no trouble whatsoever in making the transition, understanding perfectly his function in the group. "I had really locked into their way of doing folk," he says, "because what they were doing was folk music with the mindset of rock and roll—folk music with *hooks*. *Young* folk music that you could get your teeth into, as opposed to the ethnic stuff. So coming from rock and roll, I knew exactly what they were doing immediately: the banjo had to have a hook line, the chords had to be simple, and it had to be repetitive.

"Bobby and Nick were very *organic* musicians; there was nothing cerebral about their musicianship. It was totally *natural*, and that was a great part of the magic of the Trio; it was that *thing*, that natural energy, that made them connect with millions of people. It was a force that some groups have and some don't, but it is as real as electricity or running water and it translates to anybody, anywhere in the world. I've always been influenced by other people—and these guys weren't. They were totally themselves. They enjoyed singing music and playing music; but it was not so much an obsession and escape for them, as it was with me, because they had nothing to escape *from*. They were very comfortable with themselves and with the world.

After two weeks of rehearsal, the new Trio made its first public appearance, playing a benefit concert for the Boys Club in Santa Rosa, California. The audience was as enthusiastic and boisterous as ever, convincing the group that it had, indeed, made the transition to bigger and better things. Capitol Records, however, was less convinced. The Kingston Trio was big business to the label, accounting for roughly 20% of Capitol's gross profit. Millions of dollars and big salaries were riding on Stewart's ability to musically fit in and help perpetuate the Kingston Trio sound on record.

"There was a lot of pressure coming from Capitol as to whether the golden goose was going to still lay the golden egg," recalls Stewart. "When we went into the studio to do *Close Up*, all these execs were in the control booth with [producer] Voyle Gilmore. We did 'Jesse James,' and they all smiled, shook hands and left."

Capitol had good reason to smile. *Close Up*, the Trio's first album with Stewart, is as refreshing and musically stimulating as *At Large* was to the group's Dave Guard era. This is a different Trio entirely—more relaxed, more spontaneous, more "into it" than ever. Not simply the "new boy," Stewart is a full contributor to *Close Up*, taking the lead vocals on "Take

Her Out Of Pity" and "Weeping Willow," as well as supplying crisp, inventive banjo lines on "Jesse James" and "Reuben James." The influence of Guard and of Pete Seeger is evident in his playing, particularly in Stewart's melodic approach to banjo; yet Stewart's style is often much more expressive, more free-flowing.

"I always like to play what I heard in my head," he says. "If it's more melodic, it's because I didn't know *how* to play the other stuff. I was never a great banjo player. As long as it worked and did its melodic job, its job as an energy center, it was fine with me. Now, Dave Guard—*there's* a banjo player. Hooks, riffs—beautiful stuff. I don't know, maybe I was just lazy."

On both banjo and guitar, Stewart used finger-picks exclusively. In addition to a Gibson 12-string used on "O Ken Karenga," Stewart played a Martin 00-21, with its higher tone, to avoid getting lost on the bassier sound of Shane's Martin D-28. Like Guard before him, John's primary banjo was a Vega Pete Seeger Long Neck 5-string, although he later used a Gibson Long Neck 5-string briefly ("I just wanted to try something different; it didn't cut nearly as well as the Vega"). Stewart also played a Martin D-28 and several Guild 12-strings.

If *Close Up* legitimized Stewart musically to Trio fans, *College Concert* did the same for his acceptance as a personality within the group. The LP was recorded December 6-7, 1961, in the Grand Ballroom of the Student Union Building at the University of California at Los Angeles. Stewart emerges as the Trio's main funnyman, a role that Guard had played before him. Unlike Guard, however, whose wit was more satirical in the Mort Sahl vein, Stewart's humor ran closer to the Bob Newhart school of self-deprecating comedy, with a touch of sophomoric craziness added to it. Bob Shane says that none of it was rehearsed, that it came right off the top of Stewart's head, with the better lines kept in the show and expanded upon. The college audience, their toughest and most loyal cadre of fans, loved it.

Musically, *College Concert* is an interesting mixed bag containing revitalizing versions of "MTA" and "Coplas," as well as new material. "O Ken Karenga" is particularly lively, with Stewart setting the rhythm by strumming the taut string sections between the bridge and tailpiece on his Gibson 12-string, followed by Shane's strong open chording. Reynolds then picks it up on "boo-bams," a series of tuned cylindrical plastic tubes of varying lengths, designed and built by David Wheat, the Trio's bassist. The whole tune keeps picking up steam, carried by Shane's raucous baritone lead and by a spectacular Nick Reynolds drum solo.

The Trio continued a full-time nationwide touring schedule of colleges, amphitheatres, and top clubs, returning periodically to the studio to meet their three-albums-a-year contract with Capitol. If one wishes to isolate the best of the "Stewart Era" recordings, three are particularly worthy of study: *New Frontier*, *#16*, and *Time To Think*.

"Best album we ever did," says Stewart of *New Frontier*, released in November 1962. "Worked our buns off on it; brought Jerry Walters of the Gateway Singers in to help us construct some of the harmonies, and just having his presence there made us more disciplined and added greatly to the sound of that album. With *New Frontier*, we really got a feeling for what the studio was, what it could do for the music. 'Honey, Are You Mad At Your Man,' with that one-note banjo drone running through it was very Fleetwood Mac-ish, which was something we never could've done live, you needed that studio echo to give it mystery. And the overdubbing on 'New Frontier,' and the melody of 'Adios, Farewell,' *wow*—the power of that album was the studio, because of the echo and mood you could create. It was a lot different from singing 'Hard, Ain't It Hard' and 'Oh, Miss Mary' in concert."

The album *#16*, released six months later, was likewise a studio-intensive recording, with intricate vocal and instrumental overdubbing. Prior to *#16*, the Trio had done virtually all of its own instrumental work, with the exception of bass—which by this time was played by Dean Reilly (David "Buck" Wheat, the Trio's original bassist, had left the group in early '62 to join Dave Guard in the Whiskyhill Singers). For this album, however, Glen Campbell was recruited to play 6-string banjo on "Reverend Mr. Black," the first of many Trio tunes Campbell would augment over the next couple of years. There is also some very fine acoustic guitar lead work on "Run The Ridges," overdubbed by Stewart.

It is not surprising that two of the Trio's biggest singles surfaced from *New Frontier* and *#16*, "Greenback Dollar" and "Reverend Mr. Black," respectively. A minor hit, "Desert Pete," was culled from *Sunny Side*, but the Trio never again realized Top 40 success on the magnitude of a "Greenback Dollar." Paucity of material may be one reason for this; Stewart says the well was running dry, and certainly some of the weaker material on *Sunny Side* is evidence of it. But perhaps the greater reason for it was the growing social awareness of the country, and the ability of other folk groups and performers to articulate it.

Using the musical stage that the Kingston Trio had built, Bob Dylan, Joan Baez, Peter, Paul & Mary, and scores of other "Protest" singers were becoming politically relevant, siphoning off the Trio's record-buying audience in the process. And although the group had recorded such protest anthems as "Where Have All The Flowers Gone" and "Blowing In The Wind" (as well as Stewart's own "Road To Freedom"), the Trio in the summer of 1963 was in no way aligned to the protest movement. They always reflected the happier, more optimistic side of America; *New Frontier*, in fact, was a celebration of JFK's challenge for national greatness both in space and around the world, with the Trio dedicating the

**Capitol lost interest in the band after the Beatles-led British invasion of 1964, so the band signed with Decca Records.**

album to the Peace Corps volunteers. For the Trio to have jumped on the protest bandwagon would have been a betrayal to the group's instincts, although Stewart privately longed for it. By the fall of 1963, however, the group had philosophically reconciled itself to the need to put more social relevance into their music. It was to be done, however, on their own terms, through a series of introspective songs that best expressed their individual and group sensitivities. The album was to be titled *Time To Think*.

As a document of their art, proof of what tremendous emotional and musical forces could be marshalled by the Trio when it was motivated, *Time To Think* is unquestionably their finest effort. From Bobby Shane's magnificent interpretation of Billy Behen's "Patriot Game," to Stewart's snarling "If You Don't Look Around," this album did indeed give its audience plenty to think about. Never intended as a protest album ("It is not our intention with this album to try to become a voice for this generation . . . " read the liner notes), it remains perhaps one of the best examples of the genre to come out of the entire '60s.

*Time To Think* proved to be the last studio album recorded for Capitol, with a final "live" album taped in March 1964, at the hungry i in San Francisco. In their seven years on the label, the Trio had done much in establising Capitol as a major company, and

to this day several of the Trio's gold records still hang in the Capitol Tower Lobby, out of what one would hope is appreciation. Voyle Gilmore once said that Capitol did everything possible to keep the Trio after their contract had expired, but that Werber "wanted an arm and a leg" if the group was to resign. Nick Reynolds laughs at this suggestion, saying that Capitol offered no more than a 1% increase as an incentive. "You see, they had this group called *the Beatles* that was selling *millions* of records a week, so it was kinda like, 'Oh, gee, sorry you're not re-signing, bye-bye.'"

Decca records, however, was more than happy to sign the Trio to a multi-million-dollar recording and independent production contract, anxious for the prestige the group would lend to the label's somewhat stuffy, old-fashioned image. Concurrent with the Decca deal, the Trio built its own studio in the basement of Columbus Tower, their office building in San Francisco. While considered state-of-the-art by 1965 standards, it just wasn't good old Stuido B in Hollywood. "We didn't have Capitol's chambers or [engineer] Peter Abbot anymore, and we could never duplicate the power of those Capitol sessions again," says Stewart, commenting on the flat quality of the four Decca albums recorded at Columbus Towers over the next two years. Unfortunately, it was more than a change in studios that affected their sound; it was a change in attitude. While such albums as *Nick, Bob, John* and *Stay Awhile* are filled with excellent songs and polished arrangements, Stewart says that the "X" factor was missing. "When we were working hard in the studio, we were not overly concerned with the technical angle; we were concerned with the *energy*—the right attitude. It was the group's attitude that made it better, and you can't buy it, you can't EQ it in. You've either got it or you don't. After *Time To Think*, there wasn't the same enthusiasm. That was the beginning of the end."

Recording-wise, Stewart's point is well taken. But it is important to keep in mind that recording, while enormously lucrative for the Trio, was always considered a secondary activity for the group, both artistically and financially. When asked to evaluate the Trio's recorded work, Bob Shane says, "I'm proud of every damned thing we did that sold. I'm a professional entertainer, and once I've recorded something and stopped singing it, I don't think about it. Even in our peak years of selling records, we made more money and had more fun on the personal appearances. People don't realize that."

That the Trio, and *not* the concert marketplace, would determine the end of the group's career was perfectly in keeping with its history and personality. Since 1957, the band had worked constantly, on the average spending 300 days on the road—and cranking out three albums—a year. "It was never intended to go on forever," says Nick Reynolds. "We never wanted to be the Mills Brothers of folk music. We quit when it was time to quit."

The Shane/Reynolds/Stewart Trio's farewell performance, on June 17, 1967, was held where it all began, at the hungry i in San Francisco. After a short period of designing and building racing cars, Nick Reynolds moved to a ranch in Oregon where he lives today—happy, proud of his years in the Trio, still a star. John Stewart went on to pursue a career as both a songwriter and recording artist, writing "Daydream Believer" for the Monkees as well as recording more than 15 solo albums. In 1979, Stewart scored a Number One hit, "Gold," and he continues to tour extensively; he is today one of America's most prodigious songwriters. And Dave Guard is an editor in New York state, still writing and playing music, and the author of a guitar instruction book.

Had it not been for Bobby Shane, the Kingston Trio would simply have receded into musical history. When the decision was made to disband the Trio in 1967, Shane was the only member opposed to it. "I was kind of angry that the group broke up," he says, "because I felt we were finally in a position to make some improvements. It takes *years* to really feel confident, to get to the point where everything works together to make it better. It's a combination of respect, trust, friendship—it's a constant thing, and if it starts to fray, it shows up in the music."

Shane is quick to defend the present Trio, himself, Roger Gambill, and George Grove, as the equal of the earlier versions of the group. Shane, Gambill, and Grove have worked long and hard to overcome obstacles that were never placed in the way of the previous Trio lineups. Nostalgia has been the greatest hurdle.

Because Bob Shane sang 70% of the lead vocals of the old Trio's repertoire, and because the public still loves the old hits, fully half of the current Trio's concert repertoire is material from the first two Trios. This in turn, invites comparisons between today's group and the Guard and Stewart Trios. Proponents of Gambill and Grove argue that George and Roger are superior vocalists and musicians, making today's Trio a "better" group overall. It is an unnecessary argument, and one that is unfair to all concerned. From the outset, each Trio has presented its own unique sound and magic. There has been a continual evolution of the group concept, and it is within this context that today's Trio should be judged and appreciated.

"The nostalgia we do isn't *my* nostalgia," says Shane. "I went through a period when I hated doing the old songs; I was bored. But then, more and more people would tell us how much those songs meant to their lives, and that's when I became proud of doing them. I overlooked the fact that I was bored."

Today the old hits are rendered faithfully—with Shane and Gambill on guitar, and Grove on banjo—but with the added kick of drums (played by Tom Green), electric bass (played by Stan Kaess) and electric viola and tenor guitar (played by Ben Schubert). In addition, the Trio has begun an intensive schedule of concert dates with leading symphonies and civic orchestras, featuring string arrangements by George Grove.

To date, the current Trio lineup has released three albums: *Aspen Gold*, a digitally recorded and mastered "superdisc" (Nautilus) ("We wanted to be the first folk group to do it," says Grove); *25 Years Non-Stop* (Xeres S); and *Looking For The Sunshine* (Xeres S). [*Ed. Note. An organization called Kingston Korner (6 S. 230 Cohasset Rd., Naperville, IL 60540) serves as a national clearing house for Kingston Trio and John Stewart recordings, and also publishes a Kingston Trio Newsletter.*] The first two albums, while musically pleasing and professionally executed, are essentially re-recordings of old Trio hits. It is with *Looking For The Sunshine* that today's Trio finally steps out, unencumbered by the nostalgia noose, to show its stuff. And there is plenty to show.

"We went into the studio without any preconceived notions, other than to do a good album that *we* enjoyed," says Grove. "Looking For The Sunshine," the title cut, shows Gambill delivering a terrific bluesy C & W solo, counterpointed by some fine John Sebastion autoharp licks. Gambill is one of the few vocalists today that can comfortably and competently shift from country to folk to gospel to cabaret (as he does on "I Like To Hear The Rain") with total authority. Given Grove's string arrangements as a vehicle, the man soars. Gambill is an old hand at versatility, having sung everything from operetta in college, to country at Opryland, to folk in some of the best clubs in the country before teaming with Shane in 1974.

George Grove is, likewise, showcased on *Looking For The Sunshine*, both as an arranger and as a vocalist ("Easy To Arrange"). Grove, who is a classically-trained musician (Wake Forest College) as well as a seasoned Nashville session player, is the Trio's consummate musician. He is as adept at tasty single-string guitar lines as he is at blazing 5-string banjo solos. If there is a shortcoming to *Looking For The Sunshine*, it's that Grove is not featured enough, considering the depth of his talent. "Longest Beer Of The Night," from the Trio's *Alpen Gold* album, however, documents Grove's power as a blues singer/guitarist.

Throughout it all, Bob Shane's whisky baritone weaves that familiar Kingston Trio vocal sound. Shane's voice is deeper, more emotive now, a function of both time and experience; though it's tough to imagine an improvemenmt of a voice that Frank Sinatra once acknowledged as being so distinctive that even *he* wouldn't try to cover "Scotch And Soda." What's more, in much the same way that Reynolds and Shane allowed Stewart to fully contribute to *Close Up*, and therefore allowed the Kingston Trio to evolve musically, Shane steps back on this album, sharing the lead vocals equally with Gambill and Grove.

And so, 27 years after packing the hungry i in San Francisco, the magic of the Kingston Trio is still potent. The music has evolved, the personnel have changed, but some things remain the same:

"I think we're a much better musical act, and better musically in some ways," says Shane. "I think it's been a proper evolution. There is a demand for our type of acoustic music, and not just from those people who remember the Kingston Trio. With more story songs, I think we could attract listeners even among very young children. The music is timeless."

* * * *

**P**ERHAPS NO OTHER GROUP in the history of American music has done more to popularize the acoustic guitar and the 5-string banjo than has the Kingston Trio. In the original group, as with the two Trios to follow, the Martin guitar remained the staple instrument for concerts and recording.

Although Bob Shane is pictured holding a Martin 000-28 on the cover of the Trio's first album, he never owned or played one with the group. His main instrument was the archetypal dreadnought, the D-28, the first of which he purchased from Bergstrom Music in Honolulu for $180 in 1956. All other Trio D-28s, and there were many, were purchased from Harmon Satterlee of Satterlee-Chapin Music in San Francisco, or from Sid Hiller of Columbia Music, also in San Francisco.

Actually, Shane's first instrument was a Martin ukulele. He graduated to a Silvertone 4-string tenor guitar sold to him by George Archer, a popular writer of Tahitian music.

Throughout the early Trio days, Shane used heavy-gauge D'Angelico bronze strings on his guitars. In 1963, Harmon Satterlee, who did all the repair work on the Trio's instruments affixed two large, black pickguards to one of Shane's original D-28s, making it a Shane trademark of sorts among Trio fans. When asked what prompted the modification, Bob laughingly replies, "A lot of scarred wood." Shane had picked up the idea from Stan Wilson, another San Francisco folk singer (who had picked it up from Josh White), as a way of preventing a complete wearing through of the top due to heavy usage. Satterlee was also to build a custom 12-string for Shane featuring a large Guild-like body, wide neck, and a mother-of-pearl bat with ruby eyes. This guitar, which Shane refers to as "The Bat Wing Guitar," is owned by a private collector in San Francisco; his original D-28, with the wide pickguards, is owned by his brother-in-law. Shane also owned and played a Vega long-neck, 5-string banjo in the Trio.

Nick Reynolds was also raised in the Martin tradition, owning Martin ukuleles from childhood. "Martin

was *the* ukulele," says Reynolds. "In my family, it was the epitome, and they were pretty serious players. My father had Martin guitars, old ones, in fact he had an old New York Martin that I still have. In the Trio, we considered Martins real tough workhorses, like the Porsche, they just don't break down. And the way we used to beat 'em and thrash 'em, there was no delicacy involved." Reynolds first played a Martin 0-17T tenor purchased from Harmon Satterlee. He then purchased a Martin 2-18T. This guitar, serial #38023, was built in 1929 and was used by Reynolds on many of the early Trio albums. In 1961, Reynolds had it converted to an 8-string model by Harmon Satterlee who replaced the neck and bridge, removing the pickguard and refinishing the instrument at the same time.

Beginning in 1959, Reynolds added a Martin 0-18T to his road and recording instrument collection, although he continued to use the 2-18T occasionally. Nick presently has two 0-18T's, one of which has also been converted to an 8-string model; the other, Serial #191378 (1963) remains stock with the exception of Grover Rotomatic machines. Reynolds used a thick felt ukulele pick for playing the 4-string tenor, and a flexible plastic pick for the 8-string.

Dave Guard's first guitar was a Martin as well, a small mahogany-bodied 6-string model purchased when he ws 16. For his guitar work in the Trio, Guard occasionally used a D-28 and more often, a Martin 00-21. He also owned and played a Velasquez classical made for him in New York. While Guard is high in his praise for Martin ("nothing else came close"), he is equally quick to praise Gibson, owning both a Gibson 12-string guitar and a Mastertone banjo. "We were playing on a show with the Everly Brothers, and I really liked those jumbo Gibsons they were playing," he recalls. "So I asked Gibson to make me a jumbo 12-string, using the same body as the 6-string models the Everlys were playing. I think it's the first Gibson 12-string made, because the neck was way off. I had Harmon Satterlee remake the neck and it's been just a terrific guitar since then. You can play it ten hours a day and it still stays in tune."

On the first Kingston Trio album, Guard is pictured playing a Stewart banjo. This was given to him by Nick Reynolds' father, and remained Guard's recording and concert banjo until late 1958 when he purchased a Vega Pete Seeger, long-neck, 5-string model directly from the factory. Guard says the change to the Vega long-neck was because he wanted to play in lower keys. When he first began playing banjo in the Trio, Guard was using only a thumbpick and his fingers; he later switched to two metal fingerpicks.

---

## A Selected Kingston Trio Discography
*Aspen Gold*, 51 West Records (care of Columbia Records) Q-16116; (On Capitol): *Best Of The Kingston Trio Vol. I, II, III* , SN-16183, SN-16184, SM-2614; *From the 'hungry i'*, M-11968; *Looking For The Sunshine*, Xeres 10006; *Scarlet Ribbons*, SN-16186; *Tom Dooley*, N-16185; *25 Years Non-Stop*, Xeres, 10001.

# JOAN BAEZ

Eighteen-year-old Joan Baez was an immediate hit at the 1959 Newport Folk Festival. Within a few years she had several albums on the charts and was featured on the cover of *Time Magazine*. While Joan is more well-known for her voice than her instrumental talents, she was featured in *Guitar Player* in December of 1971. Her life and music have been committed to the twin aims of peace and non-violence, and in 1965 she founded the Institute For The Study Of Non-Violence.

**By Jim Crockett**

MUSICIANS HAVE BEEN ACTIVE in political struggles for centuries—probably ever since there were musicians and political struggles. In the eighteenth century, Mozart, a Catholic, included a Lutheran chorale in his opera "Magic Flute," in an attempt to resolve the religious differences then splitting European society. Toscanini refused to conduct in Nazi Germany. Polish pianist and composer Paderewski fought actively for his country's freedom, and was even a signer of the Treaty of Versailles. Pablo Casals left his home in Spain when Franco became its dictator. And in America, many folksingers of the '60s marched and sung in the struggles for civil rights and against the Vietnam war.

Which brings us to Joan Baez. Certainly it was her singing that first brought her to public attention, at the 1959 Newport Folk Festival. Her rich, traditional singing style and wide repertoire of American and British folk material, quickly earned her a wide fol-

lowing. But within a very short time her political stance came to dominate the way people thought about her. She has taken highly visible positions on dozens of issues during her career. In 1962 she toured the south on a strictly no-discrimination concert tour—at a time when blacks and whites were segregated throughout the South. The following year, she refused to appear on ABC—TV's "Hootenanny" program, since it had blacklisted Pete Seeger for his political views. In 1964 she announced that she would refuse to pay her income taxes because the money was largely used to support the Defense Department. In 1965 she founded the Institute for the Study of Non-Violence in California. Other causes that occupied her during the '60s were anti-war marches in West Germany, striking farm workers in California, and working to abolish the death penalty. In October of 1967 she, her mother, and sister (Mimi Baez), were jailed in Oakland, California, for demon-

Joan was such a hit with the Newport Folk Festival crowd in 1959 that Vanguard offered her a recording contract, which she turned down. At the time she was just 18 years old.

strating against the draft at an Armed Forces induction center.

Her political involvements have continued to the present day. She still dedicates her time, and her music, to the issues of peace, civil rights, world hunger, and economic justice. These efforts have sometimes antagonized her political enemies, but not limited her audience. For Joan, there was never any problem mixing politics and music. Though she sang mostly traditional songs in her early days, she had actually been involved in political action in high school, before she had ever sung publicly.

Joan was born on January 9, 1941, on Staten Island, New York. Her father, Albert V. Baez, a physicist, had immigrated to the United States from Mexico. Her mother, Joan Bridge Baez, was born in Scotland. Joan spent her childhood in New York and California, and also lived for nine months in Iraq, Turkey, and Switzerland.

Her music interests developed in 1954, when she was 13 and living in Palo Alto, California. Joan took up the ukulele, "conquering it in a summer. It was me and Arthur Godfrey all the way," she says. There was a period of classical piano training for her too, but the regimentation was more than she could stand. In fact, she rebelled against the entire idea of disciplined musical education, preferring instead The Sons of The Pioneers, Tex Ritter, and even Bill Haley and the Comets.

"When I was 15," she recalls, "I got a black, split, old board of a Sears guitar, and began figuring out some stuff to play on it." After that she got hold of "gigantic $50 Gibson that just hung around my knees. I was so . . . well, it never occurred to me to adjust the strap. I was going around singin' Day-O' and all those other Belafonte songs." At this time folksingers such as Belafonte and Odetta had become her biggest influence. Why folk music? Well according to Joan, "I was looking for something real, and those old songs seemed very pure and very real as opposed to the

rock n' roll . . . "

The Baez family moved south to Redlands, California, about this time. This was when Joan first became aware of the social implications of her dark complexion. Kids wouldn't have anything to do with her, and adolescent loneliness became an obsession. "I wanted friends so badly, then," she says, "that I'd do anything. At lunch I'd sit around and mimic various singers. I could carry a tune then, but it took me a year and a half to develop my vibrato."

It was in high school that Joan got her first taste of political activism. Her father, a Quaker believing in non-violence, had been a conscientious objector in the '40s, but he was against his daughter becoming too involved in social issues. Nonetheless, when Joan's high school held a civil defense drill, she was one of three students who refused to participate, choosing to remain seated in the classroom. That led to her initial appearance on newspaper front pages.

In 1958 the family moved to a suburb of Cambridge, Massachusetts. There Joan was able to visit all the folk clubs, listening to people like Eric Von Schmidt and Rolf Kahn. She had switched guitars by this time, too, and was playing a nylon-stringed Goya folk guitar, like many other folkies of the day.

After high school she had a brief fling with higher education, enrolling in Boston University's drama school. But by this time, singing and playing guitar were her primary interests. She began hanging around a club called Tulla's Coffee Grinder, adding to her folk song repertoire. Once she started performing, Joan quickly became a fixture of the Cambridge scene, playing the Club 47, Golden Vanity, and The Ballad Room. During this period she turned down an offer from Harry Belafonte to join his troupe. Albert Grossman, later Bob Dylan's manager, saw her in one of these folk clubs and brought her to Chicago to perform at a spot called The Gate Of Horn. It was there that she met singer Bob Gibson, and he asked her to appear with him at the 1959 Newport Folk Festival.

Joan was not even billed at Newport. But when she sang, the 18-year old was an immediate hit with the crowd, and also with fellow performers such as Pete Seeger and Odetta. As a result she was offered a recording contract by Vanguard but, displaying that personal sense of priorities that has marked her career, she turned it down, and went back to perfecting her act in coffeehouses. After her second appearance at Newport the following year, however, Joan did sign with Vanguard and issued *Joan Baez*. To keep that folk feeling "pure of soul" she had Fred Hellerman of The Weavers playing guitar on the album. On later recordings she was to use Bruce Langhorn for the upfront work, a man whom she considers one of her greatest musical influences. The success of the album led to a triumphant tour of colleges across the U.S. in 1961.

Joan's albums have done very well in the two decades since then, regardless of the health of the folk music scene. Though she toured frequently in the '60s, she has always reserved the greater part of her time and energy for her political activities. Throughout her career she has consistently turned down lucrative offers for TV shows, movies, and concerts, and yet remained a top folk artist. In lieu of concerts she often played benefits for charities, civil rights groups, and anti-war rallies. She was arrested for civil disobedience in 1967 during a demonstration against the draft, and spent much of her time in the late '60s speaking against the U.S. involvement in Vietnam, becoming a favored target of right-wing critics in the process.

In 1968 Joan married Stanford activist David Harris. Shortly thereafter, Harris was sent to jail for refusing to register for the draft. During this tumultuous period her album sales continued strong, as she issued *Baptism* in 1968, and the popular top-selling *Any Day Now* in 1969. She also issued her autobiography, *Daybreak*, that year.

Another record from that era, *David's Album*, is somewhat typical of her later work. It features her singing contemporary songs backed by Nashville session players like Grady Martin. This was a long way from the very traditional folk "purity" of her early recordings. She once said, "I literally thought, when I was 18, that if you added a bass and drums that you became wicked and vile."

She appeared at the Woodstock Festival in 1969. Her performance in the rain at the festival was featured on the film and record of the event. In 1970 Vanguard issued a two-record retrospective of Joan's work, *The First Ten Years*, but in 1972 she switched labels, moving to A&M. It was there that she would make some of her most commercially successful recordings, including the singles, "The Night They Drove Old Dixie Down," and Diamonds And Rust." The latter was her first self-penned hit, and signalled a new direction in her career, as she increasingly developed her songwriting skills.

In 1975 and again in 1976 she toured with Bob Dylan's Rolling Thunder Revue, which included Bob Neuwirth, Roger McGuinn, and Ramblin' Jack Elliot. She had been friends with Bob since meeting him at Gerde's Folk City in 1962, and along with Peter, Paul, and Mary, had helped popularize the young songwriter's material. She continued to record throughout the decade, and frequently toured to support her albums, including *Blowin' Away* and *Honest Lullaby*.

In preparation for *Honest Lullaby* (1979) Joan, took her first vocal lessons. She was finding it difficult reaching the higher registers and began lessons to improve her upper range. At the time she said, "That's one thing I've never done before in my musical life . . . exercise my voice."

She often displays this characteristic modesty about her vocal and instrumental talents. Because she isn't a trained guitarist, she dislikes talking about her playing technique. Though she considers her guitar work only an accompaniment to her three-octave voice, reviewers and critics have taken notice of her delicate picking style since the first record. She never learned to flatpick and contents herself with various strums and a homegrown yet effective Travis-picking style using the thumb and three fingers. She admits even she sometimes really isn't certain how she plays what she does. "I'm not even sure of the brand of strings I use," she says sheepishly. "I usually use La Bella silk-and-steel, but someone gave me a big box of some other kind and I've been playing them since."

She realizes she could be a better guitarist with regular practice, "but I simply have no discipline." Her guitar playing, like her singing is self-taught, though some critics refuse to believe it. "One interviewer really liked the Villa Lobos thing I sang on one of my earlier albums," she says, "and wanted to know how many hours a day I practiced singing. I tried to explain that but he wouldn't believe me. I finally had to say 'Oh all right. About three hours a day,' then he was satisfied."

Today, after appearing on more than 30 albums, Joan is without a major record label contract. This situation puts her in a kind of commercial exile, with no easy way to reach a larger audience. Many other performers, such as Peter, Paul, and Mary, and Arlo Guthrie, are in the same boat. And yet, like Joan, they remain terrific concert draws. When she performs it is usually for worthy causes she supports, such as nuclear disarmament, or the annual Bread And Roses Festival (Bread And Roses is a charitable organization started by her sister, which brings musicians and performers into nursing homes, drug rehabilitation centers, and other places where people normally can't get out to hear music). In a fitting tribute to her role as a protest singer, and an artist who always put political principles above monetary gain, she opened the 1985 Live Aid concert in Philadelphia. She was playing on a bill with much younger artists, some of whom weren't even born when Joan won the crowd at Newport in 1959. The chance to share her commitment with them plainly inspired Joan and she used the opportunity to pass the torch of protest to a new generation of musicians saying, "This is your Woodstock, and it's long overdue!"

## A Selected Joan Baez Discography
(On Vanguard): *Any Day Now*, Van 79306; *Joan Baez*, Van 2077; *Ballad Book*, VSD 41-42; *In Concert Vol. I and II*, Van 2122, 2123; *Love Song Album*, VSD- 79-80; *Baptism*, Van 79275; *Blessed Are*, 6570-1; *Carry It On*, Van 79313; *Country Music Album*, Van 105-6; *David's Album*, Van 79308; *Farewell, Angelina*, Van 79200; *Joan*, Van 79240; *One Day At A Time*, Van 79310. (On A&M Records): *Best Of Joan Baez*, AAM 3234; *Come From The Shadows*, AAM 3103; *Diamonds & Rust*, AAM 3233; *From Every Stage*, AAM 6506.

# DOC WATSON

Since coming to prominence through his association with Clarence Ashley in the late '50s, Doc Watson has been a major influence on folk and bluegrass flatpickers. For most of the past two decades he has toured with his son and fellow guitarist, Merle, who died in a tractor accident at the family farm in October, 1985. Doc was interviewed in the March, 1979 issue of Frets.

**By Jon Sievert**

PROBABLY THE MOST influential and commercially enduring instrumentalist to emerge from the Sixties folk experience was a blind singer/guitarist from Deep Gap, North Carolina: Arthel "Doc" Watson. Doc was not only a compelling vocalist with a rich baritone and a vast repertoire of Blue Ridge Mountain music, but a true virtuoso of the flatpicked acoustic guitar.

The effect Doc had on guitarists was immediate. Until he showed what could be done, the vast majority of budding folk guitarists were content to assume the traditional role of vocal accompaniment and rhythmic backup. When Doc turned up, flatpicking the lead to fiddle tunes at blazing speed, the fallout was immediate. Gifted young guitarists Clarence White of the Kentucky Colonels and John Herald of the Greenbriar Boys were among the most important of those immediately affected. Doc's genius estab-

lished once and for all the validity of the flatpicked acoustic guitar as a lead instrument.

Arthel Watson's story begins on March 3, 1923. One of nine children of Annie and General Dixon Watson, he contracted an eye disease as an infant that left him blind before he was two years old. Hymns he heard sitting on his mother's lap in church, and the old-time ballads she sang around the house, formed some of his first memories of music. His father was also a singer, and something of a banjo picker, and led the family every night in Bible reading and hymn singing.

Doc got his first musical instrument, a harmonica, at an early age, and thereafter received a new one each Christmas. Before long he had strung a single steel wire to the woodshed's sliding door and tuned it to his harmonica so he could provide his own bass accompaniment while he played.

When Doc was seven the musical world began to open up for him. His father bought a table model Victrola from an uncle, and included in the purchase were a stack of recordings by such groups as Gid Tanner and the Skillet Lickers, the Carolin Tar Heels, and the Carter Family. The collection soon grew to include recordings by Jimmie Rodgers, Riley Puckett, and Mississippi John Hurt.

Because of his blindness and his family's poverty, Doc did not start school until he was ten. His parents sent him to North Carolina's School for the Blind, in Raleigh. When he came home the following summer his father offered to build him a banjo. Doc accepted and took to the new instrument immediately, learning to frail several tunes.

A couple of years later, when he was twelve, Doc heard a classmate playing a guitar. Soon he had learned a few chords himself, and after he returned home he made a deal with his father and got his first guitar, a $12.00 Stella. Not long afterward he teamed with his brother, Linny, to learn many of the region's old-time mountain tunes and many of the new songs he was hearing on the Grand Ole Opry and the clear-channel bootleg Mexican radio stations. Doc's early performances were mostly limited to front-porch playing with relatives and neighbors until the pressure of making payments on his first Martin convinced him to try singing in the streets.

Doc acquired his nickname when he was 18. He and a friend were getting ready to play for a remote radio broadcast at a furniture store, and the announcer decided the "Arthel" was too cumbersome to use on the air. "Call him 'Doc,'" a lady in the crowd suggested. The name stuck (Doc says there is no truth to the story that it derives from the Dr. Watson of Sherlock Holmes lore).

In 1947 Doc met and married Rosa Lee Carlton, daughter of a fine old-time mountain fiddler named Gaither Carlton. Gaither was a walking repository of old tunes indigenous to his isolated mountain home and he passed along many that remain part of Doc's repertoire today.

Despite his blossoming talent, Doc still was not earning any money from his skills. After his marriage he took to tuning pianos to help feed his family. It wasn't until 1953, when he was 30, that he became a successful working musician. That was the year he met Jack Williams, a piano player from Tennessee who was fronting a country and western swing band. Williams was impressed by Doc's talent and invited him to play lead guitar in a the band. Shortly thereafter Doc traded in his D-28 for a 1953 Les Paul Standard and became an electric guitarist. (Even today Doc carries those '50s tunes with him, and he delights in occassionally astounding audiences with a hot encore rendition of "Blue Suede Shoes" or "Tutti Frutti.")

Because the band did not have a fiddle player, Williams called on Doc to provide the lead part on fiddle tunes for square dancing. Thus, ironically, it was on the electric guitar that Doc developed and honed the style for which he was to become so famous on the acoustic guitar.

The association with Williams lasted nearly eight years. The band toured eastern Tennessee and western North Carolina, playing VFW halls and square dances. During that period Doc continued to pick and sing old-time music with his family. He also played with a neighbor, Clarence "Tom" Ashley, who had been an original member of the Carolina Tar Heels.

In 1960, as the folk boom was just beginning, Ashley was sought out by two young musicologists named Ralph Rinzler and Eugene Earle. Anxious to record Ashley, Rinzler, and Earle happened to get Doc Watson on banjo and guitar in the bargain. The results of that meeting are still available on a pair of albums, *Old-Time Music At Clarence Ashley's* [Folkways].

Rinzler was excited by the sessions, especially by Doc's unique talent. He immediately began making plans to get Ashley and Doc to New York to perform their old-time mountain music for the growing folk audience there, but Doc was dubious. Doc simply could not believe that there was anyone there who wanted to hear it.

Fortunately, Rinzler prevailed. In the spring of 1961, Doc Watson made his urban debut at a Friends of Old-Time Music concert in New York. He was accompanied by Ashley, Clint Howard, and Fred Price. A year later he gave his first solo performance at Gerde's Folk City in New York.

Doc was soon much in demand, traveling the country playing concerts and hootenannies and making some television appearances. He was a smash hit at the 1963 Newport Folk Festival, and in November of that year he played a historic concert with mandolinist Bill Monroe at New York's Town Hall. Bootleg recordings of that concert are still surfacing.

About that time the folk music boom began to bottom out. The Beatles had arrived to breathe fresh air into rock and roll, and most of the newly discovered folk artists were returning to a subsistence level as performers. Doc himself came very close to going back to North Carolina for good, though not for lack of an appreciative public. He was homesick, and with his vision handicap traveling was very difficult.

In 1964 Doc came home from nearly three months on the road to find that his 15-year-old son, Merle, had taken up the guitar. It wasn't too long before Merle was good enough to play rhythm guitar for Doc. At 16, Merle became his father's backup guitarist, road manager, and chauffeur, and the two began spending up to 300 nights year on the road.

Because of Merle, Doc was able to continue his career, reaching a steadily widening audience even during acoustic music's leanest years.

In 1968 the father-son duo was asked by the State

**Doc's flawless playing of traditional Appalachian fiddle tunes on guitar attracted legions of fans in the early '60s. He characterizes his picking motion as three-quarters arm motion and one-quarter wrist motion.**

Department to represent the United States in a cultural exchange program with African nations. The Watsons went from snow-covered North Carolina to 100-degree temperatures in Nairobi, Kenya, playing at villages in the bush country of Malawi, Zambia, Botswana, Lesotho, and Swaziland to enthusiastic native audiences.

In 1972 Doc's music touched a new generation of listeners when he participated in the recording of *Will The Circle Be Unbroken* [United Artists], a landmark project organized by the Nitty Gritty Dirt Band. The Dirt Band gathered together and recorded with a living country and bluegrass music Hall of Fame that included Doc, Maybelle Carter, Earl Scruggs, Roy Acuff, and Merle Travis. The result was a three-record album that later went gold. Doc's warm humor, his singing, and his remarkable guitar playing sparkle throughout the album.

The burden of travel eased for Doc and Merle in the '70s. Their commercial appeal was such that they flew to their many concerts in a private twin-engine plane. The team was joined in 1974 by bass guitarist T. Michael Coleman, who still performs with Doc today.

Doc's distinctive playing starts with a Herco nylon flatpick, which he favors because of its embossed grip surfaces, its durability, and the cleaner sound it makes against the strings. The strings themselves are medium-gauge D'Addarios (Merle uses medium-light Gallaghers, from the same company that produces the Watsons' guitars). Doc likes his guitars set with an action slightly higher than normal, feeling that the extra clearance produces more punch and volume. He uses a capo—he calls it a "cheater"—occasionally, most often at the third fret. Doc also fingerpicks on occasion.

Although his right arm appears to move very little while he plays, Doc has characterized his technique as three-quarters arm motion and a quarter wrist motion. He leaves the little finger of his right hand lightly touching the pickguard as a depth gauge. Doc believes that flatpicking technique must be light and delicate to be clean, and suggests practicing scales using even up-and-down picking. On the left-hand technique, he advises guitarists against copying his use of the thumb on the sixth string for barred chords. He says that Merle has developed a better reach on the neck by using conventional barre chording.

· · · ·

**C**OULD YOU TELL US *a little about that first banjo your dad built for you?*

When I came home that first spring at school my dad said, "Son, I might make you a little banjo this summer," and I said, "I ain't never seen one of them." He said, "Well, I used to pick a little and I know where to get ahold of some of them tension hooks, so I believe I can make you one." So he commenced to

working on it. He carved the neck out of maple and made little friction tuning pegs like dulcimers have. When he got the hoop done he stretched a groundhog hide over it, but that just didn't work right. It was too stiff and didn't give a very good tone. We solved the problem, though, when Granny's 16-year-old cat passed on. That made one of the best banjo heads you ever seen and it stayed on that thing, I guess, as long as I picked it. Dad got it made and tuned it up and the first piece I ever heard him play was "Rambling Hobo." He showed me a few tunes to get me started. Then one day he picked it up and put it in my hands and said, "Here, son. Take this and learn to play it good. You might need it in this world. It's yours now." He never would pick no more after he got me started.

*It seems like your father left you with a fine legacy by giving you that banjo.*

Making that banjo and encouraging me into music, knowing that it was a trade I could learn, was a mighty fine thing he did for me. The best thing my dad ever did for me in my life, though, was to put me at one end of a crosscut saw. He put me to work and that made me feel useful. A lot of blind people weren't ever put to work. I remember the morning when he leaned back in his chair, took a big swig of coffee, and said, "Son, do you think you can learn to pull a crosscut saw?" and I said, "Yeah." I didn't know what I was getting into but I soon found out, I tell you right now.

*Could you run down a progression of the guitars you've gone through since you've been playing?*

Well, I got the Stella when I was 12. I had heard a friend named Paul Montgomery in school playing guitar and learned a couple of chords. When I came home that summer, my brother had borrowed my cousin's guitar. Daddy heard me messing with it one morning and said, "Son, if you can learn a tune on that by the time I get back from work this evening we'll go find you a guitar of some kind." He didn't know that I already knew a chord or two, and when he came home I could pick the chords to "When The Roses Bloom In Dixie Land." That's when we went and got the Stella. I kept that awhile and I worked out the price of my second guitar myself at the end of a crosscut saw. That was a Silvertone from Sears. I traded around a time or two between that and when Mr. Richard Green, an old man who ran a little music store in Boone, helped me get my first Martin.

*Do you remember what model it was?*

It was a Martin D-28. That must have been about 1940. It was a new guitar and he let me have a year to pay it off. I played on the street nearly every Saturday, when the weather was warm, at a cab stand in Lenore, South Carolina. Sometimes I'd make as much as $50.00, and I paid that guitar off in four or five months. I didn't aim to lose that thing. I kept that guitar right up until the time I joined Jack Williams.

*Is that when you bought the Les Paul?*

Yeah. I tried to use a pickup on the Martin for

awhile but I finally got up enough nerve to trade it on the Les Paul.

*Did you get into altered chords with the Jack Williams band?*

Some. Jack played pretty decent piano, mostly honky-tonk, and I'd improvise with the three-and four-note chords. I didn't worry about learning all the barre chords because we had a rhythm guitar player. The hardest chore I got into with that group was playing the lead fiddle tunes for square dancing. That man would just keep you going for twenty minutes. He'd break your arm off.

*What do you think you gained from that experience with Jack Williams?*

I still use some of the hot licks that I played on the electric, but they come out sounding a little different to the ear when you play them on the flat-top. I got a lot of technical practice with the flatpick during those years. It helped build my knowledge of using the flatpick enormously.

*Did you always flatpick, right from the start?*

I started off playing with a thumb lead, Maybelle Carter style. Then when I began to listen to Jimmie Rodgers I figured out there was something being done there besides the thumb and finger. So I got me a pick and started working on it. It was Hank Garland who inspired me to learn fiddle tunes on the guitar. I did learn some fingerpicking from a fellow named Olin Miller. I loved Merle Travis. That's who I named my son after.

*Was your work with Jack Williams your first real performing job?*

Well, of course there were the street things; and people who heard me on the street invited me to come to amateur contests and fiddlers' conventions, and I went. I began to win a few, but I found that people didn't want me in their shows no matter how good I was because I was a little trouble to them and I didn't have a flashy stage show. It just wasn't accepted then for you to just sit on the stage and pick, unless you were a super musician, and that I wasn't. I did win some contests, though, and I remember one time when I entered once in the professional category and won it. That really helped my ego.

*Your music shows a wide variety of influences. Were you exposed to different kinds of music early?*

We had the records and they were pretty varied. In 1939 we got a battery-set radio and we could pick up anything from Del Rio, Texas, to Minneapolis, Minnesota. I heard a lot of big band music. I remember getting interested in dixieland jazz. I thought that was some kind of fine. And later I began to like the Dorseys and Phil Harris. You name it and I began to like the sound. When you begin to understand music and your ear is being educated to the theory, then you can really learn to love it. You can't really love something until you can understand it.

*At what point did you start using the custom-built J.W. Gallagher [Wartrace, Tennessee] guitar you have now?*

I don't remember the exact year that happened.

After I stopped playing electric and went on the road I borrowed a Martin from a boy named Joe Cox who couldn't play a lick. He gave me that guitar to play as long as I wanted and I used that for quite awhile. Then I played some on a D-28 that Ralph Rinzler had. Merle and I both had Martins for awhile. Then one Easter J.W. and his son dropped by our house with three or four of their guitars. The house was full of people who had just come back from Union Grove [the nearby music festival]. I played all of the guitars and just before he left he came over and handed me the guitar that I'd liked the best. He said, "I want to give you this, and there are no strings attached except the ones on the guitar. We'll just let the thing endorse itself if it is any good." I used that guitar for eight years. Three years ago this September he came up to me in Nashville and told me he wanted to do something for me because I had sold more guitars than he could make, just by playing that guitar. I told him he could build me a new guitar with a neck to my specifications, and I sent him my '53 Les Paul to copy. He copied the neck and shape, the fretboard, and the type of frets, and made a guitar to suit himself. That's what I have now.

*Is that what he calls the Doc Watson model?*

Yes. He heard me playing it and asked if he could produce it and put it in his catalog. Then in January he brought me a twin to it and I've got that at home. I played it on the road for two or three months to break it in so if something happened to one, the other wouldn't have to hit the road straight brand new. When a guitar is green you might be able to hear the good in it, but they're not like they are once you've played them awhile and you break them in. They have to be played to season them properly.

*Do you ever play the banjo anymore?*

Maybe one out of ten shows I'll pick it up and play something. I've let Merle do most of the banjo work.

*Did you ever play another instruments besides banjo, harmonica, and guitar?*

I tried the fiddle for awhile but I never could get that bowing hand right. I've picked around a bit on the mandolin and I do think I could learn to play that. I never could find a mandolin that had a neck wide enough to suit me and a tone fittin' for beings, though. I did find a beautiful old Gibson A model that I done my damndest to buy, but the lady that owned it didn't want to sell.

*When did you get the notion to try to play fiddle tunes on the guitar?*

I guess I actually started trying to do that pretty early. I'd made up my mind that I couldn't play the fiddle, but I wanted to play with the same kind of bounce and rhythm that the fiddle did so I started working them out on the guitar. You can't do the same things that are done on the fiddle but you can do the tunes to where they are pretty. I spent a lot of time practicing. I hadn't heard anyone else do that on a guitar before, and I'll tell you it really surprised Bill Monroe when we played together at the Ash Grove in Los Angeles. Ralph [Rinzler] had got the idea for me and Bill to do some of the old Charlie and Bill Monroe things together as an extra short set on the shows. The first tune we did was "Paddy On The Turnpike," and all at once I took a break on the guitar. Bill came over after we got off the stage and said something like, "Mighty fine guitar playing." Then in a few minutes he said, "Do you know 'Tennessee Blues'?" and I said, "Yeah, I think I can pick it." We got back up there the next time and we flat got on it and I played just as fast as he could go with it. When we got off the stage he said, "Man, you got after that tune. I've never heard a guitar played like that before." You can imagine how I felt. I'd been listening to Bill Monroe for maybe twenty years.

*What kind of process do you and Merle go through in working out a tune?*

Well, I don't ever tell Merle how to play a tune. I might suggest something like, "Try this and see if it

> **Doc attributes much of his musical success
> to his father who "put me to work and
> made me feel useful. A lot of blind
> people weren't ever put to work."**

will work," but you can't mold a guy if he's a true musician. He's got to pick the way he picks. We'll sit down together and get the melody line straight and he will pick around a bit on it. I'll let him think about it for awhile and in the next day or two he'll sit down again and he will pick it. He does his own arrangements. He'll play a tune one way one night and a different way the next. Same with me. There are one or two songs that have definite arrangements. I play "Sweet Georgia Brown" about the same way every time, maybe adding different phrasing here and there occassionally, but basically it's the same arrangement. The country songs that I'm so used to I'll play a little different each set, depending on how I feel. "Milk Cow Blues" is one we vary quite a bunch.

*Do you consciously do things with your voice and harmonica to play against the guitar?*

I think the combination comes out according to your feelings. If you are really into a tune, not forcing yourself or nervous, and really into playing for an audience, those sorts of musical things happen as a result of your feelings. It's not a conscious thing. You may practice at something to get it a certain way but find it comes out different when you do it onstage.

*Do you use a pickup on your guitar?*

Yes. Merle and I both have Barcus-Berrys installed in our guitars. We got into that because of shoddy sound systems at a lot of the festivals. If you turned it loud enough for them to hear your guitar you got feedback. Well, if you put a padded-down signal into their board you can play as loud as you want. It might not sound as sweet and clean all the time, because of their system, but it will be the sound of the guitar.

*What kind of amps are you and Merle using?*

We've used Fender Twins for years. I don't believe you can hardly whip them for what we do. We rent them wherever we go.

*What is your general opinion of the festival circuit these days?*

I'd really rather not say what I think about some of those festivals. There's about 70 percent of them that I wouldn't take Rosa Lee or my daughter Nancy to. People go to certain festivals just because they can raise all the hell they want. The security is bad and there's a lot of drinkin'. There's too many who don't go to listen who spoil it for those that do. It's just downright rudeness. Those festivals are sure a far cry from the quiet, very attentive audiences of the 60s folk festivals. That Newport festival was something. I

remember when Clarence, Fred, Clint, and I played it in 1963. We'd go out onstage and eight to ten thousand people would go dead quiet and listen to the music. Man, you couldn't believe the ovations for those simple old tunes that Clarence did. You knew the people were there to hear the roots of their music.

*Do you hear many new pickers who excite you?*

Lord, yes. There are a lot of fine ones coming along. Norman Blake is surely one. That last album I heard by him has some licks on there I don't think I could do. The left-hand parts I believe I could handle, but I don't know about that right hand. I'm going to ask him what kind of operation he had on that wrist to loosen it up like that. Tony Rice and Dan Crary are two more mighty fine pickers. In fact Tony is recording a couple of cuts with us for this live album. There's also a real fine young fingerpicker named Guy Van Duser. He can pick himself a guitar. There are so many guitar players that play for a show and then there are some that play for the love. Man, you can sure tell the difference when you sit down and listen to them. Too many people are just trying to see how many notes they can play on the guitar. Fast and tasteful *can* be combined. Two musicians can play a riff and the choice of notes and the phrasing is what makes it tasteful or not—no matter how fast or slow it is played.

*Do you get much of a chance to jam with new musicians these days?*

Once in awhile I will if I'm rested and their playing interests me. I'm ashamed to say, though, that I don't have the passion for the music that I did at one time. I seldom jam anymore because I play so much on the road that I get it out of my system with audiences.

*How much of your musical repertoire is made up of the old-time tunes?*

I'd say about 30 percent of my music comes from family and relatives and the rest from records, radio, and what-not. One new tune we're doing for this live album is the old Everly Brothers song called "Dream."

*Do you have any ambitious concept albums that you are anxious to do? Do you still have a good backlog of old tunes to draw upon?*

Well, there are quite a few old ones that I could dig out. We've got one more album under this contract and I haven't even thought of half of that. We just kind of take them one at a time.

---

## A Selected Doc Watson Discography

**Solo albums** (on Vanguard): *Doc Watson*, 79152; *Essential Doc Watson*, VSD-45-46; *Good Deal*, 79276; *Home Again*, 79239; *Southbound*, 79213; (on United Artists): *Doc Watson Memories*, UA-LA423-H2; *Convoy*, UA-LA910-H. **With Merle Watson:** *Doc Watson & Son*, Vanguard, 79170; *Doc Watson On Stage*, Vanguard, VSD-9/10; *Ballads From Deep Gap*, Vanguard, 6576; *Lonesome Road*, United Artists, UA-LA022-F; *Look Away*, United Artists, UA-LA-887-H; *Then And Now*, Poppy, PP-LA-022-F; *Pickin The Blues*, Flying Fish, FF352. **With others:** *Greatest Folk Singers Of The Sixties*, Vanguard, VSD-17/18; *Old Timey Concert*, Vanguard, VSD-10; *Country Music And Bluegrass At Newport*, Vanguard, 79147; *Oldtime Music At Newport*, Vanguard, 79147; *Doc & The Boys*, United Artists, UA-LA601-G; *Old Time Music At Clarence Ashley's*, Folkways, 2359; *Progressive Bluegrass*, Folkways, 2370; *Watson Family*, Folkways, 2366; *Earl Scruggs, His Family & Friends*, Columbia, C-30584.

# PETER, PAUL, & MARY

Peter Yarrow, Noel (Paul) Stookey, and Mary Travers became one of the most successful folk acts of the '60s, blending intricate harmonies, with fingerpicked guitar arrangements. Though the group disbanded in 1970, they have recently regrouped and released a self-produced album in 1984.

**By Helen Casabona**

IF YOU LIVED THROUGH the '60s, you probably know most of Peter, Paul, and Mary's songs. Perhaps the most popular folk act of that decade's folk boom, Peter, Paul, aNd Mary were also one of the most long lasting. They survived the coming of the electric guitar and British rock—all without moving markedly from their folk roots. Today, 20 years later, they're still selling out their shows, which in recent years have numbered nearly 40 a year.

But despite, or perhaps as a result of their success, Peter, Paul, and Mary have often been part of a controversy between the old and the new—between those who were trying to hold on to a folk music tradition, and those keeping up with the times. By making hits of Pete Seeger's and Lee Hays' "If I Had A Hammer," and Bob Dylan's "Blowin' In The Wind," Peter, Paul, and Mary successfully blended the folk tradition with commercial sensibility. And yet this synthesis drew criticism from folk "purists," who contended that the trio was opportunistic and that its slick, professional performances bore little resemblance to the the tradition it claimed to represent.

In fact, Peter, Paul, and Mary were by no means the first folk group to find success on the pop charts. The Weavers, founded by Pete Seeger in 1949, launched a popular folk revival that would both inspire and pave the way for the Boom of the '60s. They exhumed classics like "On Top Of Old Smokey" and polished them up to appeal to audiences of the times. By 1955, their album "Weavers At Carnegie

(Left to right) Peter Yarrow, Mary Travers, and Paul Stookey, may have ridden the crest of the folk boom wave, but they also were among the first entertainers to become involved in the civil rights movement.

Hall" turned on an entire generation to this renewed folk genre.

Another commercial folk act really kicked off the folk revival of the '60s. In 1958, the Kingston Trio amazed everyone by taking a new version of the folk classic, "Tom Dooley" to the top of the charts. Three college kids made it look so easy—just learn a few chords and a three-part harmony. It was a sound everybody could listen to, and the folk craze had begun.

Forewarned perhaps by the political controversy that plagued the Weavers, the Kingston Trio changed the words of songs to eliminate all political content, even going so far as to copyright their "rewritten" versions. Criticism of the Kingston Trio was primarily focused on this apolitical stance. After all, politics and left-wing sentiments had been a main ingredient of folk music since "Yankee Doodle Dandy."

When Albert Grossman (manager of Bob Dylan, Ian and Sylvia, et al.) formed Peter, Paul, and Mary in 1961, he made it a visual/vocal combination: Peter grew a goatee to match Paul's, and Mary's ironed blonde hair became the fashion for teenage girls all over the country. But the trio sought middle ground when it came to song material: their hits ranged from sweet and innocent children's songs like "Puff The Magic Dragon" to Dylan's "Blowin' In The Wind" and "The Times They Are A' Changing."

By the mid-'60s, Peter, Paul, and Mary were the most popular folk act at home and abroad, headlining folk and rock concerts, clubs, and making appearances on TV. They were among the main attractions at the Newport Folk festivals, of which Peter was one of the founding members.

Peter Yarrow was born May 31, 1938, in New York City. He grew up taking violin and art lessons and was first exposed to folk music at the High School of Music and Arts, where he admired Woody Guthrie, Burl Ives, Pete Seeger, and Josh White. He earned a BA in psychology from Cornell University, but also taught courses on folklore and folk music. In 1960, he played on CBS's Folk Sound, U.S.A., which led to an invitation to play at the Newport Folk Festival later that year.

Noel Stookey, later to become Paul, was born Christmas Eve, 1937, in Baltimore, Maryland. Perhaps the trio's most avid instrumentalist, he started playing at 11, when his father gave him a Martin tenor guitar, which he played like a ukulele.

"My folks could tell I was busting out musically," Paul reports, "so they gave me a banjo one Christmas. But I didn't want a banjo, I wanted an electric guitar. So they got me a Kay electric with a semi-acoustic body and I reworked it, putting some long-handled volume and tone control knobs on it. "I played that thing until I was 21, when I heard Segovia play. Then I borrowed $20, sold my electric guitar and amp, and bought a Martin 0021 Classical."

Paul's first professional music experience was playing rock and roll in a band, "Bird of Paradise" for

which he wrote some original material. After college, he tried to make it working in a camera shop in Philadelphia and then as a production manager for the Cormac Chemical Corporation in New York City. But although the town was right, it didn't take him long to realize the job wasn't. So back he went to entertaining full time. He played music around Greenwich Village, but by the end of 1960, he had made a name for himself locally not as a singer but as a stand-up comic.

"It was only because I started singing in the Village and was exposed to people like Tom Paxton, Ramblin' Jack Elliott, and especially Dave Van Ronk that I became interested in doing some of those songs."

Mary Allin Travers was born November 9, 1936, in Louisville, Kentucky, and moved to New York City at age two. She attended a progressive private school where folk music came with the education and grew up in Greenwich Village.

"My life was full of people who were seriously involved in folk music. I met Pete [Seeger] when I was ten, and I also met Paul Robeson. But it never occurred to me that it would become my profession—it was a hobby, anyone could sing, even if they couldn't sing."

At 14, Mary sang with the Songswappers, a children's chorus that recorded three albums with Seeger. In 1957 she got a job in the chorus of Mort Sahl's Broadway flop, "The Next President." After that, she went through a series of jobs at literary and advertising agencies by day, while looking for music contacts by night.

Then one night in 1961, Mary met Stokey at the Gaslight in Greenwhich Village. They were introduced by Milt Okun, who encouraged them to form a duo. Okun was a singer/songwriter and music

teacher who would later become the trio's Musical Director.

The two singers started performing together and it wasn't long before they were approached by Albert Grossman, who at the time was handling Yarrow. Grossman suggested that the three form a trio. Paul initially turned down the offer, but a few weeks later Mary invited him over to sing. Peter was there and the rest is history. Stookey changed his name to Paul (to parody a line in a folk song that went, "Peter, Paul, and Moses, playing 'round the Roses") and a year later, the group had a recording contract with Warner.

Their first album, *Peter, Paul, and Mary*, came out in '62 featuring "If I Had A Hammer," "Lemon Tree," and "Blowin' In The Wind." In '63, "Blowin' In The Wind" was released as a single and sold 300,000 copies in the first two weeks—the best selling Warner release to that date—It also won a Grammy for Best Folk Music Record of the Year. Even the black rhythm and blues stations played it, a feat for any pop song, much less folk pop.

In '64 they had another hit single, "Go Tell It On The Mountain." 1965 saw three more albums: *Peter, Paul, and Mary in Concert, A Song Will Rise*, and *See What Tomorrow Brings*. That year they brought a Canadian songwriter into the American public's view by doing Gordon Lightfoot's "Early Morning Rain." Later in the decade they did a similar favor for John Denver, with a gold-record version of "Leavin' On A Jet Plane."

The early '60s folk boom, however, was short lived. Rock and roll came to town in the middle of the decade and most folk artists either joined up or got left behind. When Bob Dylan showed up at the Newport Folk festival in 1965 with an electric guitar, many saw that the end of the folk era was at hand. But Peter, Paul, and Mary kept going. In 1966 and '67, two of their singles made the charts: "The Cruel War" and "I Dig Rock 'n' Roll Music," and perhaps their best collection appeared on *Album 1700*, released in 1967. They continued to churn out albums and hit singles, year after year, culminating with two in 1969: "Too Much Of Nothing" and "Day Is Done." By 1970, they had put out ten albums: eight gold and five platinum.

Their breakup in 1970 was not because of a lack of business. They disbanded right before "Leaving on a Jet Plane" became their first No. 1 single. According to Paul, they just ran out of things to say together and wanted to strike out creatively on their own. What may have also increased the tension was that Paul had been charged with having illicit relations with a minor and the resulting court case and legal pressures proved a burden on the entire group.

After they broke up, all three stayed in music to varying degrees. Mary and Peter continued with Warner making solo albums. Neither's albums sold well, but Mary came up with one hit in the early '70s, "Follow Me." Peter's biggest accomplishment was that he co-wrote Mary MacGregor's "Torn Between Two Lovers." As for Paul, he turned to Jesus and moved to several rural locations, settling finally in the backwoods of Maine. He sang about 40 gigs a year at places like his daughter's high school and had one modest hit in '71, "The Wedding Song."

The '70s was a decade for reunions: Crosby, Stills, and Nash, Dylan and the Band, the Beach Boys and Brian Wilson, Jan & Dean. And in 1978, Peter, Paul, and Mary struck out on a 17-date reunion tour around the U.S. But when they came on stage, there were no cherry bombs, no disco fog, and still no electric guitars. Peter and Paul had traded in their goatees for mustaches and more skin was showing on their foreheads, but Mary hadn't changed a hair. Even their audience was the same, barring some mortgaged ideals and children in tow.

Peter, Paul, and Mary's reunion wasn't a one-time affair, but a renaissance, and they're playing to this day. Like many older performers, they continue to be a big box-office success, even though they have no contract with a major recording label. They went on nationwide tours in 1980 and '84 and continue to play up to 40 gigs a year.

Their commitment to social causes remains strong, as indicated by their 1983 tour which was limited to benefits and charities, including an appearance (not a performance) at the Live Aid concert in Philadelphia. They also headlined at the Kerrville, Texas, Folk Festival, along with fellow '60s performers Carolyn Hester and Happy and Artie Traum.

There's no denying that Peter, Paul, and Mary were the brain child of a market-conscious manager. But the fact remains that they popularized a form of folk music, stayed consistently with that sound, outlasted their contemporaries who tried to do the same, and are still successful.

It may have been a shock to traditionalists to see a group of college kids making money singing a Pete Seeger classic in perfect three-part harmony. But in hindsight, we see that Peter, Paul, and Mary didn't destroy a tradition; they made it accessible to a contemporary public and went on to define a tradition of their own—of the '60s—bridging a gap between the beatniks and the hippies, voicing anti-war and civil rights sentiments before it was popular to do so. Mary said, "We are the children of Pete Seeger. We came from the folk tradition in a contemporary form where there was a concern that idealism be a part of your music and the music a part of your life."

---

### A Selected Peter, Paul & Mary Discography
(On Warner Brothers): *Album 1700*, 1700; *A Song Will Rise*, WS 1589; *Moving*, W 1473; *Ten Years Together*, K-3105; *Peter, Paul & Mary*, K-1449; *In Concert*, 1555; *Reunion*, K-3231.

# BOB DYLAN

JIM MARSHALL

Early in his career Dylan carried the mantle of Woody Guthrie (even recording "Song To Woody" on his first album). But his songwriting talents served notice that he was much more than an interpreter of musical traditions. In the 25 years since he burst on the scene, Dylan has become a legend, certainly one of the most important lyricists of his generation. His records have run the gamut from highly electric rock to simple folk and country. He was recently a featured singer on the "USA For Africa" single, "We Are The World."

**By Phil Hood**

POET, VISIONARY, FOLKIE, rocker, political rebel, religious fundamentalist, blasphemer, and prophet—Bob Dylan has accumulated hundreds of labels in his long career. And he has always shed these labels as quickly as they've been pinned on him—by altering his style, his sound, and his message. Dylan's various musical incarnations—young folksinger, protest singer, symbolist poet of the psychedelic era, Nashville cat, Jewish patriarch, chief medicine man of the Rolling Thunder Revue, born-again Christian, and more—have alternately surprised and

disappointed his audience, but always challenged them. This continuous creative change has kept Dylan's career alive for two-and-a-half decades, and made him the most influential songwriter of his generation.

Dylan has been through so many changes, it's hard to appreciate the excitement he caused on the folk scene back in 1961. He was the most revolutionary performer of the era, with an originality and power that had an enormous impact on fellow performers and young audiences. When he burst on the scene,

after, the harmonica, all without formal training. When he was ten he got a cheap Sears & Roebuck guitar and an around-the-neck harmonica holder.

One of his first influences was Hank Williams, not unusual for a musically-inclined kid in the '50s. He was also fascinated by the black bluesmen—Jimmy Reed, Howlin' Wolf, B.B. King, and others—that he would listen to at night on distant southern radio stations.

Little Richard became one of his earliest heroes, as did Elvis Presley. Many years later Dylan was to say that having Elvis Presley record one of his tunes, was a great honor.

By ninth grade Bob was banging out Little Richard tunes on the piano and assembling his first garage bands. In Anthony Scaduto's book *Bob Dylan: An Intimate Biography*, one of Bob's high school pals, drummer Chuck Nara, recalls, "Of all the guys around who were playing [music], Bob was the only one with a specific goal in mind—that he was going into the entertainment business and was going to make it. He talked about having a group and getting somewhere with records.

The young Dylan also had an ear for country and traditional music. He liked a lot of old cowboy songs, and particularly enjoyed the music of Hank Snow and his Brazos Valley Boys.

It's interesting to note that for Dylan, rock came first, not folk. His sensibility and early public persona, which perhaps owed more to James Dean than Woody Guthrie, was a natural outgrowth of these early experiences. When Dylan moved to rock music in 1965, and took his generation with him, he wasn't abandoning folk so much as going back to his own roots.

By his late high school years, Bob was frequenting rhythm and blues record shops in Minneapolis, and searching out new friends in the big-city music community. He was obsessive about music. Bob's girlfriend from that era tells how on the way to their junior prom Bob drove her to the little town of Virginia, about 30 miles away, so he could visit a black disc jockey he knew there. They sat about in their prom clothes and talked music. Bob was strongly drawn to the blues, both the rural sounds of Jesse Fuller and the more urban music of singers like Big Joe Williams.

In 1959 he enrolled in the University of Minneapolis. Influenced by the music of Odetta, he had traded in his electric guitar for a Gibson flat-top acoustic. He became part of the burgeoning folk scene that you could find on nearly any college campus in those days. The intellectual and social ferment that would engulf society in the '60s was brewing in the folk music community of that era. Kids were discovering leftist politics and sexual freedom (the pill debuted in 1960), as society threw off the social and political constraints of the '50s. At college Dylan got his first exposure to radical politics, as well as a broader variety of folk music. His first folksinging gig

folk was in the process of changing from a musical style to a social phenomenon—becoming the vehicle of a political and personal youth-rebellion. Though Joan Baez had been the first of the new generation to receive mass-market acclaim in Dylan's original songs, a visionary voice first expressed the hopes, fears, and disaffection of his contemporaries.

Robert Allen Zimmerman was born on May 24, 1941, in Duluth, Minnesota, to Abraham and his wife Beatty. By the time he was six the family moved to Hibbing, out on the Mesabi Iron Range near the Canadian border. There his father ran a furniture store. Bob took quickly to music—playing the piano by the time he was nine and, shortly there-was at a small club called the Ten O-clock Scholar. When the proprietor asked his name, he replied "Bob Dylan," (He later claimed it was an unpremeditated response). The material he was playing at the time was the same mixture of Weavers, Pete Seeger, Kingston Trio material that you could hear in coffeehouses in any of a hundred college towns across the U.S.

He quickly became a mainstay of the folk scene and began working at clubs in St. Paul and Minneapolis for a few bucks a night. And he was soon to discover the artist who would have the greatest impact on his folk career. Woody Guthrie.

Dylan discovered Guthrie through Woody's autobiography *Bound For Glory*. The young Dylan was caught up not only in Woody's enduring songs of protest and patriotism, but also in the romantic hobo life he lived, riding the rails in the Dust Bowl era. This was exciting stuff for a kid who had always felt suffocated by the small town life of Hibbing. In Jonathon Cott's *Dylan*, (1984 Rolling Stone Press, New York) he quotes one of Dylan's college classmates as saying that though Dylan was the "son of a Jewish furniture dealer from up on The Range, Bob would rather have been from some place in Arkansas. He wanted to be part of another kind of romantic and glorious tradition . . . some sort of folk dust bowl tradition."

Dylan himself loved to imagine that his past was as interesting and checkered as Woody's. He would sometimes tell people he was an Okie, or from California, or that he had ridden the rails and met some legendary bluesman. To a soul hungry for authentic experience, the Guthrie legend was the stuff of dreams.

That winter Bob dropped out of school, bumming around Madison, Wisconsin (where he played with Danny Kalb, later of the Blues Project), and Chicago, meeting people and playing small gigs—trying to live the life on the road. A dream had formed in his mind by that time—he wanted to get to New York to see Woody. In January of 1961 he headed for the Big Apple.

Dylan was ready for New York. It was, as he was to say later, "a great place for me to learn and to meet others who were on similar journeys." Within a few days of arriving Bob had played at the Cafe Wha? and gone to visit Woody at Greystone Hospital in New Jersey. Soon he was spending Sundays at the Gleasons, who would take care of Woody on weekends at their East Orange, New Jersey home. The crowd at Gleason's often consisted of Pete Seeger and his wife Toshi, Ramblin Jack Elliot, Cisco Houston, Peter LaFarge (author of "The Ballad Of Ira Hayes") and others. There he sang "Song For Woody," the first of his own tunes that he would ever record. Woody took a shine to him, saying, "He's a talented boy. Gonna go far."

Bob's first public gigs in New York were at Greenwich Village coffeehouses. Usually these were non-paying, or pass-the-basket jobs, but they gave him valuable experience. Though his guitar playing was improving as he worked on his blues styles, his nasal voice was still often off-key. The sort of down-and-out act he affected, trying to sound like an old blues singer, didn't sit well with some club owners. He would assume a clowning, Chaplinesque pose, sometimes playing the mime on stage, or wearing a funny Huck Finn cap, as he experimented with various disguises on the way to forging his own identity.

In April of 1961 Dylan got a gig at Gerde's Folk City, opening for bluesman John Lee Hooker. His five-song set went over well and led to a two-week stint that fully established him as someone worth watching on the folk scene. He also began playing Monday "hoot" night at Gerde's, and singing at other venues around town. At the time Bob had no set place to call home, and would live in a variety of friend's apartments. For a while he was taken in by guitarist Dave Van Ronk and his wife. Dylan later credited him as a major musical influence, and used his arrangement of "House Of The Rising Sun," on his first album.

He was also meeting lots of other people in the folk community, such as John Herald (of the Greenbriar Boys), Ric Von Schmidt, Mark Spoelstra (whom he played with at the Indian Neck Folk Festival that May) and others. In the summer of 1961 he got a call for his first recording session—playing harmonica for Harry Belafonte. Unfortunately, Bob's cavalier attitude toward the studio cut short his career as a sideman. Belafonte was a real perfectionist who wanted to do take after take. Dylan thought playing the same thing over and over boring, so he walked out of the session after running through the tune once.

His next job was playing backup harmonica on a Carolyn Hester album. Hester was one of the most popular folksingers at the time, and was later featured on the cover of Saturday Evening Post Magazine. She had come to the Northeast from her home state of Texas in 1956 and later toured with The New Lost City Ramblers. Carolyn was married to writer, singer, and composer Richard Farina, and already had two albums under her belt when she signed with Columbia. She decided that adding Dylan's harmonica would give her new record a different sound, something to separate it from the glut of folk albums beginning to hit the market. It was at these recording sessions that Dylan met John Hammond, the legendary Columbia producer, who also numbered Bessie Smith, Bennie Goodman, and Billie Holiday among his discoveries. John was looking for someone who had a message for the kids, and somehow had a hunch that Dylan was the one. After hearing Bob play harmonica he invited him to come by and make a demo tape.

Before Dylan made his first recording with Hammond, Bob got to blow his harp on a session with Victoria Spivey, Lonnie Johnson, and Big Joe Williams. Spivey had been a best-selling black artist in the race record era of the '20s, and Johnson had been an important early blues guitarist. The three of them played a series of "reunion" shows at Gerde's. Spivey met Dylan, who hung around backstage as much as possible during their appearances and became friends with the young singer. Dylan wanted badly to be in on their recording session, and asked her many times to let him play. She consented over the objections of those who felt the work should go to a black musician. Bob recorded "Sitting On Top Of The World," and "Wichita" with Big Joe Williams, who calls out one of Dylan's solos on the record as "Little Junior" playing harmonica.

On the same day as these recordings, September 26, 1961, Dylan was billed with the Greenbriar Boys for two weeks at Gerde's. Critic Robert Shelton of the *New York Times* attended opening night and wrote a rave review, which had a great influence on bringing Dylan to the attention of a wider audience. In October, after Hammond heard Dylan's tape of "Talkin' New York," he was signed by Columbia, the same label Pete Seeger was on. Many people in the folk music community were surprised and overjoyed that he was the first of the newest generation of singers to get a contract with a major label. Things were starting to happen fast for Bob Dylan.

That first album, *Bob Dylan*, cut in late 1961, gives a good view of how Dylan's "folk" style was evolving. Most of the tunes were completed in one "take." Dylan showed an early and lasting preference for leaving mistakes and false starts in the final mix. He was a highly interpretative singer, capable of shouts, howls, and extended vocal leaps that would play with the melody and the time signature. He showed no interest in sticking to "accepted" renditions of traditional material, which had been a cardinal virtue to many, more pious, folk artists of the day.

On this album he also played several older blues about dying, a theme that Dylan has stuck with. "See That My Grave Is Kept Clean" and "Fixin' To Die" show off his deft sense of timing and emotional blues vocals. A tune he learned from Ric Von Schmidt "Baby Let Me Follow You Down," shows his finger-picking style and harmonica work to good advantage. There is plenty of strong right hand flatpicking too, particularly on rhythmic blues numbers.

Though a lot of folks felt Dylan couldn't sing, and there are moments when you have to pull for him to hit the notes on this record, what comes through *most* is his singing. He holds one note for half a minute on "Freight Train Blues," and he makes "House Of The Rising Sun" come alive with a growling, raspy vocal copied from Van Ronk, injecting new life into the old material.

Dylan's first album didn't do too well commercially, selling only 5,000 copies the first year. Nevertheless, Hammond remained high on keeping Dylan with the label. So did Johnny Cash, a force at Columbia and a Dylan fan from the first. Though some at Columbia had begun referring to Dylan as "Hammond's Folly," his position was secure. And by 1962 the Bob Dylan of fame and fortune was emerging. He began to come into his own as a songwriter, churning out the topical protest songs that would become his signature.

Dylan's political sensibilities were no doubt heightened by the involvement of many folksingers in the civil rights movement. Certainly, this seemed to be the first political issue that really moved Dylan. His songs such as "The Ballad Of Emmett Till," (the story of a black boy who is lynched for whistling at a white woman) and of course, "Blowing In The Wind," and "Masters Of War," established him as an angry voice of protest in the burgeoning students' civil rights movement that was having such an impact on a generation of young people throughout the country.

Dylan's songs were printed in *Sing Out!* and were drawing attention from other artists, who realized something unique was going on. His friend Dave Van Ronk, had urged him many times to avoid being a Guthrie clone, to forget re-creating the '30s and live in the present. Scaduto quotes Van Ronk as saying to Dylan, "Hey man, you're really getting into something. Welcome to the twentieth century."

His second album *The Freewheelin' Bob Dylan*, was released in May of 1963 and showed just how quickly the poet was finding his voice. All of the tunes but one were written by Dylan. "Blowin' In The Wind" of course had firmly established him as a major songwriter, but this album also included the classic, "Don't Think Twice, It's Alright," "A Hard Rain's Gonna Fall," and "Girl Of The North Country."

All the elements of the style were falling in place now: his fingerstyle guitar with simple blues licks, the harmonica breaks, poetic songs of vision, love songs, protest songs, and the flippant, almost throwaway "dream songs" or "talkin blues." He also cut "Corrina Corrina," on that record, backed by guitars, bass, and drums, using a Buddy Holly voice that wouldn't be heard again until the *John Wesley Harding* album. "Corrina" and "Mixed Up Confusion" had earlier been issued by Columbia on a single, and then quickly pulled from the market when the company decided the tunes were too rock & roll-oriented for Dylan's image. "Rock & Roll" was becoming a dirty word in folk circles.

It's hard to realize now just how great Dylan's impact at the time really was. Gordon Lightfoot, Phil Ochs, and other young singers of the day were heavily influenced by Dylan's presence. He legitimized the role of the artist/songwriter, while vastly expanding the subject matter of popular songs. He rejected traditional interpretations of folk material. Most importantly, he was singing about things that really mattered to his young audience. In the late '50s a generation of manufactured stars had served up a steady diet of mindless pablum over the airwaves. Dylan was doing something else, entirely. He was changing the personal and topical boundaries of the popular music.

Bob was a big hit at the '63 Newport Folk Festival,

and was beginning to receive the attention of a major star. He was booked for the Ed Sullivan show, but cancelled when they would not let him perform the satirical "Talkin' John Birch Society Blues." His album, *The Times They Are A Changin'*, released in January 1964, at the peak of the civil rights movement, was Dylan's most overtly political record, and one that established him as a "protest singer" with the public at large. His style was becoming stronger as he established strident, compelling melodies for songs like the title cut and "With God On Our Side." By this time he was a full-fledged media superstar.

What wasn't evident at the time was the extent to which he was devoted to following his personal muse, rather than following in the "folk tradition," or in the role of protest singer. His next record, *Another Side Of Bob Dylan* came out in August 1964. It offered a less political, more introspective view of the world through love songs such as "To Ramona" and "Spanish Harlem Incident," and his anthem of disillusionment, "My Back Pages." By turning to more personal material, he actually began to alienate part of his audience. This process was completed when he released *Bringin It All Back Home* in March of 1965. It featured the full range of Dylan's songwriting talent, with bittersweet lovesongs ("Love Minus Zero"), protest and humor ("It's Alright, Ma"), and variations on talking blues ("Subterranean Homesick Blues"). Not only that, a whole side of the album was electric and the songs demonstrated a hard-edged sound, and deeply symbolic lyric style that had only been hinted at in earlier work.

In retrospect, Dylan was probably doing nothing more than establishing his right to make any sounds he wanted. He was fully a part of his generation, not immune to the excitement the Beatles were generating. He once said that he kept how much he liked the Beatles to himself because his contemporaries in the folk world considered them strictly for teenyboppers. But Dylan was impressed with the energy electric bands created, and of course, he himself had started in high school with electric guitar and piano. With *Bringin' It All Back Home* he had actually gone back to his roots.

Dylan had also alienated his audience by becoming, to their way of thinking, apolitical. By exchanging his political themes for more personal ones, he had entered a phase, which continued until 1968, in which he was mainly known as a purveyor of powerful, frightening, songs that made use of symbolic dreamlike imagery. As his poetic voice expanded its range, he was still speaking to universal themes, but not on such an overt level.

With *Bringing It All Back Home* he cut his ties to the expectations of his followers, refusing to play his appointed role of folk music avatar. *Sing Out!* proclaimed he had sold out for a commercial, Top 40 sound. Dylan anticipated these reactions in the liner notes to the album. They are essentially a stream-of-consciousness poem in which he rejects the roles of

protest singer, and a singer of serious folksongs for an urban, intellectual audience. In one verse a hitchiker says he has seen him at a folk festival and Dylan protests:

". . . you must be mistaken/I happen to be one of the Supremes/"

Later on he says:

". . . I would rather model harmonica holders than discuss Aztec anthropology/"

and,

". . . I know there're some people terrified of the bomb. But there are other people terrified to be seen carrying a *Modern Screen* magazine. Experience teaches that silence terrifies people the most."

In June, 1965, he released a single, "Like A Rolling Stone," on which he was backed by guitarist Mike Bloomfield, organist Al Kooper, and others. This was his most electric tune to date and his first real radio hit. The following month he set the folk world ablaze when he appeared at the Newport Folk Festival backed by the Paul Butterfield Blues Band. Though everyone was well aware of his new rock direction, many of his fans in the audience apparently thought he would play the old stuff at Newport. The crowd heckled and refused to clap as Dylan and his band pushed through "Maggies Farm," and "Like A Rolling Stone." Bob eventually left the stage, returned with his acoustic guitar, and sang (prophetically) "It's All Over Now, Baby Blue."

Though his new act didn't go over at Newport, Dylan was on the verge of finding a new and larger audience. The following month he played at Forest Hills with Robbie Robertson, Levon Helm, (both of the Hawks, later the Band), Al Kooper, and Harvey Brooks. The set was half acoustic and half electric and went over with a minimum of protest; when *Highway 61 Revisited* came out, Dylan was fully established as an electric artist. He had three records on the chart simultaneously, and was literally as influential as the Beatles and Rolling Stones.

The music he wrote in this period created a furor that went way beyond the boundaries of folk music. His influence as a songwriter had an enormous effect on his contemporaries, spurring a stronger use of language both as poetry and as a weapon of personal catharsis. The angry, disillusioned tone of this period was, in many respects, the perfect voice for a country caught up in a decade of political assasination and campus strife.

Though Dylan was accused of forsaking folk for rock, in reality he was fusing folk with popular music. With his music he was both following and creating a powerful musical trend, and he took a large part of the folk community with him. He also had an enormous affect on rock musicians who discovered through him the folk virtues of protest, and serious, straight-from-the-gut lyrics. Dylan's tunes were recorded by dozens of young artists of the late '60s and early '70s, including the Byrds, Manfred Mann, The Turtles, Jimi Hendrix, Joe Cocker, Stephen Stills, and others.

After his *Blonde On Blonde* double LP in 1966, Dylan suffered a disastrous motorcycle accident that kept him out of the record stores for a year and a half. He returned with a new sound as different as his first album was from *Highway 61 Revisited*. While other rockers were on the verge of the worst psychedelic excesses, Dylan's *John Wesley Harding* featured a simple acoustic sound and a batch of Biblical ballads and morality tales. It was well produced, too. He had selected outstanding Nashville musicians (Kenny Buttrey, Charles McCoy, Norman Blake, Charlie Daniels, and Pete Drake) to create an impeccable studio sound.

On the surface this album is a return to folk music, and some fans saw it as a retreat from his position on the musical vanguard. Of course, in many respects Dylan was foreshadowing the softer, singer/songwriter rock sound that should soon come into vogue. His sound was actually getting stronger, and his voice was more controlled and directed than on any of his earlier efforts.

But if *John Wesley Harding* was a shock to his fans *Nashville Skyline* was an atomic bomb. It was almost pure country music, with a touch of folk and Guthrie influences. Of course, the young Dylan had loved traditional country as much as rock and roll. He was doing to his electric followers what he had done to his folk followers with *Bringin' It All Back Home*,—refusing to give them what they had come to expect. *Skyline* is filled with the kind of ditties and love songs that the younger Dylan might have sneered at, but this is an older Dylan, celebrating the joys of fatherhood and marriage. On the cover he is seen grinning, wearing a cowboy hat, and holding a big Gibson guitar in his left hand. Inside he sings the praises of "Country Pie" and staying home with the wife ("Tonight I'll Be Staying Here With You"). The album also produced the hit "Lay, Lady, Lay." Johnny Cash appeared on the album with Bob, and also featured Dylan on his television show in 1969.

His next phase, beginning with *Planet Waves* and including *Blood On The Tracks, Desire, Street Legal*, and others show Dylan as an adult artist. He is much more in control of his sound, even if he is still a producer's headache—eager to get it all in one take and not overdub. In a 1978 *Playboy* interview Dylan said "Later on [in his career] the songs got more defined but it didn't necessarily bring more power to them.

The sound was whatever happened to be available at the time. I just haven't paid as much attention to it as I should have. My recording sessions have tended to be last minute affairs. I don't really use all the technical studio stuff. My songs are done live in the studio—they always have been and they always will be done that way."

The method may be impetuous but the music is not. These albums are more rhythmically interesting than his earlier work, and they show a greater range of instrumentation than he had used before, with violins, strings, electric, and acoustic guitars.

In August of 1979, Dylan again had a surprise for his audience. He released *Slow Train Coming*, an album of unabashedly "born-again" songs, filled with praise for his new faith and fire and brimstone warnings. In many ways, this phase has been a recapitulation of his early themes and influences. He spoke with the angry defiance of an Old Testament prophet as early as his second album, and religious ideas have figured in nearly every album he has recorded. Interestingly, the sound on these albums shows greater attention to production values than on any earlier recordings. He has worked with gospel backup groups and gone to a young producer, Mark Knopfler of Dire Straits. Once again his voice is a snarling opponent of hypocrisy and complacency and once again he has confounded his followers with his born-again religious stance, and hawkish defense of Israel (on the tune "Neighborhood Bully" from *Infidels*).

In each of these phases Dylan has sustained his folk roots. To this day perhaps a quarter or more of his songs are straight 12-bar blues. He may have embellished the forms greatly over the intervening years, but the music he was learning and playing when he hit New York in 1960—gospels and blues, talking blues, traditional ballads, and rockabilly—are the same musical forms he works with today.

Perhaps his most recent records point the way toward a new synthesis of his folk roots with popular music, or maybe they are just resting stops before he makes another dramatic change in direction. We can only be sure that Dylan will remain an elusive prophet, unwilling to be pinned down or to let his listeners get too comfortable. He aims not only to entertain, but to shake us up too. He once described folk music as ". . . legend, myth, bible, and ghosts." By this definition, he has never really left folk music at all—but only led it in new directions.

## A Selected Bob Dylan Discography

**Solo albums** (On Columbia): *Another Side Of Bob Dylan*, PC-8993; *At Budokan*, PC2-36067; *Basement Tapes*, C2-33682; *Before The Flood*, KG-37661; *Blonde On Blonde*, C2S-841; *Blood On The Tracks*, PC-33235; *Bringing It All Back Home*, JC-9128; *Desire*, JC-33893; *Dylan*, PC-32747; *Bob Dylan*, JC-8579; *Bob Dylan's Greatest Hits*, JC-9463; *Greatest Hits, Vol. II*, PG-31120; *Freewheelin' Bob Dylan*, JC-8786; *Highway 61 Revisited*, PC-9189; *Infidels*, QC-38819; *John Wesley Harding*, JC-9604; *Nashville Skyline*, JC-9825; *New Morning*, PPC-30290; *Planet Waves*, PC-37637; *Real Live*, FC-36553; *Self Portrait*, C2X-30050; *Shot Of Love*, TC-37496; *Slow Train Coming*, FC-36120; *Street Legal*, JC-35453; *Times They Are A-Changin'*, PC-8905. **With others:** *Concert for Bangladesh*, Capitol, STBK-12248; *Greatest Folksingers Of The Sixties*, Vanguard, VSD-17-18; *Newport Broadside*, Vanguard, 79144; *Newport Folk Festival '63*, Vanguard, 79148.

# DAVE VAN RONK

An early influence on Bob Dylan (who stayed at the Van Ronk household in Greenwich Village), Van Ronk was a major figure in the folk revival. His mastery of blues, jazz, and ragtime styles set the standard for a generation of fingerstyle guitarists. This article first appeared in the December 1980 issue of *Frets*.

**By Mark Greenberg**

WHAT IS THE BLUES? "An infinitely long salami," according to bluesman/folksinger/guitarist Dave Van Ronk. "Most blues don't have a beginning, middle, or end. You just cut a couple of slices of blues."

Dave Van Ronk has been slicing that salami since 1957, when he decided to join the fledgling folk music revival as a throat-wrenching singer of blues and other assorted songs, and as a guitarist in the style of the black blues and ragtime fingerpickers of the '20s and '30s. Today Van Ronk is regarded as a founding father of both the blues and ragtime guitar revivals. His 1964 guitar arrangement of the "St. Louis Tickle" [*In The Tradition*], which he learned from an old piano roll, inspired guitarists to begin transposing classic rags and other contrapuntal, piano-based music to their far less expansive instruments. Yet Van Ronk does not see himself as a guitarist. "I love the credit I get for being a guitar player," he admits. "But come on, man, I'm not a guitar player. I'm a singer."

He certainly is that, though those with *bel canto* inclinations or sensitive ears might be driven back a few steps by Dave's trend-setting blend of rasp-wheeze-growl-slide-and-shout. Among the first of the white city boys to become hooked on the old recordings of such blues singers as Furry Lewis, Mississippi John Hurt, and Josh White, Van Ronk had the audacity in the late '50s to try to sound like those men. He did not try to emulate any particular one (his vocal heroes were then, and have remained, Louis Armstrong and Bing Crosby); rather, he sang as though he were one of them himself. Immediately popular at coffeehouses and on college campuses, Van Ronk, in turn, became a bridge between young, white city people and the largely ignored older black music. While Van Ronk may dismiss its importance, it was surely his guitar playing, as well as his singing and Falstaffian presence, that gave that bridge its strength.

Born in Brooklyn in 1936, Van Ronk's first musical love was jazz, particularly the traditional style of New Orleans and the later styles associated with Kansas City and Chicago. At the age of 12 he tried to learn the ukulele; but, unable to develop a decent roll, he gave it up. Later he acquired a guitar. He started with a 4-string, like his uke, and gradually worked his way up to a 6-string.

The guitar was soon supplemented by a tenor banjo, and Van Ronk found himself providing the flat-picked, four-to-the-bar rhythm in a traditional-style jazz band, an experience that he found less than fully satisfying. "Everyone else in the band was having the time of their lives," he ruefully recalls, "and there I was—chong, chong, chong, chong."

It was in the early '50s, while he was still chopping fours, that Van Ronk began acquiring old blues records, "as an adjunct to my self-education process in jazz." He began to hear a way of playing the guitar that at first he found totally baffling. "The first time I heard fingerpicking," he recalls, "I assumed it was two guitar players with flatpicks, one of them playing the bass and the other the melody. I had never seen guitar played any other way than with a pick."

That was to change one Sunday, a few years later, as Van Ronk was walking through Washington Square in New York's Greenwich Village, where the weekly gathering of folkies was going strong. Although he had liked the popularized versions of folk songs that the Weavers had turned into hits in the early '50s, Van Ronk usually walked right past the Washington Square singers and pickers. "God, I was a terrific snob," he says. "I hated all that stuff."

One day, however, something caught his ear. "I think it was [old-timey guitar and banjo player] Tom Paley that I first actually stopped and watched," Van Ronk recalls. "And I realized, 'Holy God, that's what Furry Lewis does.' So I hung around and spoke with him. He was very nice, as he always is, and he answered my dumb questions. I really wanted to sing, and the fingerpicking stuff was ideal for accompanying yourself. And I really wanted to get out of the

goddamn rhythm section."

But switching over from using a flatpick to using his fingers proved somewhat difficult for Van Ronk. "I started out with the idea that the thumb on the right hand moves independently," he says. "It does not. It moves in conjunction with either the index or middle finger. My first misconception, one that caused me a great deal of frustration, was the idea that you get the thumb alternating between bass notes—you get up a good head of steam—and then you just add the melody in with your fingers. That's just not true. It's got to be a coordinated effort between all three fingers."

It was also in Washington Square that Van Ronk first encountered the Reverend Gary Davis, whom he lists as his "strongest single influence." In the 1930s, while still in his native South Carolina, Davis had influenced many of the first-generation blues and ragtime guitarists, including Blind Boy Fuller and, through him, Brownie McGhee, another of Van Ronk's heroes. Davis, then a storefront preacher and street singer in New York, was beginning to affect a new generation of players with his searing, impassioned vocals and his forceful, complex guitar work.

Listening to and watching Davis provided Van Ronk with the key to arranging piano rags on the guitar. "There's a whole thing with rags," Van Ronk points out. "You start in a key and then there's going to be a modulation of, I believe, a fourth. If you start in *A*, that's going to take you to *D*, and if you start in *C*, God help you. That's going to take you to *F*, which is a very difficult key to fingerpick in because you don't have any open strings for your bass. I learned how to play in *F* from Gary. Once I learned a couple of his things in *F*, it was easy to figure out how to go from *C* in 'St. Louis Tickle' to the section in *F*."

The clue for Van Ronk's version of "Maple Leaf Rag" [*Sunday Street*] also came from Davis. "Everybody who was trying to do 'Maple Leaf Rag' was trying to do it in the key of *C*," he recalls. "I heard Gary messing around with it in the key of *A* and said, 'that's right, this is it.'"

Van Ronk still advises aspiring folk guitarists to pay close attention to past masters. "A lot of people who are into folk music now are into the secondary and tertiary derivations and are not familiar with the original sources, and that really hurts," he maintains. "Instead of learning 'Candy Man' from Reverend Davis, they'll learn it from me, though there's more to learn in getting it from Gary because there are all kinds of facets in Gary's [version] that aren't mine—all kinds of approaches that you can take if you go to the original source."

Van Ronk's professional folk music career got its real start as a result of encouragement from another powerful singer, Odetta. In New York, between trips as a merchant seaman, Van Ronk joined some friends who were singing at the Cafe Bizarre, "free, gratis, for nothing." The paid headliner, however, was Odetta, and, as Van Ronk recalls, "I was a big Odetta fan. I thought she was the greatest thing since bottled beer. I did my show and came off, and there was Odetta standing in the wings. She said, 'That was awfully good. Do you do this for a living?' And I said 'Nah, nah.' And she said, 'Well, you ought to.' That was all I needed. I practically tore up my union card, my seaman's book. If she had told me to jump off the Brooklyn Bridge, I would have done it."

As the folk boom swept into the '60s, Van Ronk became part of the in-group of folk-style musicians populating Greenwich Village. He spent his time in the company of such new and soon-to-be celebrities as Bob Dylan, Tom Paxton, and Joni Mitchell. "It was a ten-year-long party, and I understand we had a very good time. I really don't remember anything," he laughingly maintains, adding, "There were so many people. Some of the most talented never got to be especially well-known. It was constantly in motion—a revolving door, a kaleidoscope. You never knew who was going to turn up. Even Johnny Cash used to hang around for a while."

Though a pair of albums he had recorded for Folkways in the late '50s had begun attracting a following, it was Van Ronk's recordings for Prestige in the first half of the '60s that contained what many consider to be his classics—versions of songs such as "Samson And Delilah," "He Was A Friend Of Mine" [both on *Dave Van Ronk Folksinger*], and "St. Louis Tickle." In 1963 he joined with guitarist Danny Kalb, blues collector Sam Charters, and banjoist Artie Rose to form Dave Van Ronk's Ragtime Jug Stompers. Van Ronk attributes the formation of the band to a club owner's desire to duplicate, in New York, the crowds that were being drawn in Cambridge, Massachusetts to hear the Jim Kweskin Jug Band. The group lasted about six months, leaving behind an album on Mercury that Van Ronk likes [*Dave Van Ronk's Ragtime Jug Stompers*], and an appearance at the Newport Folk Festival that he remembers as a diaster.

The jug band was followed by an attempt at a rock band, the Hudson Dusters, which Van Ronk credits to his own mercenary ends. "A lot of people I knew were getting rich and famous—and that really hurt," he states, letting out one of his combination cough-laughs. "I've always been a sensualist, always liked the good life. Nothing is too good for the working class. So we put together a rock and roll band. Trouble was, we couldn't do it right." When the band's "polytonal rock and roll" fell on its musical face, Van Ronk packed it in and decided to stick with his solo career.

He's still sticking with it, playing colleges, clubs, and folk festivals, and making records. In the '60s, he extended his repertoire to include songs by such writers as Joni Mitchell and Kurt Weill, along with some original tunes. His most recent album, *Somebody Else Not Me* [Philo], is vintage Van Ronk, with material ranging from blues by Jelly Roll Morton and Brownie McGhee, to songs by Woody Guthrie and Bob Dylan.

Through it all, Van Ronk has continued to finger

pick. His earliest struggling efforts were on a Gretsch f-hole arch-top with heavy strings. ("It was sort of like pressing down the transatlantic cable.") More appropriate later guitars have included a pre-War Gibson J-45 and a Gibson J-200. ("If Gary Davis played a J-200, then, by God, I was going to play a J-200.") For the past ten years he has been playing a Guild F-50, which he likes for its evenly balanced tone. He currently owns two such guitars, which are "as near to identical as I could get them to be. If one happens to be in a shop, I can pick up the other and, with a minimum of adjustment, pretty much get the same effects."

Despite the guttural nature of his singing and the firmness of his guitar playing, Van Ronk's fingerpicking retains a softness in its sound. In part, this is due to his dislike for new strings, which he says "sound metallic. I like a string that's been played for a while. I only change them when I have to." He currently strings his Guilds with Bozo lights (he likes to call them "Bonzos"), which give him "a long ride" despite the fact that he plays hard and leaves a lot of "nail grunge" on the strings.

The soft quality is also due to his employing neither thumbpick nor fingerpicks, but rather his nails alone. He uses two fingers along with his thumb, and deplores what he sees as his severe lack of proper technique. "I anchor my ring finger," he points out, "which you shouldn't do. The right hand should float. Similarly, I never could learn to play with a thumbpick because of the way I hold my hand. I use my thumb as if it were another finger pointing downwards, and thumbpicks don't work that way. I could never change my right-hand position, and God knows I've tried. People tell me I have a very characteristic sound—and sometimes they mean that in a positive way. I suppose it's due to my hand position."

Attributing this point to "ignorance," Van Ronk further explains that when he began to learn fingerpicking he "wasn't looking at the way the hand was positioned" but, rather, was "watching what the fingers were doing."

Later, as a guitar teacher himself, Van Ronk tried to steer his students clear of his own bad habits and toward developing their own resources. "The way I taught left an awful lot of responsibility on the shoulders of the student, which is where I think it should be," he says. "You don't teach guitar. You teach people how to teach themselves guitar. I think most guitar teachers know that, but they just don't say it."

As a fingerpicker, Van Ronk favors dropped D, or what he refers to as "English D" tuning (D-A-D-G-B-D, sixth string to first string), which provides three open strings on the bottom for his thumb. Occasionally, he uses a fully open tuning, such as the unusual open C (C-G-C-G-C-E, sixth string to first string), or the more common open D (D-A-D-F#-A-D), and open G (D-G-D-G-B-D). The last of these is not one that he particularly cares for, however, because its root (G) is not on the bottom. "I don't use open tunings too much," he says, "because I've got to be onstage, and when you start retuning you break strings." He flatly rejects the possibility of using differently tuned guitars, considering them as too much baggage.

"I used to go around with a guitar, 12-string guitar, dulcimer, autoharp, and banjo," he recalls, "each of which I could coax some kind of noise out of. I would not go out on the road now with so much as a guitar and a ukulele, even if I could fit the ukulele in my vest pocket."

Although he laughs at his ability as a traditional jazz rhythm player, Van Ronk credits the experience with helping him develop skills that proved quite useful later, including using his thumb to fret up to three bass strings. "All of that rhythm guitar stuff stood me in pretty good stead when I did learn to fingerpick," he maintains, "because I was all over the neck compared to most other fingerpickers at the time, who were stuck with the cowboy chords in the first position. I could grab a C7 fingering up the neck [at the 5th fret] and play it as an E7, or have a three-note bass line that I could move around, and a spare pinky to pick out individual notes. I didn't see any fingerpicking guitarists who did that sort of thing until I ran into Gary Davis, who also used his left thumb a lot."

Futhermore, traditional jazz provided Van Ronk with a background in harmony that he could use in his guitar arrangements. "I still like to use the cycle of fifths, the occasional diminished and augmented chord," he says. "I think it adds more individual flavor to each tune." He warns, however, that such embellishments "should be used with some discretion. You have to bear in mind that songs have their own character, and you want to make your arrangement consonant with the character of the song."

Van Ronk works out his arrangements entirely by ear. "If it is beyond the ability of my ear to deal with it in terms of chord progressions and harmony, it is beyond the ability of my ear to play it well," he contends.

He also concludes that there is a danger in striving for overly literal guitar transcriptions of piano music. "Past a certain point of accuracy you start to hit diminishing returns," he punningly cautions. "The capabilities [of guitar and piano] are so different that getting too literal with a classic rag on the guitar usually means sacrificing musicality. Thus, I've heard arrangements of 'Maple Leaf Rag' that are much more literal than mine and that require a great deal more technique than I have, but I'm not satisfied with them. In order to get notes that are in the piano score, you very often have to chop notes too short in order to get on to the next damn note.

"What is required when you're faced with a dilemma like that is to paraphrase the melody in such a way that it sounds good for the guitar. When you take too literal an approach, you're sort of abdicating your own musicality for someone else's. That's okay in one sense; nobody means any disrespect to Scott Joplin, and I'd be only too happy to abdicate my musicality for his, if it were possible on the guitar. But I can't. It's not going to sound all that good. You have to use your own judgment in order to get a piece that sounds good as music. Too often it becomes sort of an exercise in virtuosity for its own sake. This happened to ragtime piano, too."

At the same time, Van Ronk is free in his praise of the generation of sophisticated fingerpicking guitarists that emerged in the '70s, singling out Dutch ragtime player Ton Van Bergk and American "stride" guitarist Guy Van Duser for special praise. "They're terrific," proclaims Van Ronk. "Man, they make me feel very incompetent."

Van Ronk himself is primarily concerned with guitar in its relationship to his singing. "There are," he says, "two fundamental approaches. One is where what you're playing on the guitar and what you're singing are going more or less with one another, and the other is where you use contrast, though very few arrangements are entirely one or the other." As an example of the first, he cites gravelly voiced Texas gospel singer and haunting slide guitarist Blind Willie Johnson; for the second, "where you're playing a counter melody or some sort of repeating riff against what you're singing," he mentions Louisiana blues extemporizer Robert Pete Williams. "Or," Van Ronk adds, "you can use the guitar to play fills between the phrases when you sing. [Texas bluesman] Lightnin' Hopkins is the classic example of that."

And what of Dave Van Ronk? How can he best be described? "I never argue with people who call me a folksinger," he says, "though I'd much rather be called a 'jazz musician' or 'song stylist' or some crap like that. But that's not going to happen. I don't think of myself as a musician, really. I do music. I sing. I play. I read books. I smoke the odd cigar. I do this, that, and the other thing. I'm just living my life the best I can."

## A Selected Dave Van Ronk Discography

*Black Mt. Blues*, Folkways, 31020; *Blues At Newport*, Vanguard, 79146; *Blues Project*, Elektra, 7246; *Dave Van Ronk*, Fantasy, 24710; *Dave Van Ronk And The Hudson Dusters*, Verve (dist. by Polydog), 3041; *Dave Van Ronk Folksinger*, Prestige (dist. by Fantasy) 7527; *Dave Van Ronk's Ragtime Jug Stompers*, Mercury (dist. by Phonogram), 20864; *In The Tradition*, Prestige, 7800; *Inside Dave Van Ronk*, Prestige, 7716; *Philadelphia Folk Festival*, Flying Fish, 064; *Somebody Else Not Me*, Philo, 1065; *Songs For Aging Children*, Chess-Cadet (dist. by All Platinum), 50044; *Sunday Street*, Philo, 1036; *Van Ronk Sings*, Folkways, 2383. **Out-of-print:** *Just Dave Van Ronk*, Mercury; *No Dirty Names*, Verve; *Our Singing Heritage*, Elektra.

# TOM PALEY

Tom was an original member of the highly popular and influential New Lost City Ramblers. Born and bred in New York, Tom was steered toward the classics by his mother, a piano teacher, but he soon developed an interest in banjo and guitar. He joined the Ramblers in 1958 and departed from the group in 1962. He still records and tours in the U.S. This interview first appeared in *Frets* in February of 1980.

**By Mark Greenberg**

ALTHOUGH HIS NAME might not evoke instant recognition among today's legions of guitar and banjo pickers, Tom Paley has been, for nearly 30 years, one of the most highly respected revivalist performers of old-time music. Best known as a founding member of the premier urban string band, the New Lost City Ramblers, Paley was among the very first northern folk musicians to master the virtuoso instrumental techniques of such rural southerners as guitarist Sam McGee, banjoist Uncle Dave Macon, and guitarist Mississippi John Hurt.

Born in New York City in 1928, Paley was in high school when he first became interested in the folk music of Woody Guthrie, Pete Seeger, Huddie "Leadbelly" Ledbetter, Josh White, and Burl Ives. His infatuation with old-time music began when a chance turn of the radio dial landed him in the middle of a program—Tom remembers its name as "something like the Hometown Frolic or Bunkhouse Jamboree" —that featured occasional folk material by such artists as Seeger, along with popular country and western music of the day and "once in a while some other music that sounded interesting: people like the Carter Family, the Blue Sky Boys, Uncle Dave Macon, and the Mainer brothers, and sometimes a Charlie Poole thing. I began to hear some of that old-time stuff and decided I was even more interested in it [than in citified folk music]. So I started listening to those programs all the time. My parents began going crazy because I'd have the radio on six or seven hours a day when I wasn't in school."

Paley bought his first guitar and banjo in 1945. He then started searching through secondhand stores for what were already old 78s, so that he could learn to play this otherwise virtually inaccessible music. A few years later he bought the guitar that remains one of his principal instruments today, a 1929 Martin 00 40H. He paid what seemed to him "an enormous price"—$55.00. "I dithered for a month before I finally decided to buy it," he remembers, laughing. "Am I glad I did!"

At the same time Tom was becoming more

involved in the New York folk music scene centered around Seeger, Guthrie, and the Peoples' Songs organization. "I was one of the young folk-song enthusiasts who hung around and got to sing at a concert or a rally or a picket line," he recalls. Through a friend, Vic Traibush, he met both Leadbelly and Woody Guthrie. "In fact," Paley stated, "Woody and I performed together for a while. But we stopped getting jobs after a short time because Woody didn't always show up; sometimes it turned out that he had gone away on his rambles—God knows where—without notifying me or the people we were going to play for. One of our very first public appearances together, if not *the* first, was at the [1950] Leadbelly Memorial Concert."

Tom spent much of the Fifties studying and teaching mathematics at a succession of schools. Those included Yale University, where he met Rambler-to-be John Cohen: and the University of Maryland, which brought him in touch with such Washington/Baltimore folk music enthusiasts as Mike Seeger—likewise destined for Ramblerhood.

In 1958, Paley, Seeger, and Cohen ended up playing the same tune in the same place at the same time, and the Ramblers were formed. Old-time music had begun its campus-and-coffee-house-based comeback. The Ramblers, however, were increasingly plagued by internal conflict, and in 1962 parted company.

After a short stint with Artie Rose and Roy Berkeley as the Old Reliable String Band, Tom decided to try life in Europe for a while. That "while" continues today, with Paley currently living in London.

In Europe Paley has continued to play his old-timey music, touring the continent, Scandinavia, and Britain, performing both solo and with other musicians. In 1966 he formed the New Deal String Band. The group included banjo player Joe Locker, who appears on Paley's most recent Kicking Mule album, *Hard Luck Papa*. In recent years, Tom has begun making occasional appearances back in the U.S.

Those appearances, as well as the Kicking Mule album, reveal a Tom Paley who still radiates what Mike Seeger has called "an overpowering instrumental ability;" and they also reflect a set of personal quirks that have justly earned him a reputation as a character—a kind of Victor Borge of old-time music. His lengthy bouts of tuning onstage are practically his trademark. Both onstage and off, his irrepressible wit finds constant expression in punning introductions to songs and in free-associative quips. Often his humor is self-directed. He is fond, for example, of quoting Roy Berkeley's assessment of his vocal abilities; "We all know that Tom Paley is to singing what Albert Einstein was to figure skating."

Paley's voice is, of course, an important part of his music, lending a plaintive, homey quality to the blues, ballads, and songs that—with instrumentals and dance tunes—make up his repertoire. But it is as a guitarist and banjo player that he has earned his reputation as a real master. (He also plays dobro, man-

dolin, autoharp, and harmonica, and recently added the fiddle to his musical arsenal.)

Paley's current passion is playing the fiddle, which he refers to in performance as "the questionable part" of his program. "I'd vaguely thought about starting on fiddle for years," he says, "but when I'd pick up somebody's fiddle and try to scratch out a tune it would always be so awful that I just didn't get around to continuing it." Then, in 1975, while buying a fiddle for his son Ben, Paley decided to pick one up for himself. Now he can hardly put it down. "It's a fascinating instrument, the fiddle—even just as a work of art," he says. "But trying to play the damn thing is quite a task, a challenge. It's the thing that's exiting for me now. I enjoy playing the guitar and I enjoy playing the banjo. But I've been playing them for years, and I sort of expect that when I get up and play something on them, I'll play reasonably well. But on the fiddle, I never know what's going to happen."

• • • •

**Y**OUR 00-40 MARTIN GUITAR *is your most familiar instrument; but what other instruments do you own?*

In Europe I use the Martin and a B&D [Bacon & Day] Silver Bell Style 1 banjo, though it doesn't have a Bacon neck. I bought the banjo for about $20.00 in 1950. I use any of several fiddles—mostly either an old Stainer copy; or a Mittenwald with a lion's-head scroll, which was probably made before 1850; or a Maggini copy. In the States I keep a fairly new Martin D-35 and an Arthur E. Smith banjo, one of the cheaper models. I also have a guitar, something like a Martin 00-40 or 00-42, and there's a metal bar—or more accurately, tube—running lengthwise through the body under the soundhole. I have no idea what it's for; maybe it muffles the tone, which is not bad but doesn't project much at all. I also have a strange Clifford Essex Paragon guitar, which has a carved top and back, an oval soundhole, a tailpiece, and a moveable bridge. The top is of thin wood, unlike the Gibson models of the same vintage, and the tone is good, though odd, with a powerful bass—the effect being something between a dobro, a D-28, and an f-hole guitar. I have a Windsor [Whirle] Ambassador Supremus banjo, too, with the fifth string passing through a tube from the peghead to the 5th fret.

*What are your string and pick preferences?*

On banjo I tend to like light-gauge strings, Black Diamond by preference, though the wound fourth strings wear out too quickly, and I may start using heavier-gauge fourth strings. In any case, I don't play as much on the fourth as on the others, so a heavier string shouldn't hamper my playing much. On guitar I prefer medium-gauge Mona-steel or nickel strings. For years I used Gibson, but—at least in England—they're so expensive that I've shifted to D'Addario. I prefer tortoise shell flatpicks—not very large and of medium thickness. Nothing else seems to have the same snappy action and clear tone. But I'm using flat-picks less and less. I like a large-size dobro thumb-pick and either National or Jim Dunlop fingerpicks, which I straighten out so that the part that strikes the strings is flat. On fiddle I use either Pirastro or Thomästik chrome-steel strings. The former seem to give a prettier tone, but the latter are louder. I also have one fiddle strung with Fisoma gut-core strings.

*Would you describe the styles you play on banjo, and identify who influenced them?*

I do some three-fingered banjo picking, some-times with thumb lead but more often with first-finger lead. Sometimes the lead moves between the thumb and the fingers. Even when I use my fingers in perhaps the same way as a bluegrass picker would, the sound is different. I attack the strings differently, and don't use picks. Some influences on my three-finger picking come from Charlie Poole, Uncle Dave Macon, my own guitar picking, and to a limited extent, bluegrass banjo pickers. I used to do a great deal of what I call "Pete Seeger style" picking [Seeger's basic strum—pick up, strum down, and hit the fifth string in a one, two-and rhythm]; and some of my own variations on it, like letting the middle finger pick up after the first finger, breaking the first beat into two half-beats. Most of my banjo picking, particularly when I'm on my own, is some form of frailing, usually with the thumb dropping in to pick notes on the first four strings; that is, what most people nowadays call "clawhammer" style. It's inter-esting. When I was first playing, I used to hear the expression "clawhammer" used to describe every fingerpicking style on the banjo *other* than frailing and "classical" style, including Scruggs style! Influ-ences on my frailing style include Uncle Dave Macon, Clarence Ashley, Wade Ward, and Hobart Smith.

*What about your guitar styles?*

I play with either bare fingers, with thumbpick and two fingerpicks, or with a flatpick, though I seem to be using a flat-pick less and less as the years pass. For the most part, I can do similar things with the thumb and fingerpicks. I never did much of the mod-ern cross-picking stuff, in any case. My style was more a mix between Maybelle Carter's and Bill Carlisle's, sometimes applied to songs and sometimes to fiddle tunes. I tend to use fingerpicks when I want a hard-driving, thumb lead style, and to use bare fingers for most of my other finger-style playing. My accompani-ment style on guitar—the way I back up fiddle and banjo—is basically a combination of Riley Puckett and the two guitarists that Charlie Poole had, Norman Woodleaf and Roy Harvey. As for my solo fingerpicking on guitar, I'd say that Sam McGee was an important influence, along with Mississippi John Hurt and Brownie McGee.

*Do you have any techniques that seem peculiarly your own?*

Sometimes when I'm fingerpicking on either guitar or banjo, one or both of my fingers may pick *down* as well as up [on individual strings] in order to simplify getting certain notes at specific times. Exam-ples of that on my Kicking Mule album are in "Franklin Blues," "Early Morning Blues," and the Rev. Gary Davis Medley.

*Do you ever use any altered or special tunings?*

Most of the time on guitar I play in standard tuning, but once in a while I tune the sixth string to *D,* or use open *G* [*D-G-D-G-B-D* sixth through first] or open *D* [*D-A-D-F♯-A-D,* sixth through first]. On banjo, my principal tunings are open *G* [*G-D-G-B-D,* fifth through first]; Standard *C* [*G-C-G-B-D,* fifth through first]; open *C* [*G-C-G-C-E,* fifth through first]; *G* modal [*G-D-G-C-D,* fifth through first]; and open *D* [*F♯-D-F♯-A-D,* fifth through first]. There are a few others that I use for one or two seldom-done tunes, such as *G-D-G-C-E* for "Turkey In The Straw." Strangely, I never use "double *C*" tuning [*G-C-G-C-D,* first through fifth], which is very popular among drop-thumb frailers. I find open *C* tuning more useful. On fiddle, I play almost exclusively in standard *G-D-A-E* [bottom-to-top] tuning, but I have experimented with *A-D-A-E* and *A-E-A-E* a little. Sometimes I use an adaptation of *D-D-A-D* by raising it a whole tone to *E-E-B-E;* or more commonly, altering that to *E-E-B-F,* in which case the first three strings are just one step up from standard tuning, so that one can play them in the normal way—getting the keys of *E* and *B,* while using the fourth string as a bass drone.

*Just what was it that attracted you, a city boy, to old-time and traditional country music?*

I suppose it sounds a little trite to say it, but it sounded genuine, as opposed to how pop music sounded, which seemed to be artificial, and—well, trashy, really. There was just something catchy about it. It was also partly because I was in with a crowd that was going folk dancing and listening to folk music, and within that field the traditional stuff sounded right to me. I was particularly interested in instrumental sound—the way banjo, fiddle, and guitar fit together. It was pretty nice. I still think so after all these years.

**A Selected Tom Paley Discography**
**Solo albums:** *Folksongs Of The Southern Appalachians,* Elektra, EKL-12; *Hard Luck Papa,* Kicking Mule, KM 201. **With The New Lost City Ramblers** (On Folkways): *American Moonshine And Prohibition,* FH5263; *Earth Is Earth,* FF869; *New Lost City Ramblers, Vols. 1, 2, 3, 4, & 5,* FA-2396, 7, 8, 9, 5; *Old Timey Songs For Children,* FC7064; *Songs From The Depression,* FH5264. **With Others:** *Folk Festival At Newport,* Vanguard, VRS 9083-4; *Newport Folk Festival 1959-60,* Folkways FA2432; *Old Reliable String Band,* Folkways, FA 2457; *Songs Of The Civil War,* Folkways, FH5719; *Who's Going To Shoe Your Pretty Little Foot,* Topic, 12T113.

# JOHN HERALD

As the founder, with Eric Weissberg and Bob Yellin, of the Greenbriar Boys, John Herald was a leader of the urban bluegrass renaissance in the '50s and '60s. Today, he is recording and touring as leader of the John Herald Band. He was interviewed by *Frets* for the December 1979 issue.

**By Art Edelstein**

LARGE CITIES PROVIDE excellent breeding grounds for musicians. It is no wonder, then, that intensely populated New York City has been among the most fertile for folk musicians. An early influence on budding city flatpickers during the late 1950s and early 1960s was John Herald, himself a Greenwich Village native. Herald's bluegrass-influenced guitar style brought about a necessary link between popular Southern players, like Doc Watson and Don Reno, and the resurgence of traditional music in the urban areas of the North. Herald's music, influenced by the playing of Watson and Reno, was accessible in live and recorded performances for guitarists interested in learning bluegrass and traditional playing styles.

In 1958, along with banjoist Bob Yellin and mandolinist/banjoist Eric Weissberg, Herald formed the Greenbriar Boys, one of the first northern bands to feature bluegrass, old-time, and original tunes. For nearly a decade, the Greenbriar Boys were the toast of new York City and Philadelphia audiences.

Herald, it appeared, was headed for a promising career. Multi-talented, he played cleanly and energetically, sang lead tenor, and wrote original material. His guitar work became a mainstay at Vanguard records and it graced many of the albums cut by folk-singers Ian and Sylvia. He also recorded with Ramblin' Jack Elliott.

When the folk revival of the 1960s waned, Herald himself seemed to disappear from the professional music scene. Rather than stay with bluegrass music, he chose to move from New York City to the Catskill Mountains in New York state, where a burgeoning music community was taking root around the town of Woodstock.

An expected one-year stay in Woodstock stretched to three years, and only the need to earn a living got Herald out on the road again, this time with a band called the Honkies.

During the early 1970s, Herald moved to California, but he was never successful in getting a toe-hold in the music scene there. Nor could he find musicians who would play with him on more than a casual basis. His only solo album, recorded during that period, sold poorly, and he admits it suffered because of his heavy drug involvement at the time.

He returned to Philadelphia in 1976 and formed an electric band. He spent two-and-a-half years playing mostly on the East Coast, hitting the New York City/Philadelphia bar circuit. While trying to build a reputation with this band, John also became part of the Woodstock Mountain Review, a congregation of friends from his Woodstock base. Three albums resulted from that collaboration.

In 1981 he reorganized his band again, forming the John Herald Band. Today its members include Caroline Dutton (fiddle); George Quinn (bass); and Cyndi Cashdollar (doborist, who performed with David Bromberg, Levon Helm and Rick Danko, and others). The band's eclectic mix of material helps them avoid being pigeonholed as a bluegrass act, and they cross the line between pop and traditional music with ease. "The musicians in the band are marvelous pickers," John notes, "and this is especially important in bluegrass shows where instrumental virtuosity is so important."

The group's "acoustic country" sound has won them a good regional following. They have recorded two well-received albums for Rooster Records and performed with artists such as Vassar Clements and John Sebastian.

. . . .

*COULD YOU TELL US something about your early musical influences?*

In my last year of high school in New York I learned a little guitar. I was originally interested in rhythm and blues. This was in the late Fifties—I'm not really sure of the year. The next fall I went to the University of Wisconsin and met Eric Weissberg and Marshal Brickman. The two of them were actually the first ones to educate me. Eric showed me a few chords. I used to follow them around like a puppy dog. I was in awe of them. They played Flatt and Scruggs and Don Reno tunes; they would play all the time, and I would just watch them. I got my first guitar after that first year at college. I never took lessons. That same year I went to Nashville, heard Bill Monroe, and picked up some Don Reno records. Some of the hottest guitar picking to this day is on some of those Reno and Red Smiley records.

*How did the Greenbriar Boys form?*

Somewhere around 1960 Eric, myself, and Bob Yellin formed the group and played just for fun. We got a few concerts with the American Youth Hostels and played Washington Square [a park in New York City] on Sundays. The group of people interested in old-time and bluegrass music only numbered about 20 in those days. Shortly thereafter we got hired to play at Gerde's Folk City [in New York] as one of its first acts. I was selling dictionaries at the time, but I would practice up to eight hours a day and I listened to a lot of records. We didn't rehearse a lot until we started working with Ralph Rinzler. We got Ralph when Weissberg left to play with the Tarriers. Right about then Vanguard Records said they would call us. Rinzler had a big effect on my music. I had just gotten an apartment in Greenwich Village and he came up and helped paint the whole place. It took about a week, and during that time he brought down all his tapes of old-time musicians. We would listen to hours of tape. I love Riley Puckett, Charlie Poole, and Uncle Dave Macon, I hadn't heard any of that before. I especially like the singing and guitar picking of Riley Puckett. Ralph also introduced me to Eugene Earl, who has one of the biggest old-time record collections. He used to let me come up and listen, and I'd stay for six hours at a time. On all those Greenbriar records there's from one to three Puckett songs.

*In the early Sixties bluegrass was virtually undiscovered in New York. What sort of direction did the Greenbriar Boys take?*

When we first did those early records, I wanted to do all types of music. Country music was in me from as early as I can remember. I guess I tried to emulate it at that time. We didn't try to copy anybody then, except Puckett. I would play the guitar and pick it the way I thought a fiddle or banjo would sound. I chose the majority of the tunes because I was the lead singer, but Ralph picked a few. Of course, when Frank Wakefield replaced Rinzler he had a full background. I wasn't trying to change the music even at that time. If I heard a tune and noticed a little flat spot I would think, "Well here we could do a modulation or go to a different chord."

*How many albums did the Greenbriar Boys record?*

Vanguard put out four and a half. One was a sampler of a few groups. Then we did *Dion And The Greenbriar Boys* for Elektra. The band stayed together from about 1960 to 1967.

*At that time were you also doing session work for Vanguard in New York?*

I used to be a lead guitar player for Vanguard.

Whenever they needed a lead player, Maynard Solomen—the head of the label—would give me a call because he had taken a shine to me. I did a lot of session work in the '60s. I'm not innately a lead guitarist. What I used to do was ask the artist for a tape a week or two ahead of time so I could go through the songs and work out breaks at home. I couldn't just go into the studio and knock off a great break. I'd work off of chords, learn them, and just start fooling around with whatever ideas came to me. Most people who know me mention my leads on Ian and Sylvia recordings of "The Little Beggarman" and "Four Rode By" as some of my best playing. At the time I was listening to a lot of bluegrass. Ian and Sylvia wanted me to do concerts with them, but I was too nervous at it onstage. To this day I still get a little stiff; the harder I want to please the stiffer I get. When I'm really trying to please a particular person in the crowd, I'm not thinking of the music. It just happened to me the other day; there was someone from a record company there, and that's all I had on my mind. I just did the worst I've ever done [laughs]. I do my best playing and singing when there's no one in the audience.

*What did you do when the Greenbriar Boys broke up in 1967?*

After I moved to Woodstock, I needed some money so I put together a group with Bob Stoner, Alan Stole, and Bob Tanner. I've always wanted to appeal to the masses. I've always liked rock and roll. I love it all and back then in Woodstock they were all there—Van Morrison, Taj Mahal, Dylan, Koerner Ray and Glover, Mark Spoelstra, the Traum brothers, Maria Muldaur. I used to play with them and Amos Garret. We didn't play much with the Band; they stuck with Dylan. In 1970 I formed a group called John Herald And The Honkies. It was just a little too strong a name for the public. I was playing bluegrass, Cajun, and country-rock. We traveled all over and cut an album for Paramount. It didn't come out too well 'cause I was doing a lot of drugs at the time and I didn't see things too clearly. That was in 1972. Then I went to California. It was a different territory. It was a very lonely type of place and I couldn't get a full-time band together. I moved to Hollyood, but couldn't find the musicians that could play with me. I didn't like the California personality; it was hard to break into the camaraderie of the place. I did play some with Linda Ronstadt and Jackson Browne. In 1976 I got a chance to come back to Philly and I did it.

*You recorded an album for Bay Records in 1978. How did that project originate?*

All my life I've been known as a bluegrass picker, but bluegrass isn't the only music I like. I like folk-rock, hard rock, African, Katmandu—anything, lots of kinds of music. I realize in this day and age you can't be too eclectic. People want concept albums, a sound like the performer is putting across a certain soul, not two souls. I don't like that. I hardly understand those concept albums, and when I hear one it kind of bores me. Well to get back to the Bay album,

a committee in San Francisco—Bread And Roses, run by Mimi Farina—offered to pay me and my present band to get us out there for a benefit concert; though then they said they would just pay our fares. At the same time Nancy Covey, who runs McCabe's Guitar Center in LA was trying to get us a tour out there. She had lunch one day with Mike Cogan from Bay Records and my name came up. Mike said he wanted to record us and he would pay the plane fare to get the band out there. The album took a week to make. It wasn't too well thought out; we just did it live with a few overdubs. I had never intended to record a strictly bluegrass album again, but in this case I had some tunes I was singing, so I thought I might as well get them down. I've always been dying to appeal to the masses, and I knew that album wasn't going to do it. That's why I wasn't intending to record bluegrass. But even when I was in the Greenbriars, we'd sing something like "Ragged But Right" or "Roll On John," and people would be screaming "bluegrass!" So even then they thought we were ruining bluegrass music.

*How do you expect to break away from the bluegrass stereotype?*

I have an electric band now. We play mostly in Pennsylvania, New York City, and the New Jersey bars. We have to bring a whole new set of fans to this music. It's a case of making money and we're getting serious about it. We do Cajun, country, electric grass. Three performers I'm excited about now are Rod Stewart, Joe Ely, and Gary Stewart. I want to get into that mood—that's what I'm trying to shoot for. If you listen to Rod Stewart, he has country songs on each album. He comes from a folk base. I even like his "Do You Think I'm Sexy?," and that's not close to folk.

*Can you see yourself doing that type of material?*

I would like to try. I don't know if my voice can carry it. I'm finding out now what my voice can carry—what a thin, high voice can do with electric music. But it's fun trying.

*Why not opt for a "newgrass" band and stay closer to your roots?*

I think newgrass has peaked. Those bands in general did not get anywhere. Maybe the New Grass Revival and my band are trying to do something different with bluegrass. [David] Grisman is doing acoustic jazz. If the Dillards couldn't get anything going I don't know who can. Tunes like [country singer] Conway Twitty's "Boogiegrass" could almost get something started. You can clog dance as well as disco to bluegrass. I love to see people dance when we play. So if we can get a term that people can dance to, then that's the direction I want to go. I think I want to appeal to new bluegrass people who are a little more open-minded. Country people don't like their bluegrass messed with, but if you're from a city you become more openminded I made [fiddler] Richard Greene a bet years ago. He said, "I'll never play anything but Bill Monroe." I said, "Richard, in three years you'll be doing it all," and that's exactly what he did. And some of the music I'm doing now, like "Levee Breaking Blues," suits my ears very well in an electric context. Anyway, I want to make the band as much a whole unit as possible, though I want to remain the front man. Rock audiences call us bluegrass right away, though bluegrass fans find us hard to label. I've been eclectic all my life, and people never know what I'm playing, so I'd like a label.

*How do you fit in with the Woodstock Mountain Review?*

Right now it's a very part-time thing. Like the record liners say, it's a meeting of friends. We play songs in all kinds of different conglomerations. The set band is me, Roly Sally, Artie and Happy Traum, Bill Keith, Jim Rooney, Pat Alger, and Larry Campbell—who also plays in my band. We go out from ten days to three weeks twice a year. It's up in the air whether we'll do another album. I think Rounder wants to see how well we'll stick to it.

*The group doesn't want to keep playing as a band?*

I personally wouldn't mind if I could make a living at it. Our tastes are almost exactly similar; we all like the same rock, bluegrass. It's like a vacation. I make more money with this than my own band, it's just fun, and we don't rehearse that much.

*You are also known for your songwriting. Have you been writing much in recent years?*

More this year than ever before. Usually I'd write seven to ten songs a year; this year it's been maybe 15 to 20. I'd like other artists to do them, but I'm a very bad businessman.

*What themes are you writing about?*

If I feel very emotional about my love life, it's very easy to write a song. If I'm in a bland state in my love life, which is usually where I am [laughs], then they don't come that easily. If the song comes from reality, then I find it very easy to write. But the majority of my songs are not from reality. I'm naturally inclined to writing a silly song like "John The Generator," it's easy to create in that vein. I've been doing this for a while now, and last summer I got my first car for $200. I've never had any money, and now I'm going to make damn sure I make some, so I'm going to write about love now. I'm 38. I've been a musician for 20 years so now I'm writing love songs; that's where the money is. I'm not writing complicated songs; some of the best songs have simple chords. But I have this nervous, eclectic nature, which usually means I have a lot of chords in my songs. A lot of people think I'm a speed freak—which I'm not! My problem is that I need to mellow out a little.

*What guitar do you play now, and what other guitars have you owned over the years?*

I play a 1950 Martin D-18 that I bought from Matt Umanov in New York City nine years ago. It's perfect for me. The action is very low; it's like butter. Onstage I use it with a Barcus-Berry pickup. The guitar I had before that was also a D-18, from 1939, but that was destroyed in a fire at my Woodstock home in 1970. I played that one from about 1964 to 1970. My first guitar was a small, sunburst Gibson—I'm not sure of the model, probably a J-45—that I bought in a pawnshop on Third Avenue in New York City in 1959. That one cost me $50, and I used it for three or four years. It's on the cover of the first Greenbriar Boys album. I also owned a De Lucia that was made in 1914, a real antique. It was bigger than a D-45 and very light; but I needed money, so I sold it in 1969. That guitar is on the cover of the *Dion And The Greenbriar Boys* album.

*What strings do you use, and how often do you change them?*

I use Darco medium-gauge strings. I've used them for about eight years. Before that I used Gibson Mona-Steel strings. Usually I change strings before every performance; if I don't, then I often break a *G* or *D* string onstage. Most of the flatpicks I use don't have a brand name, but they are all mediums. I've tried the Ovation 7mm plastic pick, and I like it. I have some on order. I used tortoise-shell picks in the early days but found them too scratchy; and anyway, I'd rather that we let the turtles live.

*How do you record? Do you use any different guitars or microphones?*

In the studio I just use my Martin—same strings and everything. The nicest recorded sound I ever got was on a demo tape done in the Record Plant in Sausalito, California. The engineer, Tom Flye, taped a microphone right into the soundhole.

*Where exactly do you want to be as a musician?*

My trouble has been that I've never really stuck to anything. Even in the Greenbriar Boys, everybody had different ideas. Now I'm doing exactly what I want to do, and I'm going to stick with it. When I was with the Honkies, for two-and-a-half years we didn't have drums. It wasn't folk-rock or rock, and without a banjo it wasn't bluegrass. I had an idea at the time I might have used cello. I have my own idea on what I would like to do with music, and maybe sometimes I'll do it. Right now I'd like to make people cry on sad songs, laugh on the funny songs, make them dance on other songs. And I guess I'd like to get to the point where I'm making a lot of money but not so much that I can't be invisible on the streets.

**A Selected John Herald Discography**
**Solo albums:** *John Herald*, Paramount, PAS 6043; *John Herald And The John Herald Band*, Bay, 213, *The Real Thing*, Rooster Records, RSTR126. **With The Greenbriar Boys:** *Better Late Than Never!*, Vanguard, 79233; *Ragged But Right*, Vanguard, 79159; *The Greenbriar Boys*, Vanguard, 9104. **With Ian and Sylvia:** *Four Strong Winds*, Vanguard, 9133; *Ian & Sylvia*, Vanguard, 9109; *Northern Journey*, Vanguard, 9154. **With the Woodstock Mountain Review:** *Mud Acres*, Rounder, 3001; *Pretty Lucky*, Rounder, 3018. **With others:** *Ramblin' Jack Elliott*, Prestige, 7721.

# BOB YELLIN

Bob's parents were professional musicians, and he brought a classical music background to bluegrass. His 25-year career has given ample evidence of his songwriting and banjo talents. Now performing with his own group, Bob reflected on his career and instrumental techniques in the December 1984 issue of *Frets*.

**By Mark Greenberg**

**B**LUEGRASS WAS JUST a distant speck on the urban folk-music horizon in 1960. And that year three young men from the New York City area—the Greenbriar Boys—became the first northern group ever to win the band competition at the solidly southern Union Grove Old-Time Fiddlers' Convention in North Carolina. The next year the Greenbriars' banjo player, Bob Yellin, became the first Yankee ever to walk away with the coveted first prize for his instrument.

The Greenbriar Boys—at that time Yellin, guitarist/singer John Herald, and mandolinist Ralph Rinzler—went on to play a leading role in the traditional side of the '60s folk revival. Along with the old-

time oriented New Lost City Ramblers, they helped introduce authentic mountain string music to new, eager, urban audiences.

"They must have been the first bluegrass group I ever saw live," recalls mandolinist David Grisman, then an East-coast neighbor of Rinzler. "We were just amazed at that music. We used to go over to Ralph's all the time and watch them practice." By the time the Greenbriar Boys disbanded in the late '60s, bluegrass had become a vital part of the urban folk music scene.

Bob Yellin was the group's banjo player for most of those years, leaving only when his marginal musician's earnings proved inadequate for supporting a family. Two attempts at folk-rock-pop groups, the Swingin' Six and the In Crowd, proved artistically unsatisfying, and Yellin left the world of professional music. He also left the United States, and moved his family to a kibbutz in Israel. They lived there for 14 years (and Yellin eventually started a bluegrass band: Galilee Grass).

Today Yellin is back in the U.S., working in the wire and cable industry. He is also playing music whenever the opportunity presents itself. For a while he worked with his ex-colleague John Herald in the John Herald Band, making the summer round of festivals, clubs, and bars. Since then, he's concentrated on his own, family-based group, now called Yellin Grass.

The group originally consisted of Bob, his wife Yona (on vocals), his son Eric (electric bass), and his brother Gene (guitar). Eric has since returned to Israel. He was replaced by Neil Comaty, while Marty Laster has joined the band on fiddle.

So far, Yellin Grass has taken a relaxed attitude towards performing, occasionally appearing at such well-established New York-area venues as the Eagle Tavern and Town Crier. They also appeared in the 1983 New York Bluegrass Festival. Yellin Grass currently is working on a demo.

The 48-year old Yellin's involvement with music began with his family. "It's in my blood," he says, pointing out that his father was a pianist and his mother a concert violinist.

In keeping with his parents' classical tastes, young Bob studied violin, piano, and harmony before entering New York's High School of Music And Art, where he majored in trumpet. He was totally unaware of the banjo.

That changed in 1954, during the summer between high school and college, when Yellin heard Flatt & Scruggs' recording of "Flint Hill Special" at a party. "That was it," he laughs. "Fate cast a shadow over me that summer. The sound of the banjo was imprinted in my brain, and my soul."

A ten-dollar cowboy guitar got him started learning Hank Williams songs and such guitar pieces as "Jimmy Brown The Newsboy." About a year later, a girlfriend gave him a cheap Kay banjo, and Yellin was off and picking. Bob got Pete Seeger's *How To Play The Five String Banjo*, and turned immediately to the three-finger section, since his sole interest was in Scruggs-style picking. He also began recording bluegrass songs off the radio, and listened to them over and over as he tried to absorb the elements of bluegrass-style playing.

"One of the first breaks I learned was from Flatt & Scruggs' 'Take Me In Your Lifeboat,'" he recalls. "It's still one of my favorites. And some of the backup on that is just unbeatable. For me, Scruggs is *the* master of backup. He's in another dimension, another order of magnitude, separated from any other banjo player I've ever heard.

"I seemed drawn to a certain kind of music that centered around the Stanley Brothers, the Osborne Brothers, Reno & Smiley, Jimmy Martin, Flatt & Scruggs, but also Johnny and Jack, and Roy Acuff. I guess I liked the old-time sounding bluegrass. That's what drew me into the music. The first time I saw Flatt & Scruggs in person I just went through the back of my seat."

Yellin, however, had no one with whom to share his enthusiasm. His friends weren't interested in bluegrass. That changed one Sunday afternoon when Bob happened upon the weekly gathering of folkies in New York's Washington Square. Among them were young banjo zealots Eric Weissberg, Marshall Brickman, and Roger Sprung. "I couldn't believe what I was hearing," says Yellin. From then on, Washington Square was sacred. "Sunday from two to six I was in Washington Square, period. That's where I got into it."

Yellin also met his future partners, John Herald and Ralph Rinzler, at the Square. He likewise made the acquaintance of Mike Seeger. In 1958, he traveled with Seeger to the Old-Time Fiddlers' Convention at Galax, Virginia, where he got his first taste of the banjo's natural habitat. He also received second prize, along with Seeger, for a double-banjo version of "Old Joe Clark." (That tune can be heard, with Yellin picking and Seeger frailing, on the classic album, *Mountain Music Bluegrass Style* [Folkways].

Back in New York, Yellin joined forces with Herald and Eric Weissberg (who also played mandolin) to form the Greenbriar Boys. Weissberg soon left to join the Tarriers and was succeeded by Paul Prestipino, who was subsequently succeeded by Rinzler. It was during Rinzler's tenure that the band gained its festival-contest victories and then established itself through its Vanguard records and concert appearances as the country's leading urban bluegrass band.

"Each of us had our own love," Yellin says of the group's members. "Mine was traditional bluegrass music. Ralph's first love was Bill Monroe, but also what they called 'that old-timey music.' Ralph introduced the repertoire to both of us.

"Things sort of happened by themselves," Yellin continues. "It wasn't that we consciously tried to do something. We knew that we were probably one of the only so-called urban bluegrass bands at the time. I think we were the first. But we didn't know what was going on in all the cities. We got to LA and found that there were bluegrass bands out there. But they were mostly made up of people who came from the South. Clarence and Roland White had the Kentucky Colonels, and it would be hard to say whether they were urban or country. They were both from Maine. Roger Bush, their bass player, was from LA. But you can't get more urban than being New Yorkers, so I guess we might have been the first real urban bluegrass band."

Still, being a full-time band seemed more of a dream until 1962, when the Greenbriar Boys were invited to audition for Vanguard Records. Their first

effort for the label was a sampler album called *New Folks*, to which they contributed four songs. One of those was a version of Bill Monroe's "Rawhide."

I had heard Monroe's original recording, but I didn't try to copy it," Yellin recalls. "I did sit with records in order to learn the style, but not to learn the tunes. So I don't know anyone else's banjo tunes note-for-note.

"No one had ever played 'Rawhide' the way I did. I went high up on the neck, which wasn't done. And I made up two different breaks where I took inversions of the four chords in the bridge [*E-A-D-G*] up the neck. A few people then took off from that and developed it much further."

At the time of the Greenbriar Boys Vanguard audition, another new folk artist, Joan Baez, was working on her second album. She heard the group and asked them to back her on two songs, "Pal Of Mine" and "Banks Of The Ohio." That led to a concert tour with Baez and a booking arrangement with her manager, Manny Greenhill. "The tour went real well," recalls Yellin. "We just enjoyed the hell out of it. So the three of us decided we'd try to make a go of it, and I left my job, and that was it."

All along, Yellin was consuming as much bluegrass as possible. In addition to the trips to Union Grove and Galax, he made frequent pilgrimages to Sunset Park, in southeastern Pennsylvania, whenever one of the front-line bluegrass bands was playing. He did his share of parking-lot picking there, and he met such banjoists as Bill Emerson of the Country Gentlemen. And Yellin always went backstage to talk banjos. His calling card was his original Gibson RB-4 flat-head, which he bought in a New York music store in 1958 (for $125) on a tip from Roger Sprung. He still plays that banjo today. "I knew that if I went backstage and opened my banjo case, I'd always get a good conversation out of the musicians," says Yellin. "Don Reno had the exact same banjo, and so did J.D. Crowe."

"I think my two favorite banjo players are Scruggs and J.D. Crowe, and I suppose that my style is pretty close to J.D.'s. But I didn't really model my playing on anyone's. Every time I heard a break that I particularly liked, I'd work on it. After a while you get a repertoire of certain breaks and instrumentals and they all blend together to form your style. I also listened to a lot of Sonny Osborne."

Despite his triumphs at Union Grove and Galax and a third-place finish in the annual Sunset Park Banjo Contest, Yellin describes himself as "not really technically a very good player."

"For me, the banjo is a soul kind of experience," he says. "It's a feeling kind of thing more than a technical kind of thing. I never really concentrated on the technical side. I play more by feeling."

In line with this philosophy, Yellin displays a casual attitude towards his instrument. Except for having Gibson reconstruct the neck after the banjo was run over in a festival parking lot, he has had nothing major done to it. "I haven't touched the tone ring," he states. "I was talking with Sonny Osborne once and I noticed that his banjo—he has a gold-plated Granada—was getting green and kind of funky inside. I asked him about it, and he said 'I never touch it. Don't fool with it.' I'm absolutely one hundred percent in agreement with him. I don't change the head or anything. And I try to change the strings as little as possible." Yellin estimates that he's had the same head on his banjo for about 13 years.

For strings, Bob generally prefers Gibsons—a .009″ first, .010″ second, .011″ third, .010″ fifth, and a plectrum second or third string for the wound fourth. He likes to play hard, and breaks a lot of first strings. For a capo, he used a Grover with double elastic. He dislikes fifth-string capos, which he says get in the way of fretting the fifth string with his thumb. Instead, he has model railroad ties at the seventh and ninth frets. By hooking the string under the tiny spikes, the fifth string is effectively capoed without the nuisance of a bulky capo. The ties were installed by luthier John Monteleone, and were angled into the fretboard slightly so Yellin wouldn't hurt his thumb.

The Greenbriar Boys at the 1964 Newport Folk Festival. (Left to right) Bob Yellin, Frank Wakefield, and John Herald.

For the bridge, Yellin prefers a standard three-legged, ebony-topped Gibson or Grover, and rounds off any sharp corners. His tailpiece is angled down, with its leading edge a little bit up from the head. "That definitely sharpens the sound on my banjo," he points out. He likes "fairly high" action.

Bob is somewhat more particular about his picks. "I have four or five National fingerpicks from the old days. You can't get them anymore. They're wearing down slowly, but I just keep using them." For a thumbpick, he switched from white plastic Nationals to custom-made tortoiseshell picks that were prepared for him by a craftsman in Singapore. "They don't wear out and they have a very beautiful sound, a very clear tone. I watch my picks—never let them out of my sight," he says laughing.

Although he favors the older Scruggs style, Yellin rules nothing out. He admits that "melodic" licks occasionally find their way into his playing. Among the newer crop of banjo players, Bob singles out John Hickman as particularly enjoyable. "I like his playing very much and think that he, more successfully than any other banjo player, had combined the Scruggs style and the Keith or melodic style."

"I don't think that the banjo lends itself as well to jazz or rock as it does to more traditional-sounding music. But I certainly wouldn't try to discourage anybody from experimenting. Who knows what you'll come up with. For myself, the band that I had in Israel and Yellin Grass have departed from traditional bluegrass music in the direction of pop singers like Paul Simon, Loggins & Messina, the Eagles, and Crosby, Stills, and Nash. There are a lot of good songs for the banjo that don't come from traditional bluegrass. We're adding them to our repertoire because traditional bluegrass is limited in its quantity." Still, Yellin Grass' style remains close to traditional bluegrass.

Yellin's own experiments actually go back to his Greenbriar Boys days. An early innovation was the use of a mute to achieve a harpsichord-like sound. That effect is evident on "Roll On, John" from the *Ragged But Right* LP [Vanguard]. Yellin attributes his development of that effect to his father's classical tastes. "He just couldn't stand to hear me play the banjo. My brother played the saxophone in one room and I played the banjo in another room, and my father nearly went insane. So I went to a music store, but they didn't have a 5-string mute. They only had a 4-string mute, so I used that. But it didn't dull the fifth string. So I put an alligator clip on that side of the bridge, and it sounded so nice."

He also experimented with different tunings, particularly for the minor-key tunes that he was beginning to write. His "A Minor Breakdown," on *Ragged But Right* used a conventional *G*-modal tuning (*G-D-G-C-D*, fifth to first), with the banjo capoed at the seventh fret. For "Russian Around" on *Better Late Than Never* [Vanguard], he devised an open *D* minor tuning (*A-D-A-D-F* capoed at the seventh fret).

The latter album also featured a new Greenbriar Boy, mandolinist Frank Wakefield, who joined the group when Rinzler left to work for the Smithsonian Institution. "It was a very big change," Yellin recalls. "We had never worked with a southerner so closely, and Frank added a certain sound to the group which we liked very much. It made us sound much more authentic."

The addition of Wakefield also allowed the group to move in a *new* direction. The group's final album, *Better Late Than Never*, with both Wakefield and bluegrass fiddle ace Jim Buchanan, had a decidedly contemporary feel to it. One of the songs on the album, Mike Nesmith's "Different Drum," was eventually picked up by a young singer named Linda Ronstadt and recorded by her group, the Stone Ponies.

Yellin looks on the Greenbriar Boys' recordings with great fondness. "They weren't on a very high level technically," he points out, "but they conveyed a certain spirit, an enthusiasm for the music you rarely see these days. Even the southern people don't seem to have that kind of enthusiasm. We were just crazy about bluegrass."

Although they were a staple of the Folk Revival, influenced a generation of city-bred bluegrass devotees, and appeared on television's "Hootenanny" program, the Greenbriar Boys never achieved the popular success necessary for financial security. The band lasted for a while after Yellin's mid-'60s departure, but eventually the players went their separate ways.

Today, Yellin finds the bluegrass scene a little disheartening. "Some of the older, name bands just don't seem to have their hearts in it anymore. It's not like it used to be. I think that in the days when I used to go to Sunset Park these guys were really hungry, and their music sounded hungry. It sounded great. Now it's just another show.

"My favorite kind of performance used to be a college, or a folk festival, or a club. I like places where people know the music and appreciate what you're doing. But in 1982, when I came back to play with John Herald, I realized that's changed also. In order to make a living, John had to play for a lot of audiences that knew nothing about bluegrass music. But—every now and then—we'd play at a small club somewhere where the audience really knew the music. That was great. You don't know what you're missing sometimes until you get it back."

## A Selected Bob Yellin Discography
With The Greenbriar Boys (On Vanguard): *The Greenbriar Boys*, VRS-9014; *Ragged But Right*, VRS-9159; *Better Late Than Never*, VRS-9233; *Best Of The Greenbriar Boys*, VSD-79317. **With others**: *Joan Baez, Vol. 2*, Vanguard, VRS 9094; *Mountain Music Bluegrass Style*, Folkways.

# MIKE SEEGER

The name Seeger is almost synonomous with the development of folk music in America. Four of folklorist Dr. Charles Seeger's seven children have played important roles in the folk movement. Mike, born in 1933, is the eldest child by his second marriage (Pete is Mike's half-brother). He grew up around folk music and has had a tremendous impact as a musician, song collector and conserver, and writer. As a founder of the New Lost City Ramblers, Mike was a cultural hero to hip college kids of the late '50s. Today he continues to pursue his love of traditional music, and is a columnist for *Frets Magazine*. He was featured in the March 1979 issue.

**By Mark Greenberg**

DURING HIS 20 YEARS of performing, Mike Seeger has become widely known as an accomplished singer and instrumentalist. He has dozens of recordings to his credit. He has won recognition as a founding member of both the New Lost City Ramblers and the Strange Creek Singers, and as a lecturer who has given concerts and demonstrations of folk music at over 30 colleges and universities. But there is a private side of Seeger, an intensely personal side, reflected in everything he does. Seeger is a collector who has built a library numbering thousands of records and tapes, and who has acquired more than a score of banjos, guitars, mandolins, fiddles, and other instruments. It is his continuing fascination with the colors, moods, and relationships of the instruments and music he treasures that has made Mike Seeger one of the most respected folk artists in America today.

Seeger was born in New York City on August 15, 1933. His parents, Charles Louis Seeger and Ruth Crawford Seeger, were composers and teachers, and Mike grew up surrounded by music. The family moved to Washington, D.C. in 1935, when Mike's father got a job with the New Deal-era Works Progress Administration (WPA), and it was there that Mike's career as a musician began.

"There was a fair amount of ferment around Washington, politically and musically," he says of the family's early years in the nation's capital. "Leadbelly and people like that were beginning to be known in the urban musical circles. I remember very little about it, but I was singing that kind of music from the time I was three or four. My parents encouraged us to learn songs like 'Black-Eyed Susie' and 'Three Nights Drunk' with them. We would sing as a family group. It was clear to me that my parents were both completely dedicated to their music and to one another. I learned to use the phonograph when I was six or seven—aluminum records with cactus needles, the field recordings of the Library of Congress. I always really enjoyed playing those recordings and listening to them, singing some of the songs. From the earliest that I can remember, that music intrigued me."

Seeger's parents both played piano and his father also played guitar, but Mike was slow to learn an instrument. "When I was five my mother wanted me to start taking piano lessons," he recalls, "but I didn't want to. I had the concept that I could never play anything—that I was some kind of a klutz. So I just sang."

He began accompanying himself on the autoharp when he was 12, but he didn't begin any serious instrumental studies until his late teens. Seeger got a job in a bicycle shop when he was about 13, and that started the period he calls his "bicycle phase." He neglected music until he was nearly eighteen, concentrating his energies on bicycles instead and winning two Maryland state cycling championships. It was 1951 before he took up the guitar.

"My mother made an appointment for me to take guitar lessons with Sophocles Papas, a classical pupil of Segovia's," he says. "To learn the beginnings of chords and so forth he assigned me to Charlie Byrd, which was a nice coincidence. Unfortunately, I didn't learn very much from him [Byrd], although I got to enjoy his music later. He and Zeb Turner, I believe it was, jammed during one of my lessons, which was the high point of my study with him. I never thought I could play until I went to take those guitar lessons, but once I had the first one I was off and running."

Seeger started learning on his own, getting much of his early material from Weavers records that were around the house. His older half-brother, Pete, had helped form the group several years earlier. Pete was the youngest of the three children from Charles Seeger's first marriage, 14 years Mike's elder. The childhood ties between the two were not close, but Pete still had some influence on the development of Mike's playing.

"We had his records more than we had him," Mike recalls. "He was in the Army, and then he was married and living in New York. Occasionally he and my older brothers would come and visit, but during the early '40s we had more contact with Pete through radio."

Within six months of starting on guitar Mike began playing banjo under the influence of recordings by Pete, Earl Scruggs, and Lily Mae Ledford (of the Coon Creek Girls). He soon began diversifying his interests further.

"I had flunked out of college while trying to learn to play the banjo," he says. "I took up the mandolin within a few months of that, and then the fiddle a few months from that, and then the mouth harp a few months later."

Mike began sitting in with a local square dance band to develop his timing, and he also started to search out old-time black musicians in the Washington area. The discovery of guitarist Elizabeth "Libba" Cotten, literally in his own backyard, was a revelation for him. "Libba Cotten was working in our house one day a week," he recalls, and as I started to learn to play she began going in and kind of playing the guitar—getting to know it again. One day somebody said, 'Oh, she can play,' and she sat down and played the most incredibly beautiful piece that to that time I had ever heard. It was 'In the Sweet By And By,' and she did it first very much on the beat, then ragged it a little bit. From then on we devoted ourselves to Libba's music."

Mike formed a duo with his younger sister, Peggy, while he was still living at home. As he began to think seriously about making music a profession, he immersed himself in the traditional songs that had been such a significant part of his upbringing, and at the same time he began honing his skills as an instrumentalist.

"I used to go down to a friend's house and listen to old-time records—that was in '52 or '53—for as long as I could," he says. "I was soaking up the music in a very intense way, playing the instruments ten or twelve hours a day sometimes, and going out and seeing what few traditional musicians I knew in the area."

The seminal period also included Mike's first exposure to bluegrass music, an event that made a lasting impression on him. "In 1952 I first heard Lester and Earl [Flatt & Scruggs] out at the country music park not far from where I live now," he recalls. "Incredible! It was like a religious experience."

A conscientious objector during the Korean War, Seeger was assigned to service at Mount Wilson State

Hospital in Baltimore. His experiences there laid the foundation for his career as a folk performer. "I met some people from Tennessee and Virginia and Kentucky who really got me into singing—into trying to sing country music and really knowing country music," he says. "While I was at the hospital I would spend every spare moment singing in somebody's apartment until we got kicked out, which was usually the same night. The neighbors didn't want to hear music beyond 10, so we'd go to somebody else's house and play a few bluegrass tunes."

Though he was growing as a musician, Mike developed some doubts about the feasibility of a career in music. "It had become clear to me that I wouldn't ever be able to make music for a living," he says. "About halfway through my time at Mount Wilson it occurred to me that the best thing to do would be to go to electronics shcool to get a first-class license, and then go south to my favorite area, which was Galax [Virginia]. I'd work for a radio station and do collecting and playing—which was really what I wanted to do. I got hold of that idea from Pete Kuykendall, who runs *Bluegrass Unlimited*. After I got out of the hospital I began going to electronics school."

Seeger's detour into electronics was actually what set the stage for his life as a musician. Through his collecting activities he found he could make a living in music after all. "About that time," he says, "Moe Ash [the founder of Folkways Records] dropped me a letter saying, 'Hey, how would you like to do an album for us on Scruggs-style music?' I'd been talking with Pete Kuykendall about where all this music came from—we sat up one night and figured out all the elements of Earl's music, and what made it distinct from Snuffy Jenkins's music, and so forth. So I lit out doing the album for Moe Ash. It really changed my life—putting together an album of musicians that I knew were all around me, who couldn't be heard any other way."

Mike quit electronics school and began working as a recording technician. In the meantime, his circle of acquaintances widened to include Tom Paley and John Cohen, two musicians he met at folk gatherings in the Washington area. One day in 1958 he heard that Paley and Cohen were going to appear together on a local radio show. He invited himself along.

"I just decided to try and butt in," he says, "and I did. I think the fiddle is what did it. We had about halfway run through a tune and we went on the air. Afterward John said, 'Well, that sounds pretty good—why don't we do us a little concert in the fall and make a record?' After about a year and a half in one place with the Ramblers, it appeared that I could make a living if I could combine solo jobs with Ramblers jobs. In 1960 I started doing that, and I've been doing it ever since."

After the trio's initial concert and recording date Cohen coined the name "New Lost City Ramblers," inspired by names of old-time string bands like the

New Lost Train Blues. There was some friction within the group, and Paley departed in August of 1962. He was replaced by Tracy Schwarz. With the Seeger-Cohen-Schwarz configuration, the Ramblers became a folk institution.

Apart from working with the Ramblers during the Sixties and Seventies, Mike has performed alone and with quite a few other artists. In 1970 he married Alice Gerrard, and the two have frequently appeared together as a duo. With Tracy Schwarz, Hazel Dickens, and Lamar Grier the Seegers made up the Strange Creek Singers. Mike also worked with his sister Peggy, and has appeared in programs with his mentor, Libba Cotten, and other traditional musicians.

A trademark of Seeger's performing is instrumental versatility, but his use of many instruments is not intended as a show in itself. "We like a lot of different sounds," he says of his playing with the Ramblers. "There are many, many different sounds in old-time music and we like to show that. There isn't just one sound, like there is basically in bluegrass." A typical Seeger solo program might run through autoharp, banjo, guitar, unaccompanied voice, jews-harp, fiddle, and dulcimer before an instrument is repeated.

His fascination with different timbres and tonal qualities is as much an element of Seeger's love for music as it is a factor in his selection of program material. "I get very intrigued by the different sounds that different instruments make," he says, "and so I have a fair variety of guitars and banjos and mandolins and fiddles because of that. Certain sounds go with certain songs. I have been a collector of sound recordings on tape since 1952. I've taken my recording machine to all kinds of interesting places, and I have well over a thousand tapes now—anything from fiddle players, jews-harp players, unaccompanied singers, or bluegrass groups to a guy telling a story. I've done 20 or 25 field recordings for Folkways, and I've participated in another 15 or 20. I think over the next 10 or 15 years I'll gradually come out with a collector's choice—sounds that I've recorded just because I felt they should be recorded. Sometimes I just recorded whatever sounds were around, like the sound of a calliope, or of a guy who had a set of doorbell ringers hooked up to a keyboard and did Gospel songs with a tenor banjo accompaniment."

Seeger likes the scope of traditional music because it allows him to give free rein to his interests. "I like all the instruments or I wouldn't have learned how to play them," he says. "That's one thing about this music—you don't have to do anything you don't want to. Of course, you can starve too." He was so accustomed to the freedom of his particular art that he was astounded to learn that performers in other areas had to work under tight restrictions. "A friend of mine who is an opera singer once told me, 'Well, you have to do what you're told to sing,'" he recalls. "He was a lead singer, and it

**Mike Seeger has dedicated his life to collecting, researching, learning, playing and recording folk music. He is a highly accomplished banjoist, fiddler, and autoharpist.**

absolutely shocked me to think that I could be told by somebody what song to sing or what instrument to play. I only learn what I want to play on the instrument that I want to learn it on."

Seeger finds that he sometimes has to guard against playing at home for enjoyment because he tends to get caught up in the music. "I have a hard time making myself rehearse," he says. "I play at home much more than I play onstage, and I do it absolutely for pleasure. The biggest thing I have to do is *keep* from playing, because I don't get other things done. By far the largest amount of music I've played has been for myself. You get a different kind of pleasure from playing in front of people than you do on your own; onstage I can't stop if it's not going right."

Sharing that kind of personal enjoyment is, to Seeger, much of the essence of old-time music. "Old-time music can be any number of things—perhaps that's what I like about it," he says. "It can be a display music or a show kind of music, but looking back, I think its origins were in its being social. There's the aspect of getting together and playing for a good time, which is social; and a lot of music is for dances, which are social events." Seeger avoids categorizing old-time music as folk music. "I don't use the term 'folk music' anymore because it's too confusing," he says. "A lot of people consider folk music as Peter, Paul, & Mary—urban people playing a folk song. It even goes into playing contemporary songs other than popular songs. That's the way folk music is thought of today in some circles, so I tend to get away from the term entirely. I have very little to take its place except 'traditional music'—banjo music, fiddle music, accompaniment on singing, even up through the songs Alice and Hazel write, because they have the feeling of an extension of tradition." By the same token, Mike classifies himself as an urban traditional musician, as opposed to what he calls a *traditional* traditional musician.

One of the things that moves Mike Seeger to continue touring and giving lecture-demonstrations at college campuses is a concern that too few people have opportunities to experience traditional music today. He says he would like to see broadcasting companies make airtime available to musicians, provided that the musicians recognized a responsibility to offer more than a narrow selection of material, and he notes that a television station in southeastern Kentucky is currently donating time to a local co-op.

"I believe that the mediums of radio and television belong to a larger segment of the population than the small segment that now dominates them," he says. "If a large majority of the American people are denied access to the public airways, then a large number of musicians are denied that access, and I think they really deserve it. A real problem that we have in this country, and therefore in the world, is the problem of one thing predominating over all others. It's what happens in today's music, which I think is very sad. There are so many good musicians in this country that you've never heard of, and most of what you hear is manufactured music. That's what we thought we were fighting when the Ramblers got started, and I think I'm part of what the fighting is about, too—to regain an audience for lots of traditional musicians, not only the older ones, but some of the good younger musicians who are learning from the older ones and now have something very strong to offer."

**A Selected Mike Seeger Discography**
*American Folk Songs*, Folkways, FLW 2005; *Animal Folk Songs For Children*, Folkways, FLW 7551; *Anthology Of The Banjo*, Tradition, 2077; *Feudin' Banjos*, Olympic Records, OLR 7105; *Newport Folk Music Festival 1959-60*, Folkways, FLW 2431; *Old Time Country Music*, Folkways, FLW 2325; **With The New Lost City Ramblers:** *Country Music & Bluegrass*, Vanguard, 79146; *On The Great Divide*, Folkways, FLW 31041; *Remembrance Of Things To Come*, Folkways, FLW 31035; *20 Years Of Concert Performances*, Flying Fish, 102.

# HAPPY TRAUM

Happy, and his younger brother, Artie, played an important role in the New York folk scene as singers, songwriters, and instrumentalists. Today, they run Homespun Tapes, producing instructional materials for a variety of stringed instruments. In 1985, the brothers re-formed for a tour of Australia and the United States. This *Frets* interview with Happy dates from June 1981.

**By Mark Humphrey**

GUITARIST HARRY "HAPPY" TRAUM has been a mainstay of the East Coast folk music scene since the early Sixties, when New York City's Washington Square echoed with the sounds of a new generation of musical talent. Like so many others from that historic period, the 46-year-old New York City native has taken his art to new heights and has carved a comfortable niche for himself in the musical world.

In addition to performing and recording, Happy has written numerous guitar instruction books, as well as columns for *Guitar Player* and *Frets*. He is a former editor of *Sing Out!* magazine; and he operates his own mail-order instructional tape business, Homespun Tapes.

Happy's first encounter with an instrument came "from being in summer camp and picking up the ukulele," he recalls. When he attended New York's High School of Music and Art, "there was a group of kids who sang folk songs inspired by Pete Seeger and that whole New York left-wing folk-song movement. It was a very exciting change from the pop music that I'd been hearing; suddenly here was this music that was *saying* something. So I jumped right on it, got a

guitar, and started to play."

Happy studied for about a year with Walter Raim, "a folkstyle player who taught me how to flatpick," he recalls, "and who today is an arranger. He had some notion of the music I wanted to play—Woody Guthrie, Pete Seeger. I had a terrible guitar at the time, a Harmony, with the action about an inch off the fretboard—horrendous."

Happy quickly got involved with the folk scene that was burgeoning in the mid-'50s. "I'd go down to Washington Square, where all the kids went, and I started hanging out with people like Tom Paley, already a fine fingerpicker, and banjoist Eric Weissberg, he recalls. "Washington Square was a melting pot of all styles of playing so you could get different insights into what people were doing. There was bluegrass, old-time music, jazz, calypso, a little rock and roll. There were a lot of musical ideas to learn from."

He especially admired the music of Tom Paley, whose fingerpicking style had been influenced by Hobart Smith. "Smith was an old-time guitar and banjo payer who made some 78s of early anthologies of country music," says Happy. "Eric Weissberg was the first person I ever heard play bluegrass banjo, and he heightened my interest in banjo playing, even though I never became a Scruggs-style banjo player."

Happy's interest in traditional music received a great stimulus in 1957 when he became a student of blues guitarist Brownie McGhee. "I was going to college," he recalls, "and I had been listening to one of his albums, *Brownie McGhee Blues* [Folkways]. A couple of songs I was able to pick up just by listening to the record, but a lot of it seemed very mysterious. I was talking to a friend in the college cafeteria, and he said, 'I think Brownie lives in New York somewhere. Why don't you look him up?' So I went to the phone booth in the student union, picked up the phone book, and there he was! I got up all the nerve I had, phoned him up and said, 'Would you give me some guitar lessons?' And he said, 'Sure, come on down.' So for about two years, I'd finish classes in the afternoon, pick up my guitar, and take the subway down to Harlem to his apartment on 125th Street. Sonny Terry [blues harmonica player] would come and they'd play together; and I also met [guitarist] Big Joe Williams there. It was an amazing experience. It gave me a real in-depth look at the blues."

Having studied country flatpicking with Walter Raim and blues fingerpicking with Brownie McGhee, Happy next decided to take classical guitar lessons from Gustavo Lopez, a Mexican guitarist who had studied with Andrea Segovia. "Around 1960 I took a year's worth of classical lessons," Happy recalls. "I had been teaching guitar since the end of high school, and I realized I needed more musical background. I learned the proper hand positions—which I never use anymore. I also learned basic classical guitar repertoire: pieces by [Fernando] Sor, [Francisco] Tarrega, and Segovia. That was the end of my formal training."

Happy soon discovered that "there was no money to speak of in performing, so I became a teacher right away. I set up a teaching studio in my apartment in New York, and had quite a lot of students. I was teaching primarily folk styles. It kept me busy." He also maintained his interest in performing, and in 1963 joined a group called the New World Singers that was loosely based on the Weavers, an early folk music group that included banjoist Pete Seeger, Bassist Lee Hays, guitarist Fred Hellerman, and vocalist Ronnie Gilbert. "The New World Singers consisted of [late banjoist] Gil Turner, [guitarist] Bob Cohen, [singer] Dee Dixon, and myself," Traum says. "We were on a record called *Broadsides* with an impressive roster of musicians: [late singer/guitarist] Peter LaFarge, [guitarists] Tom Paxton, the late Phil Ochs, and Bob Dylan, among others. I did a Bob Dylan song with Dylan backing me up and singing harmony. Then the New World Singers made an album [*New World Singers*, Atlantic, out of print] and Dylan wrote the liner notes. We also put out a single of 'Don't Think Twice, It's All Right' [Atlantic] which was the first recording of that song."

When the New World Singers broke up in the mid-'60s, Happy became increasingly involved in his teaching career and began to write his first instruction book. "In 1965 I decided to transcribe my favorite fingerpicking tunes and put them in an order that people could learn from," he says. "So, I took the simplest ones like 'Spike Driver Blues' and 'Stack O'Lee,' and worked my way up to the more difficult ones. My book, *Fingerpicking Styles For Guitar* [Oak Publications, New York, 1966], was the first book to transcribe any kind of traditional playing." Since then, Happy has authored no fewer than 15 guitar instruction books.

The mid-'60s was the heyday of the "folk-rock" era and Happy left teaching and writing to enjoy the forming life full-time. Happy joined his brother Artie and some friends to form the Children Of Paradise. "I was in it for about two years," he says. "It was a creative band, but it never took form, partly because rock was just not my field. The Village [Greenwich Village, home of Washington Square] at that time was really changing its focus from the folksinger/songwriter protest."

Happy's next move was a geographic one. "I had three children at this time," he recalls, "and in 1967 I decided to get out of the city and move up to Woodstock, New York. It had been a kind of bohemian artists' colony in 1902, and there had actually been a folk music community there since the 1920s. Charles Seeger, Pete's father, lived there at one time, as did folklorist Sam Eskin. Toshi Seeger also lived there before she married Pete. 'Leadbelly' [Huddie Ledbetter] did a concert there in the '30s. So there was quite a bit of variety."

During this period Happy and Artie recorded two albums for Capitol, and they opened for many of the major acts of the day. "We went on the road a lot with [pop/rock group] Seatrain, [guitarist] Tom Rush, and the Paul Butterfield Blues Band," he recalls. "Artie and I did it for about eight years."

Happy became editor of *Sing Out!* in 1968, and at about the same time he started Homespun Tapes. "I got the idea of putting together a series of tape lessons. Because I was on the road so much, I wasn't able to maintain a regular teaching schedule," he explains. "So I thought I would put some lessons on tape, and see how they went. I based them on my first book. I started putting ads in places and sending the tapes out through the mail, and it's gradually built up over the years. We've got a whole faculty, really.

In 1972, Happy and some of the Woodstock gang cut the album *Mud Acres* [Rounder]. He also gave his first overseas performance at the Cambridge Folk Festival in England, and since the mid-'70s has traveled abroad quite frequently. "I'm touring Europe three or four times a year now," he says, "and have been to every Western European country except Germany.

"In Belgium I play in small bars that double as folk clubs, and in Spain or Italy I play in large halls for 1,000 people. The Swiss audiences are the best. Switzerland has a very avid folk following, and when you go and do a concert there, they listen, and they appreciate it. In Spain, I played at a folk festival in a soccer stadium for 8,000 people and the response was unbelievable. Besides a Spanish song, I had learned an American song from the Spanish Civil War that had been sung by the Abrapham Lincoln Brigade. That was a very moving thing; people lit torches and candles and sang with us."

Happy's touring guitar is a Cat's Eye that he got in Japan. "My brother Artie and I went to Japan in January of '79," he recalls, "and the Tokai Gakki Company invited us to see their factory. They have two operations; one is an assembly setup for fairly cheap guitars, and the other is for very fine handmade guitars. They presented my brother and me with two beautiful handmade copies of 000-28 Martins. It's become my main touring instrument. It's a small, light guitar that has beautiful action and a nice fast neck. It has a Brazilian rosewood back and a spruce top. It's also inlaid very nicely."

The pickup built into Happy's Cat's Eye was made by John Dalzell, "a very fine repairman in Woodstock," he says. "He put together a combination of a FRAP [piezo pickup] and a little microphone that's wired right into the guitar with a FRAP preamp."

Happy uses light-gauge bronze or phosphor-bronze D'Addario strings and changes them whenever they sound dead. "If I'm playing a lot, that's around once a week," he says. He picks with his thumb and two fingers and wears plastic fingerpicks and a plastic thumbpick.

"Sometimes when I'm playing in a nice, quite setting, I won't use picks," he adds. "I sometimes slip in the ring finger on the first string, but I don't wear a pick on it. I do, unfortunately, anchor my pinky on the top of the guitar. I think that in some ways that's a hindrance, but I can't get out of the habit."

Though Happy sees himself primarily as a fingerpicker, he occasionally uses a flatpick to "get more of a country rhythm, to help strum a lot of chords, or to play a break in which a lot of fast single-string notes are used. But that's not my strongest point. My fingerpicking style has developed more into what I have to say as a guitarist."

In working out accompaniments, Happy says that "the song's the most important thing, so the accompaniment obviously strives to enhance it. I try to either harmonize a lot with the melody of the song, or pick counterpoint—rhythmically or melodically—to the song I'm singing. If I take a lead break during a song, I stick reasonably close to the melody, although a lot of times the fingerpicking style itself tends to move you a little bit away from the tune, especially rhythmically, and develops a kind of life of its own. And I really like the aspect of the style; it allows you to follow the melody and at the same time leads you slightly astray of it."

Happy describes his style as a synthesis of "just about every picker I've ever heard," though he says that some influences predominate. "There are strong elements of Merle Travis, John Hurt, Brownie McGhee, and Leadbelly in my playing. Ideally, these influences are fused in my playing, and it all sounds like me."

Happy doesn't use open tunings much, though he frequently drops the bottom $E$ to $D$. "I use open $G$ [$D$-$G$-$D$-$G$-$B$-$D$] and open $D$ [$D$-$A$-$D$-$F\#$-$A$-$D$] some," he says, "but only a few songs in open tunings.

Having been on the folk scene since the Weavers era, Happy should be a good judge of the changes that have taken place in the genre, and of its current state of health. "In the old days," he says, "the places folk musicians played were coffeehouses and listening rooms. Nowadays, if you don't have a bar, you can't make any money. Generally, bars are noisy; so the musicians who play there have got to be electric bands. Consequently, what's happened is that the few places that still support the music can't pay very well and are always struggling. The musicians end up vying for the few gigs that there are. Unlike almost any other field, musicians on that kind of circuit are probably making the same or less money than they were ten years ago. With inflation, if they're making the same money as they were ten years ago, that's half as much. It's very common to be invited to play somewhere for $250.00 tops. You've got to travel there, you've got room and board to consider, and you're lucky to come home with $100.00. If you broke that down to an hourly rate, including travel time, you're not doing too well. There are people who are doing better than that, but there are also people who are doing worse—people making $40.00 a night, and glad to get it. Musicians are usually paid on a percentage basis, and audiences often don't realize that their participation is going to determine whether that musician goes home with any money."

Despite the grim odds against making ends meet playing non-commercial music, Happy doesn't discourage anyone from trying it. "If you believe in yourself," he says, "you've got to do it—take your knocks. If you have real talent, it'll come through and eventually you'll get some recognition. You've got to keep at it."

---

## A Selected Happy Traum Discography

**Solo albums:** *American Stranger*, Kicking Mule, KM301; *Bright Morning Stars*, Greenhays (dist. by Flying Fish), GR703; *Relax Your Mind*, Kicking Mule, KM110; *Silly Songs And Modern Lullabies*, Briar Records, BRI 4213. **With others:** *Black Forest Bluegrass*, Vanguard, 79427; *Broadsides*, Folkways, 5301; *Double Back*, Capitol, ST799; *Happy And Artie Traum*, Capitol, ST586; *Hard Times In The Country*, Rounder, 3007; *Mud Acres*, Rounder, 3001; *Friends And Neighbors*, Vest Pocket Records, VP-001.

# GORDON LIGHTFOOT

Gordon's songs have been recorded by everyone from the Carter Family to Bob Dylan and Barbra Streisand. He appeared at many of the major folk festivals in the '60s and hosted the BBC-TV show "Country And Western." He is one of the few folksingers of that era who has continued to have hit records without compromising his music. In a May 1985 interview in *Frets*, Gordon discussed the instrumental techniques that go into creating his trademark sound.

**By Rick Gartner**

S INGER, SONGWRITER, recording artist, balladeer. Those are some of the labels that have been used to typecast Gordon Lightfoot. But to describe Lightfoot that way is like saying the Mona Lisa has a nice smile.

How many "folksingers" get Grammy nominations in the pop/rock vocals performance category? And how many artists who emphasize acoustic guitar rhythm tracks have their tunes nominated for best

rock song, and song of the year? Those, and a bounty of other honors have been awarded to Gordon Lightfoot: ASCAP awards of merit (16 times), Juno awards (Canada's equivalent to the Grammy—16 times), and for his contributions to his country's artistic and cultural heritage, the prestigious Royal Order Of Canada membership (an honor bestowed on about 100 citizens in Canada's entire history). He's recorded five gold albums and three platinum LPs, and he's written virtually all the songs on those discs.

During his 20 years of recording and performing, Lightfoot has penned over 160 songs. Some of his melodies are direct and simple; others are sophisticated and ornate. His lyrics reflect the thoughts and feelings of an adventurous, sensitive man who has sometimes taken it on the chin but always kept his chin up.

And with the way Lightfoot's songs can spellbind the listener, it's easy to overlook his technical skills. As a vocalist he displays exceptional range—from a chesty baritone to a vibrato-edged tenor. On the guitar, he is a master of accompaniment. With his 12-string Gordon lays down a full, crisp rhythm sound. In his fingerstyle 6-string work he brings out the essential bass lines and complementary chord voicings that constitute an *arrangement,* a distinct cut above random first-position extractions.

Lightfoot's innate talents were nurtured early in life and developed over the years through study, practice, and a wide range of onstage experience. Born November 17, 1938, in the small rural community of Orillia, Canada, Gordon first showed his gift of song as a boy soprano, singing in various choral groups and winning several contests as a soloist. By the time he was seven, his parents got him started with piano lessons. He continued his study on that instrument until junior high school. By the time he was 14, the guitar lured his attention.

While he learned what he could from other guitar players and through experimentation, Gordon furthered his vocal abilities and sight-reading skills by participating in school musicals. As his high-school days drew to an end, Gordon began to write songs, and by the time he graduated he had decided to pursue a career in music.

He sensed that it was time to leave the nest. He was fascinated by the big-band sound of such groups as the Stan Kenton Orchestra, and he wanted to study the craft of the music trade. Articles in *downbeat* magazine piqued his interest in the LA music scene, and specifically in the Westlake College Of Music, which offered courses designed for aspiring studio musicians.

It was no small step for the small-town kid from Canada. But he talked it over with his parents, and they supported his decision to venture forth. Gordon enrolled in the theory course at Westlake in 1958, to learn the craft of composition and orchestration. After a couple of years in LA, Gordon decided to return to Canada. He moved to Toronto, where he saw opportunities to begin his career as a professional performer.

Gordon found that his talent as a singer was much in demand. He worked in the television industry as a backup vocalist, virtually full-time, for the next few years. He also began to perform his own tunes in bars and coffeehouses. In 1963 he went to England, where he hosted a TV series for the BBC.

His timing was perfect. When he returned to Toronto from England, the folk boom was rolling, and with his growing reputation as a singer/songwriter, Lightfoot was right in step. Albert Grossman, a prominent American music career-shaper (Bob Dylan's manager), recognized Gordon's potential and got him started on the U.S. concert circuit. American audiences were already familiar with Lightfoot's songs ("For Lovin' Me" and "Early Mornin' Rain"), which were early hits for such groups as Peter, Paul, And Mary.

Gordon signed with United Artists and made his first recording for that label in 1965. He recorded three more LPs for UA by 1970 (as well as a live album and several "best hits" reissues). What might be considered the "folk" phase of Gordon's recording career (records that were fundamentally guitar and vocal) ended when he left the United Artists label and signed with Warner Brothers in 1970.

By the early '70s the folk boom had gone bust. Only the strong survived; but Gordon Lightfoot thrived. With the full backing of a premier popular label—Reprise (Warner Brothers)—Gordon didn't just adapt to the new musical environment, he became one of the innovators.

Lightfoot's classic hit single "If You Could Read My Mind" (1970) is a model for the tasteful blending of acoustic guitars and studio orchestration. It became increasingly clear that Gordon Lightfoot was more than a great folksinger. His true gift for creating exquisite melodies and sentient lyrics became increasingly apparent as the '70s rolled on. His powerful songs and evocative vocals lent themselves beautifully to the increasingly sophisticated environment of popular music.

The hits kept on coming. "Sundown" (1973) was his next big single, and that tune illustrates another Lightfoot trademark: The crisp, driving rhythm of his acoustic guitar. Even though he has utilized (and continues to utilize) every studio tool from orchestral strings to electric guitars, he has always relied primarily on his 12- and 6-string acoustic guitars for the basic rhythm tracks. And he has always played those rhythm lines himself, both on record and in concert. His recordings also include the skills of such acoustic notables as David Bromberg, Ry Cooder, and John Sebastian.

During the first decade of his career (to 1975), Lightfoot recorded ten albums, including over 100 of his own songs. The double-album anthology of those first ten years, *Gord's Gold* (1975), is still one of the best record values on the market. It's packed with gems, and there's so many that *aren't* included.

In 1976 Lightfoot hit the charts again with "The Wreck Of The Edmund Fitzgerald." But just like the mighty freighter that went down in that haunting tune, the record industry suffered the most catastrophic decline in its history over the next few years. Nobody was ready for it, and everybody suffered. Lightfoot continued to write and record quality material. Still, as was the case with so many other

Gordon was originally a discovery of Ian Tyson (of Ian & Sylvia). He has penned nearly 200 songs in his 20-year career.

long-established artists, the recession years were lean ones for Gordon in terms of record sales.

But the demand for concerts by Gordon Lightfoot has always been strong. He and the band are regulars at such prestigious venues as Avery Fisher Hall in New York, the Greek Theater and the Hollywood Bowl in Los Angeles, and the Royal Albert Hall in London. They do about 70 dates a year, and most of those bookings are in major United States concert halls or outdoor theaters.

On tour with Gordon are Terry Clements (lead guitar); Rick Haynes (bass); Barry Keane (percussion); Michael Heffernan (keyboards); and Pee Wee Charles (steel guitar and dobro). This is the same lineup that has also been featured on most of Gordon's recordings since 1970. They put on a show that is musically studio-tight, and one that includes a wealth of material from all the stylistic phases of Gordon's prolific 20-year career.

Lightfoot continues to experiment with new modes of expression, including the electric guitar (a Gibson SG). But his classic '50s Gibson sunburst 12-string still plays a major role in his show, as does a handmade 6-string dreadnought (built by Ed McGlincey). Onstage he divides his time equally between the three guitars. Lead guitarist Terry Clements—the picker who's come up with those classic lead lines on Lightfoot's recordings—is equally facile on acoustic and electric guitars.

If you're wondering what the Lightfoot of the '80s is all about, you've got a really pleasant surprise in store for you. His 1982 LP *Shadows* is an exteremely strong record. Beautifully produced, with just the right touch of studio magic, this album features the songs of an immensely talented musician at the height of his powers. And at the writing of this article, Gordon is recording a new album that will be released in late 1985.

. . . .

*H*OW DID YOU DEVELOP *your style of rhythm guitar? Was there any one artist who strongly influenced the way you developed your own techniques?*

At first I tried to play it like Bob Gibson, a guitarist who was a major figure in the folk revival. He actually did his rhythm work with his fingers, something like a frailing banjo player. I tried to work that out on the 12-string, but I was playing so much that my fingernails would break, and so I decided to start using a flatpick. Ian Tyson of [folk duo] Ian & Sylvia helped me learn to play rhythm with a flatpick, although I ended up playing much differently than Ian.

*What is the key to playing solid rhythm guitar?*

You've got to keep in mind that you're laying down a pad for your voice and the band, if you're playing with a band. Playing rhythm is almost like

being an orchestra conductor—you're laying down something that the other guys in the band have got to get behind. That means giving them a consistent beat, but at the same time the rhythm part has to breathe. In a way, it's really very simple. You've got to play it *clean.*

*How do you learn to play it clean?*

You've got to play it light. You can't try to drive the nail in. But at the same time, it's got to be firm. You've got to develop a feel for the instrument, and that takes years of practice.

*What makes up a good acoustic rhythm guitar part?*

Well, chords and just playing across the instrument might get you by, but the difference between a really good rhythm player and a hacker is in how crisp his chord sound is, and in how clean and subtle he is about mixing in the bass notes. You can't have your bottom string rumbling in there all the time. A good case in point is something that happened to me in recording this new album. On one of my real good takes, I struck a low *E* bass note on an *A* chord, and I had to go back and punch in the right note. It might not sound like much of a screw-up, but when you're making a record everything has to be *perfect.* So you

**Gordon is a talented guitarist on 6- or 12-string, but he has also had talented accompanists over the years in guitarists Red Shea and Terry Clements.**

might as well develop good habits right from the start.

*What else should a player learn, in terms of matching the chords to the structure of the song itself?*

When I'm working out an arrangement I'll use the basic chords where they fit, but I also like to shop around for other voicings and inversions to give character to the rhythm line. There's lots of stuff available if you take the time to look around for it, and if you know a little bit about chord theory. Over the years I've learned to work right up the neck with different inversions of chords, and I think that's really important. If you use them properly, that makes the difference between something that sounds like it's just thrown together, and a rhythm line that sounds like it really fits the song.

*So the variety will help the song "breathe," as you say?*

The basic chords can sound much more effective

if you have a series of different inversions and then resolve into the regular chord shapes. I'd also like to mention that although I use a capo, I wouldn't recommend it. Back in the folk revival days, it was often done to put you in the right key for your voice and still leave you the open strings for your rhythm guitar. But especially when you get into playing with a band, using a capo can make it rough on everybody. It changes the fretboard positions for the lead guitarist, and if you move the thing around you have to re-tune your instruments. I'm pretty much stuck with it now, but I would advise people to avoid using it.

*When you work out the bass for your rhythm guitar parts, what are some of the main considerations?*

The root of the chord is not necessarily the bass note you want. You have to use your ear, and it really helps if you know some basic music theory when you're putting together your final rhythm arrangement. You've got to consider the chord you're com-

ing from and the chord you're going to, not just the chord you're playing. Again, the difference between a really good rhythm part is subtle, in choosing the passing tones and runs between chords. And then you've got to be sure you don't *overplay* the rhythm by putting too much stuff in there.

*Why have you chosen the 12-string for so much of your flatpicked rhythm work?*

Because it gives you a much fuller sound for playing flatpicked chord-and-bass accompaniments. Especially as a single performer, which is how I started out, you need a bigger sound to project better. It brings the energy level up for those songs that really need a strong rhythm. But I've also used the 12-string for fingerstyle work on some of my more romantic tunes.

*As a musician gets further along and starts performing, what are some of the factors that become more important in rhythm playing?*

You should become more conscious of dynamics. First, don't attack too hard, and be sure you don't play at the same volume all the time. Vary the intensity with the feeling of the music. And you have to be conscious of not only how you're playing, but also of how that sound is coming out through the PA.

*Even though you perform with a five-piece band, you still use just a mike to amplify your acoustic guitars. Why don't you use a pickup?*

A couple of reasons. You get a clean, natural sound with a mike. Also, I like to work the mike for dynamics. I have more control that way. I play from different angles and different distances. By moving an inch here and there, or changing the angle a few degrees, I can really get some nice variations in shading and dynamics. I'm not just moving around up there—there's a *reason* for every little movement onstage. I use a high-quality Shure mike for concerts. I try to keep the rhythm where it should be—underneath the lead, but still solid enough for the band to work around. Another thing, especially when you work with a mike, you've got to be careful to hit your bass notes *clean*; otherwise they'll come sloshing through the PA like crazy, and the guitar will sound muddy.

*When you're playing fingerstyle accompaniments do you also go for shading by moving your right hand toward the bridge or toward the soundhole?*

Yes, I do—especially when I'm recording. Usually I like to play near the soundhole, but I find that in the studio you can get a cleaner sound by moving back toward the bridge.

*In the studio, how do you position the mikes, and what kind of mike do you prefer for the guitar?*

We place the guitar mike—A Neumann U-87—about three inches above the soundhole, about a foot below the vocal mike. That way, the guitar mike is between the vocal mike and the soundhole, and it seems to take the guitar sound out of the vocal mike. The guitar mike has the live side facing down, and it picks up the sound as it projects up and out from the soundhole. With the guitar mike positioned that way, it seems to act as something of a baffle that prevents the guitar sound from leaking into the vocal mike.

*So you sometimes lay down your guitar and vocal tracks live, instead of overdubbing them?*

That's right. I come up with a real strong vocal right out of the box, with the guitar and the whole band, and quite often I'll go with that original vocal. Practically everything I've done has been cut that way. Sometimes I've been criticized for it, but it's a damn honest sound. Unfortunately, honest isn't always what makes it these days. A record has to be so perfect that you always have to at least consider redoing the vocals if you think you can get them better on another take.

*On the recording of some of your ballads, you play a second guitar line on the "high-strung" guitar. Explain that.*

It's a guitar that's tuned up an octave on the bottom four strings—using much lighter-gauge strings, of course. The top two strings are tuned normally. Then I overdub that guitar on top of the normal six-string and it gives you a sort of 12-string sound, but you can do a little more with it. It works well on tunes where I do a Travis-style fingerpicking line.

*In arranging parts for two guitars, what gives you the clear, harmonious texture that characterizes your music?*

I've always been careful to make sure that there aren't any holes in the chords, that the voicings are filled up—unless I'm after an open, more airy sound. The harmonies and different voices need to flow in a consistent way, not just come out in random licks. You have to construct the parts so that if you're playing a *Bm7* chord, the seventh will be heard. So the interplay between the two guitars is very important, and a lot of thought goes into that.

*What kind of thought, for instance?*

If one of the lines you're playing doesn't fit, you have to find out why, and put in that missing note—or take out the one that doesn't fit. Often, you find that someone is playing the wrong inversion, and you can fix it if you know what you're doing. I do most of that by ear, but if I have to I can sit down and write out the parts to figure out why something isn't working. And I've often used my knowledge of theory to determine whether a bass note is in place.

*You mentioned that knowing music theory, and being musically literate, helps in putting together your guitar arrangements. Has that also come in handy in other situations?*

You bet it has. All through the years it's come through in such smashing style for me. For example, sometimes when I'm getting ready to record an album I'll hear in my head ideas for string lines and orchestrations. I know the chord structures, the transpositions, and so forth, and when I get these ideas, I can write them down. Then I can give them to the arranger, who is really the expert, and he can take it from there. Another way theory has helped me is in writing songs. I've just run into a lot of musical problems that I couldn't have handled if I hadn't gotten the training early in my career. It's an enormous advantage to have that basic knowledge of the craft of music.

*You studied piano both as a child and later at the Westlake College Of Music. Has that played any role in your songwriting process?*

Not too much, actually. The piano just gives you a good hands-on illustration for theory ideas. Up to my ninth or tenth album I wrote most of the songs on the 12-string. Most of the songs have taken shape initially on the guitar.

*Do you have a method in writing songs, or is it something that just comes together in its own way?*

It really varies. But it's good to get a solid chord progression mapped out first, and then think about the melody and the lyrics. For me, songwriting is something that's on my mind all the time. If I come up with something positive, I'll make a note of it—whether it's a progression, a melody, or lyrics. Sometimes those ideas can be developed into songs.

*Is there a point where you just sit down and get to it?*

Absolutely. There comes a point when I sit down and confront the fact that I'm going to record an album, and I've got to work on the songs until they're finished. But there are those times when I run into a brick wall with a song, and if both my inspiration and my expertise fail me, I'll just throw the song into the wastebasket. It's no big deal for me to scrap a song. Then there are those times when I really get on a roll and I write a couple of songs in a day.

*As a writer of a lot of hit songs, have you been careful to maintain control over your creations, or did you sign away the rights to get your career moving?*

I've kept all of my songs under my own cover for the last 14 years. I formed my own company and I have those songs in my own satchel. Those are my songs and I want to keep them that way. I think that's fair. And that's sort of how I look at my whole career. I do have a manager who runs the ship, but I don't ever want to have an official show-biz type manager telling me what I ought to be doing. I like my profile the way it is. I've probably made a lot less money that way, but I'm happy with my career, and with my life.

*It seemed on your* Salute *[1983] LP your voice got buried in the mix, and that the tunes and lyrics were obscured by over-production. What's your feeling about that?*

You're right. The album had a few faults, I have to take the heat for that. These days you're not allowed to be anything less than perfect or your record just won't get played. I was sort of feeling things out with some new sounds. You've got to grow, and I've always been a guy who is willing to take a chance. I will continue to take those chances, because I'm really into what I'm doing. On this new record we've got those problems ironed out. And the new songs I've written for this record are really good—strong tunes and positive lyrics. They reflect how I'm feeling now. I'm really *enjoying* working on this album and I'm excited about touring with the new material.

*What do you do to get away from the demands of performing and recording?*

There's really no way to get away unless I clean out about six weeks, which I do at least once every two years. Then I go on canoeing trips up toward the Arctic. I've done ten of those over the years, and on some of those trips we've made it all the way up to the Arctic Ocean. But on a regular basis, to balance things I run and work out. I'm in good shape and I feel good. But as busy as my career keeps me, it really eats up most of my time. I'm not complaining, mind you, because I really love doing it, and I'm enjoying the new directions I'm going with my music. I like to keep moving forward. But thank God that I made a good living in this business, because I honestly don't know what else I could have done if I hadn't made a go of it with my music!

*If you were just getting started in the music business today as a solo performer, how would you go about it?*

Practice, man. Practice and more practice. And learn all you can about the craft of music and the business of music. Hunt out the jobs, pound the pavement. Now one thing I'd probably do differently is I'd go with a pickup on my guitar, as a practical matter. I think these days a lot of the places you'd be playing are pretty noisy, and you'd be ahead of the game if you got your axe wired. Back when I was cutting my teeth, audiences tended to listen. For the acoustic guitar, I prefer the natural sound of the mike, and I especially like the control that I have in working the mike; but it just doesn't get it if you're playing in a noisy room with a lousy PA. It's better to be heard than to sound natural and be ignored. Also, I'd say you should write as many songs as you can and work them into your act. You don't want to be playing all the same stuff as everyone else; you've got to give the audience something to remember you by.

## A Selected Gordon Lightfoot Discography

(On Warner Brothers): *Salute*, 1-23901; *Shadows*, BSK 3633; *Dream Street Rose*, XHS 3426; *Endless Wire*, KBS 3149. (On Reprise): *Summertime Dream*, MS 2246; *Gord's Gold*, 2RX 2237; *Cold On The Shoulder*, MS 2206; *Sundown*, MS 2177; *Old Dan's Records*, MS 2116; *Don Quixote*, MS 2056; *Summer Side Of Life*, MS 2037; *Sit Down Young Stranger*, 6392. (On United Artists): *A Lightfoot Collection*, UALA 189-F; *The Very Best of Gordon Lightfoot, Vol. I, II*, UALA 243-G, 445-E; *Sunday Concert*, 6714; *Back Here On Earth*, 6672; *Did She Mention My Name*, 6649; *The Way I Feel*, 6587; *Lightfoot*, 6487.

# JEAN RITCHIE

Sixty-three year old Jean Ritchie remains a steady performer at traditional music festivals throughout the United States. She was first recorded for the Library of Congress by Alan Lomax, and became one of the seven original members of the board of directors of the Newport Folk Festival. Her greatest impact has been in popularizing the mountain lap dulcimer, an instrument she learned from her father at the family homestead in Viper, Kentucky. Her honest, untrained voice retains the authenticity of her Appalachian roots. Her career was profiled in the *Frets* September 1980 issue.

**By Alanna Nash**

WHEN JEAN RITCHIE walked out on stage at a folk festival several years ago, at least one member of the audience had difficulty believing it was Ritchie herself. "I think that's Jean Ritchie," a woman said to her female companion. "Oh, no," replied her friend. "She must have died a long time ago."

I've been around so long, I guess some people do think that," laughs Ritchie, who's over 60 now but still very much alive.

On first listening to Ritchie's lovely album *None But One*, which won *Rolling Stone* magazine's Best Folk Album Of The Year award, some of Ritchie's longtime fans thought she was perhaps too much alive. *None But One* featured the Eric Weissberg

band, with instrumentation including pedal steel and electric guitars, electric bass, drums, synthesizer, and phase shifter, in addition to banjo, mandolin, and Appalachian dulcimer. Although Ritchie says most of her fans came to like the album after repeated listenings, the fear remained with some that she was moving away from her traditionally based music toward a more progressive sound. They felt Ritchie had some explaining to do.

"Really, that was just an experiment," says Ritchie, the foremost female performer of pure folk or mountain music. "I'm not a leader in those things. I tend to follow three or four years behind all the other trend-setters. But we thought, 'Well, let's try it.' Lately we've just built a house out of old logs, yet we're going to put in gas heat and all modern equipment to keep ourselves comfortable. And I think music is the same way. You sing the old songs, and they sound good with dulcimer or even unaccompanied, the way they used to be sung. But they sound equally good with modern instruments. I believe in using what's around you at the time."

For all the success of *None But One*, Ritchie returned to more traditional instrumentation on her next album *High Hills And Mountains*, the first release of her own Greenhays label. While Ritchie and her husband, George Pickow, explain that Jean always had complete freedom on her recordings ("I think they sometimes leave too much to me, because maybe if they did interfere some, my records might be a little more professional"), one reason for starting their own label is to ensure that Jean's records will stay in print.

"This album is in a different direction from the last," she says. "I haven't decided to expand into electric instruments and go into progressive music. There's no electricity on this record." Accompanying Ritchie on the album, which includes new recordings of some of her best-known songs, "The Cuckoo" and "The L&N Don't Stop Here Anymore," in addition to old Kentucky favorites such as "The Royal Telephone" and "Old Daddy Grumble," are a group of musicians Ritchie refers to as the Fresno Friends: Kenny Hall on mandolin and guitar; Frank Hicks on guitar and bass; Harry Liedstrand on fiddle; Gene Bluestein on banjo; Evo Bluestein on fiddle, autoharp, and guitar; and Jemmy Bluestein on flute and mandolin. The majority of the album was recorded last spring when Ritchie was the artist-in-residence at California State University, Fresno.

The old-timey music earned Ritchie her initial reputation. Her repertoire of songs about a time and way of life that, for the most part, is no more, has made her almost legendary in some circles. Even persons outside the realm of music recognize her as one of the major influences and contributors to the folk music boom of the 1950s and 1960s, an artist who came to be known throughout the country along with Pete Seeger, Woody Guthrie, and Huddie "Leadbelly" Ledbetter. What made her an integral part of the folk movement was her effort to bring music out of her native Cumberland Mountains, and through concerts, records, and books, represent it in its pure and original form to a public that knew little about the oral tradition of the mountain people and their music. And largely through Ritchie's influence and popularity, the mountain dulcimer gained prominence as something more than a regional folk instrument.

While Ritchie's allegiance is with the past, she has an open mind to everything that is happening today. "That's what I keep telling people, because all the time everybody accuses me of being a purist, and there are many people who just learned to play last year who are much more purist than I am," Ritchie says. "I taught an 18-year old boy out in California who wanted a dulcimer, but he insisted he had to have the hearts [soundhole cutout] upside down, because to him, that was traditional. Most everybody makes them now with the hearts going the other way, but this kid said, 'Oh, no, that's not traditional.' I don't ever insist on anything like that."

Nor does Ritchie object to the changes in dulcimer construction over the last 15 years, such as the replacement of the old-style wooden friction pegs with tuning machines. "I think that was bound to come," says Ritchie, "because so many people are playing now, not only solo, but with other instruments, and playing in bands, and they have to be able to tune quickly. And I guess that was the best answer. I still like the looks of the old wooden friction pegs better. One thing I do object to these days is the use of the big chromium things that stick up in the air. I think that looks ugly on a dulcimer. But the little black banjo-type things that you screw in the end, that's the kind we use. I think that is sort of in keeping with the look of the dulcimer. In general, though, I think the construction of the dulcimer is vastly improving. People are getting to be a little more demanding when they go to buy a dulcimer, and they know more about what to look for in the tone, and whether it's true in the bass range as well as the treble, or whether the action is nice and low."

Jean learned to play the dulcimer from her father, Balis Ritchie, when she was four or five. Having almost single-handedly revived interest in the instrument, she has seen the dulcimer go through several cycles of popularity. Today the dulcimer is enjoying an upswing.

Ritchie is a born-and-bred authority on the instrument. Before her birth, her family had already earned a reputation for singing and preserving old mountain songs, and was occasionally visited by folk music collectors. Jean was the last of 14 children, and as a girl she spent her evenings as many of the people in the mountains did; sitting on the porch as the moon came up, sharing the events of the day with family and friends, and singing the ballads, folk songs, love songs, lullabies, and work songs that the immigrants (including Jean's great-great-grandfather, James Ritchie) had brought over from the British Isles. But even then, not everyone in the mountains loved that kind of music. Many of the young people there wanted to discard Elizabethan ballads for the new "hillbilly" sounds heard on the radio. Had the women at the nearby settlement schools not encouraged children to take pride in their music, Ritchie says, the authentic mountain music might have died out. An ultimate irony, Ritchie adds, that today there are people in the mountains who never saw a dulcimer, who—in keeping up with the modern world—abandoned many of the mountain traditions, and are just now rediscovering the dulcimer along with the world at large.

While such dulcimer masters as John Jacob Niles seem to make a mystery of the instrument, Ritchie has always stressed how simple a dulcimer is to play. "I did a lot of missionary work in the old days," she says, "trying to get people to realize what a great little instrument it was, how much fun it was, and how much you could do with just going off in a corner and sitting down and amusing yourself and playing tunes. A lot of people who felt that they couldn't play anything would get all excited about playing the dulcimer."

As for Ritchie's own particular technique: "I favor simplicity. Simplicity, I guess is my trademark. I play like my dad did, with the pick." But Ritchie's pick is not an average pick. "I make them myself," she says, "out of coffee can lids. I find that the best thickness for a pick is one of the plastic can tops that has writing on it. The ones without writing are flimsy. But the ones with writing on them are a little bit heavier. Or you can use credit cards, but you have to trim them down to a long point. Collar stays are good, too." Ritchie also uses a thumb pick to strum with, but buys her thumb picks out of bins in music stores rather than making her own. "Not the stiff, brown tortoise-shell ones," she notes. "I use the white, thin plastic ones that are very flexible. You just sort of rake them across the strings, and they don't give too much resistance. I use that kind of pick for the autoharp, too."

The autoharp is Ritchie's second or third instrument, sharing a supporting role with her guitar. "Actually," she says, "my voice is my principal instrument. I rarely play a dulcimer piece without singing. I play instruments mainly to accompany my voice." Currently, she's playing an Oscar Schmidt International "Berkshire" Autoharp model, having given her Appalachian autoharp to a girl who fell in love with the instrument during Ritchie's tour in Japan. "I plan to turn this one into an Appalachian model as soon as I get around to it, by moving the bar over," she says. "Strangely enough, I think the autoharp is less well known than the dulcimer around the country. Because sometimes I go and play before a group of people, and they will have heard of the dulcimer before, but some of them will come up afterwards and say, 'What was that other instrument you played? That's really pretty! And they get all excited over the autoharp."

Her principal guitar is a top-of-the-line Goya, given to her by the company years ago. She uses an Aria model #HFAC50 for her second guitar. "They're both nylon string, because I don't play the guitar very much," she says. "I just use it for an occasional song. And I'm not a good guitar player. I don't have very tough calluses. As for make of strings, the ones I like the best I can never get a hold of. They're Thomastik, a German string that some English performers gave me as a present. They're very hard to find in this country. One man took the strings off my guitar to repair it one time and said, 'What have you got on

here? It looks like twine!'" She laughs heartily, adding "They're different colors, you see. There's a red one and a green one and a blue one. I can't use the bass ones, but I can use the trebles. They're great. And you never have to change them. They just ring and ring and ring." *Never* have to change them? "Well," she says, blushing, "no, that's not true. I play the guitar so little—two songs per performance—so I change them maybe three times a year."

Ritchie may not be interested in doing much experimenting with the autoharp and the guitar, but she has varied her stringing pattern on the dulcimer. "I play homemade dulcimers," says Ritchie. "There's no brand to them. I'm using one dulcimer that my husband George Pickow and his uncle made about 20 years ago, and another instrument that was sent to me as a gift from a man named William Docherty in Melbourne, Australia. He makes beautiful, fancy dulcimers. He's a harpsichord maker, so he really finishes them nicely, with inlay. And I also play the Musical Traditions dulcimers. For stringing, I like four separate strings evenly spaced. The next popular way of stringing is to put the first two strings together, and then another treble in the middle, and then the bass. My favorite pattern uses three [5-string] banjo strings. Two trebles are seconds, and the third is a wound fourth from the banjo. But my fourth string is a guitar third, tuned down an octave lower to make a deep, bass tone."

For the dulcimer, Ritchie favors D'Addario strings. "You can go into a store and buy dulcimer strings singly, and buy just the treble or bass, because they're usually banjo strings," she says. "But now people are putting them together for you, and they're assembling four banjo strings into a group called dulcimer strings. I change my strings maybe every two years, since the nature of the instrument is that you just slide the bar [wooden noter bar, a fretting aid] up and down, and I only make the note on one string. The other is a droning chord that goes along. I use a noter almost all the time. Once in a great while I'll just use the fingers. But I use a noter almost exclusively, and I haven't experimented with that much at all. I've experimented a lot with different tunings, just by ear, for my own amusement, but I've written most of that down in my books. I don't think I use any tunings that nobody knows. I love the tuning that I call half mixolydian and half dorian, but it turns out to be a regular minor. The harmonizations are really pretty."

By "wandering around and finding pretty harmonies" and tunings, Ritchie often finds the beginnings of a new song. "It happens with different instruments sometimes—the autoharp and the guitar—but mostly with the dulcimer, I guess. And then I'll have the tune in my head, and after a while, I'll make up a few words for it. Many of the songs that I write are based on older songs, or older tunes, and I start with that. But by the time it gets finished and I put a set of words to it, the tune has changed and

Jean Ritchie was one of many folk performers
first recorded by Alan Lomax. Her many
tours and records have helped to
popularize the mountain dulcimer.

altered so much that you usually can't recognize the
tune it comes from."

Ritchie says she varies her picking strum three or
four different ways during the course of one song,
just for variety. But again, simplicity rules, and no one
is about to catch her practicing a fancy lick. "Actually,
I play a little descant when I play a slow song or a
love song," she explains. "And then, when I do a fast
song, or one that needs rhythm, I use the coffee can
lid, or a goosefeather. I just strum it back and forth.
I've listened to people in dulcimer gatherings, where
different stylists come together, and they've all got
different ways of playing. As long as you watch them,
you think they're doing fascinating things. But if you
close your eyes, it all sounds like a dulcimer being
played. I can't see much point in getting all worked
up over getting your fingers tied up in knots and
crossing your hands and standing on your head. My
way of playing is simple, but people think I'm doing a
lot more than I am. Just the way the dulcimer is set
up, with that chord that goes along all the time, it has
great variety, just in playing it simply. If you want to
get into it as an instrument and show off your
instrumental technique, I can see how you could get
all worked up with it, but I just want to accompany
songs. I don't need all the other things, and I don't go
in for them."

In keeping with that thinking, Ritchie says she has
no elaborate miking setup. For her last two albums,
she used both contact pickups (Barcus-Berry on
*None But One*) and regular mikes together. "But in
performance, we just slap some mikes on," she says.
"I like one microphone very close to the voice, on a
boom. The dulcimer mike must be on a boom, too,
and placed in the curve in the middle, so I don't hit it
with my hands. The voice mike usually picks up the
autoharp, and for the guitar, I just raise or lower the
instrument mike. My needs are very simple onstage."

The year 1950 was a significant one for Ritchie, in
several ways. That September she married George
Pickow, a New York photographer. Pickow has contributed greatly to the high-quality look of Ritchie's
last two album jackets, and in the past has shot
photos for such artists as Theodore Bikel, Josh White,
and the Chad Mitchell Trio (when that group
included John Denver). "I also did Mercury's country
stuff, and I did all the early Elektra Records covers,"
says Pickow, a friendly, outgoing man. But then,
Pickow had an "in" with the latter company. Three
months after Ritchie and Pickow married, Ritchie
met a Haverford college student named Jack Holzman, who told her he and a friend had just started a
small record company they called Elektra. Holzman
asked if she would consider launching their folk
music division. The result—the first record for
Elektra and for Jean—was the ten-inch LP *Jean
Ritchie, Singing Traditional Songs Of Her Kentucky
Mountain Family*. Since then, Ritchie has done more
than 30 albums for different labels, including one
early, budget LP, *Hootenanny At The Limelight*,

which didn't credit its principal artist nor its background singers—one of whom was a young woman named Judy Collins, then struggling to make a career for herself in folk music. (A few years later, Pickow was to shoot the jacket photo for Collins's second album, *Golden Apples Of The Sun.*)

Ritchie was in constant demand for concert college appearances when she received a Fulbright scholarship in 1952 to study folklore in the British Isles. Part of her quest was to try to uncover the origin of Appalachian music. Through the years, a false impression has remained that Ritchie found the music had been "re-invented" in the Appalachians. "Well, I don't think I'd use the expression 're-invented,'" she says. "It was combined. The three main elements there were Scottish, Irish, and English, and they all brought music with them. Just as people would intermarry, sometimes the songs would get intermarried, too. A person would hear two or three different people in his community sing a song a different way. he might like the tune to one and the words to another, and put an Irish tune to a set of English lyrics, and start singing it that way. But Appalachia was a melting pot for the music. That was beginning to happen in England, Ireland, and Scotland, too. The old versions visited back and forth. But more so in Appalachia. Of course, with the advent of the banjo, that changed a lot of songs and made them sound typically American."

Upon returning to the United States, Ritchie appeared on a number of major television shows. She continued touring and recording after the birth of her first son, Peter, in 1954. another son, Jonathan, was born in 1958. Today both brothers are musicians and have appeared on their mother's last two albums, as well as on an early album, *Jean Ritchie At Home.*

The end of the 1950s saw the Pickows designing and building their own dulcimers in between Ritchie's appearances. In 1959, she sang at the first Newport Folk Festival. She became one of the festival's directors in 1963, as well as a member of the folklore panel of the National Endowment for the Arts.

The fact that she is not now—nor ever was—a "star" of the magnitude of say, Joan Baez, seems to cause Ritchie no concern. Rather, she appears almost relieved about it. "I was never on top of the boom," she says honestly. "When Pete Seeger would introduce me, he'd say, 'Now we're going to have a quiet moment.' I was there for contrast, serenity. So I wasn't diminished or uplifted by the boom, and my work has built steadily through the years. I really detest the star system. I didn't want to be a star, and I've been successful. George doesn't like me to say this, but I have avoided it. He says it sounds like sour grapes, like I really wanted to be a superstar and nobody ever asked me. But it's true. People used to try to push me to do things, and get me on television shows. I want to be able to go to the supermarket and not be stared at and pulled apart. I really hate that kind of thing. And I hate the star system for what it does to people on both sides. I guess that's one reason I'd have to say that the dulcimer players I admire most are Mary Faith Rhoads, Roger Nicholson, and Holly Tannen. They're all good players, but they all have another dimension beyond that. They're all sympathetic people who have heart and care about other people, which to me symbolizes where the music comes from. And it comes across in their music. There are some good players that I don't admire because they get all lost in flashy technique and nothing comes across that's human.

"I like being just an ordinary person," she continues. "One of the good things about being ordinary is I never feel that if I don't do something and keep my name before the public and sing every week somewhere, people are going to forget me. I mean, I couldn't care less if they forget me, and of course, many people have never even heard of me. Speaking of which, let George tell you a story."

Pickow picks it up. "This was really funny," he begins. "The FM station connected with Hofstra University recently started a folk music program, three hours a day for six days a week. Hofstra is rather close to where we live in New York, and after it had been on about a week, I called up and asked how it was going. The girl who was running the program said, 'Oh, great. We've had lots of requests.' And then she said, 'Can I play something for you?' I said, 'Well, the only thing you could play for me would be Jean Ritchie.' And she said, 'Jean Ritchie? How do you spell that? I'll see if we have anything by her.' And as it turned out, they didn't."

Probably by now, the young woman has found out who Jean Ritchie is. "One great thing about the folk music field is that the older you get, the more admired and revered you are, instead of having to keep young and beautiful," says Ritchie, smiling. "A rock singer, being a part of the youth cult, has to keep really beautiful and eternally 18. But people such as Lilly Mae Ledford and myself can grow older and become grand old dames, and it's great!"

---

## A Selected Jean Ritchie Discography

**Solo albums** (on Folkways): *British Traditional Ballads In The Southern Mountains*, FA2301; *British Traditional Ballads In The Southern Mountains*, FA2302; *Children's Songs And Games From The Southern Mountains*, FC7054. **With Others:** *Jean Ritchie And Doc Watson At Folk City*, FA2426; *Jean Ritchie And Oscar Brand At Town Hall*, FA2428; *Precious Memories*, FA2427; *The Appalachian Dulcimer*, FI8352; *The Ritchie Family Of Kentucky*, FA2316; *A Time For Singing*, Warner Brothers, WS1592; *High Hills And Mountains*, Greenhays (Dist. by Flying Fish), GR701; *American Folk Tales And Songs*, Tradition, TLP1011; *Carols Of All Seasons*, Tradition, TLP1031; *Courtin's A Pleasure*, Elektra, 122; *None But One*, Sire, SA7530; *Riddle Me This*, Riverside, RLP 12-646; *Shivaree!*, Esoteric ES-538.

# RICHIE HAVENS

With his unorthodox barre chord playing style, and highly rhythmic right-hand technique, Richie Havens added a unique dimension to the folk music of the '60s, and he remains a popular performer today. Though his early gigs were at such small Greenwich Village spots as the Cafe Wha?, by the end of the decade he was headlining at the Fillmore East and West, at a time when most acoustic performers were having difficulty finding commercial acceptance. This *Frets* interview dates from October of 1983.

**By Mark Humphrey**

**W**OODSTOCK, NEW YORK, was more than a geographical location for the generation that came of age in the late Sixties. It came to represent an ethic, a lifestyle, and a music that, for a brief season of idealistic innocence, seemed capable of transforming the world. If that transformation never took place, it wasn't for want of naive belief in its inevitability. And it wasn't for lack of charismatic power in the music of Jimi Hendrix, the Who, and other major rock performers of the day.

Whatever guitarist Richie Havens lacked in terms of wattage, in the company of those giants, was more than made up for by his spellbinding intensity. The image of Havens, eyes shut in an apparent trance, spinning like a dervish and thrashing at his guitar as he sang "Freedom" (*Woodstock*, Cotillion) is one of the strongest in the film of the epic rock festival. And while the intervening years have not always been kind to the participants or ideals of Woodstock, Havens still expresses the same innocence, enthusiasm, and intensity that characterized his performance at the 1969 concert.

Havens was born Jan. 21, 1941, into a musical family. While growing up in the Bedford-Stuyvesant area of Brooklyn, New York, Richie organized street-corner gospel groups. In the early '60s he began singing at nightspots in Greenwich Village; and in 1963 he was part of a Ford Motor Company-sponsored tour that included such artists as vocalist Nina Simone, flutist Herbie Mann, and percussionist Mongo Santamaria. His reputation grew to the point where he was signed by the Verve-Folkways label, and in 1966 he released his first album, *Mixed Bag*. His popularity as a major folk-rock artist culminated in 1971 when his version of George Harrison's "Here Comes The Sun" reached the Top 200 on *Billboard's* pop charts.

With crosses and amulets dangling from his neck and a dagger tattooed on his right forearm, the tall and angular Havens is a striking figure. In conjuring his hypnotic and ecstatic music, he vaguely resembles a West Indian Voodoo priest. The heavy Afro-Cuban beat in his music accentuates this, as does his appearance onstage: eyes shut, body swaying, sweat pouring down his face as his furious right hand turns his guitar into a rhythm machine. His idiosyncratic guitar playing (open *D* tuning typically fretted with his thumb) is more percussive than melodic; his gruff, heartfelt vocals owe much to the streets and churches of his native Brooklyn. His interpretations of such songs as Van Morrison's "Tupelo Honey" and Dylan's "Just Like A Woman" send the melodies to church and punctuate the rhythms.

The originality of Haven's approach (strong, rhythmic dynamics and melodic invention within a context of overall simplicity) does not, like some innovations of the Sixties, sound quaintly dated. Far from being a sentimental journey, a Havens performance is filled with an exhilaration and fire that is too seldom heard from solo acoustic performers. The man whom John Lennon, in an early *Rolling Stone* article, called "a really funky guitar player," is still that.

. . . .

**W**HAT WAS YOUR INITIAL *involvement with music?*

Kids who didn't have jobs or who didn't finish school ended up singing together. This provided some base of reality, which was basically non-violent. That's what I was doing when I was 13. In the 1950s, everybody did that to stay out of trouble. There was nothing else to do. It was a very subtle social phenomenon for young people. We all sang together in Brooklyn. Through music, young people found their initial camaraderie with people from other areas and other cultures. There wasn't a lot of craziness or prejudice in the 1950s.

*How did the gospel influence enter your music?*

One of the kids who sang with us had a mother who was very involved in the church, and so in order for him to sing rock and roll with us, we had to sing in the choir. It was a trade-off. It worked out, because we ended up liking both.

*Is it true that you sang baritone?*

Yes. I sang baritone at 13 [*laughs*]. I wrote a lot of songs, and did a lot of the hair-tearing, trying to get the guys to hit the right notes. I've probably been through 500 groups. It was a passport, to a certain degree, because when the street gang thing came along in the later 1950s, the only people who could traverse those barriers were the people who sang on street corners. Every neighborhood had them, and everybody knew each other in that society, so it was kind of a protective thing. Socially, it served a lot of purposes in the 1950s.

*What brought you to the guitar as opposed to, say, a horn?*

That's a good question, because I've always liked horns. I've always wanted to play a horn: a saxophone or a trumpet—anything that was airy. When I first started playing a guitar, it wasn't for myself; it was because I sang with a cappella groups. I had a girlfriend who had two younger brothers, 11 and 13. They had a little group, and they were dynamite. I used to do rehearsals with these kids, and a friend once loaned me his guitar. This was the time of the hootenannies in Greenwich village, so I took the kids over there one day. They killed everybody. It was a phenomenon, because they were so very young. What I didn't intend to do was sing again. I wasn't really into jumping up on anybody's stage and singing by myself. But once I started fooling around with the guitar and doing songs that I liked, it was fun. I started doing hootenannies.

*How old were you when you got really interested in the guitar?*

I didn't start playing guitar until I was 24. That's when I learned my fourth chord. Everybody knows that with three chords you can sing a million songs, but I found my fourth chord, and that changed my life [*laughs*]. Then I could sing things that I really liked, more intricate things. And I learned how to make a minor without tuning to a minor. That changed my life again.

*Didn't anyone ever show you an open tuning?*

No. I inherited that ability from my father, who played piano by ear. The structure of how I tuned it came from the church, actually. They used to have a lot of programs with gospel groups that had one guitar player. He'd play a chord, and everybody would

Richie learned his unique barre chord style of playing because when he first started learning the instrument, it was difficult for him to play with regular guitar tunings.

hum to that, tune up their voices. That's the chord, the structure that I tuned to. I never knew what key it was in [*laughs*]. That's it. I've been doing that all along.

*So the way you play evolved naturally?*

It just happened. I couldn't get anybody to teach me how to use my fingers, so I tuned to a chord, set the guitar on my lap, barred it with my thumb, and played it like a dulcimer. To keep time, my right foot learned very early to run 90,000 miles faster than my left foot [*laughs*]. It was automatic. My metronome was there.

*Have you always played in* D *tuning?*

Yes. *D-A-D-F♯-A-D,* which I sometimes turn into a minor or a minor seventh. I'll tune the third string a whole tone down, which makes it a minor, and I'll tune the high *E* down, which makes it a seventh. Those are the only strings I change. Paul Williams, my lead guitarist, changes his third string and tunes it up a tone in the same tuning.

*How long have you been playing with Paul?*

Since 1963. We grew up in the same neighborhood. He plays in the same tunings, but he uses his fingers too. I use mine very little. Most of what I do is accompaniment.

*You have a very driving right-hand style. Is that hard on guitars?*

I go through at least one and a half a year. I play a Guild D-40. I've always played them; I'll never play another guitar. They're the best.

*What sort of strings do you use?*

D'Angelico medium, and I change strings every set. I have to, because my hands sweat, and they get rusty. I use large triangular picks from Manny's in New York City. I think they're bass picks.

*When you recorded the album* Richie Havens 1983 *in 1970 weren't you a little premature?*

It was obvious then what would be happening in

'83, so I wanted to get that one out of the way [*laughs*]. Now I'm starting to get the year 2000 on my mind. It's already here: It's ready to come out of the closets into the streets. We're in for a lot of changes. We're finally going to look like Buck Rogers country.

*You were recently involved in a collaboration in Italy. How did that evolve?*

I actually got into it through a need for inspiration. I was in Italy about three years ago and heard an artist, Pino Danielle, who seemed to be saying something important. I ended up getting together with him in '82 to record. We got together for ten days just to see if it could work, and in those ten days, I ended up writing eight songs, which I hardly ever do. Pino doesn't speak English, and I don't speak Italian, so we spent a lot of creative quiet time. It was sort of psychic. Language is no real barrier when feeling is involved. I was inspired, and it all came right out. He arranged and wrote some of the music; I put lyrics to some of the melodies, and some things we wrote together on the spur of the moment.

*What do you see as the legacy of your generation's music?*

We had a vision in the Sixties of how it could be, but most of us never got together to form the foundation of how it could be. We overextended our musical projection. The few who tried on their own either failed or are still holding on. But I think that attitude of evolutionary change has finally permeated the globe. We have a global consciousness among young people. In other countries, young people have been listening to our music.

*Do you see your music, with its various influences, as an international music?*

For me it's always been that way. I was fortunate enough to grow up with everybody, thank God. My father's side is American Indian, and my mother's side is West Indian, and my name is Dutch, so it's all wrapped up. A global collaboration in music is beginning. Everyone is moving toward that.

*What do you see happening musically in the future?*

The cycle always goes back to the beginning. The root musics are coming back, because the young people want to know where all of that middle ground came from. What caused it? Each generation has to start again, go right back to that base of the trunk, looking up at the tree.

*Do you have any advice for the next generation?*

You've just got to keep playing. You can't play and think you're going to get there by impressing anybody. You've got to impress yourself, and then everybody else will be impressed, and you'll get wherever you want to go.

## A Selected Richie Havens Discography

*Mixed Bag*, MGM, 4698; *Richie P. Havens*, MGM, 4700; *Festival Of Acoustic Music*, Fantasy, 79009; *Alarm Clock*, MGM, 6005; *Stonehenge*, MGM, 6001; *Connections*, Elektra, 6E 242.

# ROGER McGUINN

With the release of "Mr. Tambourine Man" and "Turn, Turn, Turn," the Byrds (whose original members included songwriter Gene Clark, drummer Mike Clarke, vocalist/guitarist David Crosby, and bluegrass mandolinist Chris Hillman on bass) almost singlehandedly invented folk-rock music. Prior to forming the group, McGuinn had been a backup banjoist and guitarist for the Chad Mitchell Trio and Bobby Darin. He recorded dozens of American and British folk songs on the various Byrds' albums. Since the group disbanded in the '70s, McGuinn has recorded several solo albums. He was interviewed in the August 1983 issue of *Frets*.

**By Mark Humphrey**

FLOWER POWER WAS just blossoming when Roger McGuinn, wearing dark granny glasses and a medieval tunic, startled the pop music world with an electric version of Bob Dylan's "Mr. Tambourine Man." With its ethereal harmonies and jangly electric 12-string guitar, the song became an instant hit, and a fledgling LA band called the Byrds entered the

pantheon of Sixties innovators. The year was 1965, the same year Dylan was booed offstage at the Newport Folk Festival in Rhode Island for appearing with electric instruments. The controversial marriage of folk roots with contemporary instrumentation and lyrics came to be called "folk rock." The Byrds exemplified this fresh sound, and the group would break further new ground before the decade ended. Their album, *Sweetheart Of The Rodeo*, in 1968, brought country elements to a rock audience, and the country rock sound continues to influence pop music.

Roger McGuinn stood at the center of this adventurous band for nearly ten years. Since 1973 he has worked with former Byrds bassist Chris Hillman and singer/songwriter Gene Clark, has appeared in Dylan's legendary Rolling Thunder Review, and has made many solo albums. Most recently McGuinn has toured as an acoustic solo act, returning to the roots he helped transform in '65. Those roots reach back to Chicago, where McGuinn first played folk music in the Fifties. Today, the songs are his, not public domain, but the accompaniment is very much the same as it was in his early days: a banjo and an acoustic 12-string guitar. Enthusiastic about his shift from rock star to modern-day troubadour, McGuinn feels that his new acoustic incarnation may "be the way of something to come." Having been in the musical vanguard more than once before, he could be right.

• • • •

**W**HAT PROMPTED YOUR RETURN *to acoustic music after you helped pioneer the folk-rock sound of the '60s and the country-rock sound of the '70s?*

It's kind of an instinct, a gut feeling that this is where I want to be now. I'm tuned into something; I get these waves of what's going to happen, and I act on them. A couple of years ago I started hearing in my head sounds like the Weavers. I wanted to make that sound, be around that sound, hear that sound. It wasn't happening, but I just had a longing for it. I'm really not attracted to rock and roll anymore. I think it's just spinning its wheels; it doesn't say anything. The fact is, in the '60s, rock and roll was really doing something—I liked it then. Of course, I've made some changes, too; I don't stand for the same things I used to. I feel good about that, though.

*Are you encouraged by the current acoustic music scene?*

I don't know much about it, frankly. I don't know where it stands. All I know is that I like it, and I'll have to do some investigating to find out what's going on. There are certain things that give me a spark of encouragement. There's an undercurrent.

*What sparked your interest in acoustic music, to begin with?*

I was turned on by Elvis right around "Heartbreak Hotel" time, and I got my first guitar in '56, when I was 13. The first one was a big harmony f-hole that I couldn't play because the action was about an inch high. I finally found out that it was supposed to be lower, so I went and got another guitar, a Kay. I was listening to a lot of the rockabilly stuff that was going on—Gene Vincent, Carl Perkins, Johnny Cash, and the Everly Brothers. When that started to fade and the Philadelphia Sound, the greasy kid stuff, took

over, I got into folk music. I started going to Weavers concerts, hanging out at the Gate of Horn in New York, and going to Chicago's Old Town School of Folk Music, where I learned banjo from Frank Hamilton. it used to be my main instrument, but I really let it go in the past 15 years.

*When did the 12-string guitar enter the picture?*

I got my first 12-string in '58. They were very difficult to get at the time; the major companies weren't in production. The one that I got was an old Stella, a rosewood model. It was actually a pretty nice guitar. I loaned it to Hoyt Axton one time, and I never saw it again.

*Didn't you work with the Limeliters at one time?*

I was only with them long enough to record their first RCA record. After that they said, "OK, thanks a lot," and that was it. I then went to work with the Chad Mitchell Trio, for about a year and a half. Bobby Darin saw me with them, liked me, and hired me as his accompanist on banjo and guitar for his Las Vegas show. He would do 15 minutes of folk music in his set, and I was his backup. What he did was pretty authentic, and he hired me to give it [even more] authenticity, since I had a folky background. I liked working with Darin; he was a real dynamo, a real wildman. His voice gave out and he stopped working, so he went into the [music] publishing business and he hired me as a writer. I was working in the Brill Building in New York for $35.00 a week. He had me listening to the radio and copying stuff, trying to write songs like those songs. The Beatles came out at that point, so I started writing Beatles-like songs and putting a Beatles kind of sound to folksongs that I knew. I'd put a 4/4 beat to songs that were normally in 3/4 or 2/4. That's the basis of what the Byrds did, really.

*How did the Byrds evolve?*

When I got out to LA, I was working at the Troubadour as a solo artist. Gene Clark came in and said, "Hey, I like what you're doing, let's write some songs together." We wrote a couple of songs, started singing 'em, [guitarist] David Crosby walked in, started singing harmony, and pretty soon we had a trio. We got a drummer [Mike Clarke] and a bass player [Chris Hillman], and we had a band. That was '64. By '65 we had a record deal with Columbia. We recorded "Mr. Tambourine Man" and in June they released it and the song was a hit in a couple of weeks. It was a shock, because we were just on the street before that. In fact, I remember being on the street, broke, when "Mr. Tambourine Man" was No. 1, hearing cars go by playing it on the radio, and going, "Wait a minte!" I didn't have a penny, but I was a hit.

*Part of what made that record so distinctive was the electric 12-string. Do you think this was an instrument that most people were then unfamiliar with?*

Well, actually, people *had* heard it, they just didn't know. The Beatles were using it; that was the sound

**The sweetheart-era Byrds (including
Clarence White) paved the way for many
of the country-rockers of the '70s.**

on a lot of the early Beatles records, especially the ones used for the soundtrack of the film *Hard Day's Night*. George Harrison was given one of the first Rickenbacker 12-strings; it was Rickenbacker's bid for the folk market. Actually, they had pretty good insight in thinking that the folk market might go electric, which it did. They created the perfect electric folk instrument. That's what I played, but I used it a little differently from the Beatles. They were doing just single-string licks with it, and I started playing fills with it and doing rolling patterns. I was fingerpicking, which is folk stuff, and they came from a rock and roll background, where everything is flatpicked. I was fingerpicking with a flatpick and my second and third fingers. I used to fingerpick with a thumbpick and two Nationals, but I had to stop that, because I wanted to flatpick at times and fingerpick at other times, and I couldn't change picks.

*Wasn't there quite a bit of personnel change in the Byrds?*

The band started in '64 and lasted as a five-piece group til '66, when Gene Clark left. In '67 Crosby left and in '68 Chris left—everybody left but me. Then I hired new guys, including [guitarist] Clarence White, and that group lasted til '73. I disbanded it because I was going to do a reunion album with the original Byrds and I didn't want there to be two sets of Byrds around. I gathered Clark, Hillman, and myself, and we made two albums. Then Clark left again, and Hillman and I made one album, and now it's back to McGuinn.

*Of these various groups, which was your favorite lineup?*

My favorite was the original, the first five-piece band. I liked the band with Clarence White as a performing band maybe the best, because the original band wasn't ever that great onstage. They were always out of tune; there was just total discord going on all the time.

*Didn't the original band have the most striking vocal harmonies?*

On record, but if you ever heard it live, you'd be disappointed. I was disappointed every show. It was a hair-pulling experience to get up there and try to do these sounds that were great on record. The audience would start out at a really high level of appreciation when we walked onstage, and by the time we got off, they'd be groaning. We'd just let 'em down flat every time. But that wasn't the case with the Clarence White band. That would start out pretty good and get better.

*Do you feel your* Sweetheart Of The Rodeo *was the beginning of country rock?*

We actually didn't make up the first country rock; that was Gram Parsons' work with the International Submarine Band. He was the influence on the Byrds that led us to do the *Sweetheart* album. He joined the Byrds in '68 as a piano player [*laughs*]. When I hired him, I thought he was a jazz piano player, because he played that to audition. I asked him if he could play

**McGuinn's picking style, using a flatpick and two fingers, allowed him to execute banjo-like rolls on the 12-string in creating the unique Byrds sound.**

any jazz on the piano, and he did, so I didn't know he had a country background. But Gram really had done country rock before anybody that I know of. It was kind of his idea. We popularized it to a point, but then I'd say other people popularized it more, like the New Riders Of The Purple Sage, Commander Cody, all the way through the Eagles.

*Through the years, have you found any instrument that you especially enjoy playing? What type of guitar are you using now?*

It's a Valdez 12-string that was kind of custom made for me. I had a new top put on it; the original top was Spanish pine, and it was too light. It had a really good sound but it pulled up. The guitar has a pinless bridge, or rather little pegs that stick out, so you put the string balls on them. They're really a breeze to change. When one breaks, it falls on the floor. When a string breaks onstage, I don't stop to change it; there are quite a few expendable strings. You break a top *E*, and there's another *E* there. The high *G* does break quite often, but it sounds okay without it. The guitar's a little "high endy," and it's got some overtones. I've been experimenting with

some different strings to see if I can get over that. There's a slight buzz on the *B* string; I can probably fix that with a matchbook. That's how we used to do it, stick a matchbook cover under the nut to raise the action.

*Your Valdez doesn't have a pickup, does it?*

No, it's not in any way an electric guitar. That drives some places crazy—a lot of places I play don't know what to do with an acoustic guitar. They can't deal with it if it doesn't have a pickup.

*What sort of strings are you using?*

It's a mixed set, basically light-gauge. From bass to treble the gauges are [*E*] .046″ and .036″; [*A*] .026″ and .020″; [*D*] .026″ and .020″; [*G*] .013″ and .019″; [*B*] .013″ and .013″, and [*E*] .010″ and .010″. I change the strings when they sound really dead to me, or when a bunch of them break. I'm not really thrilled with changing strings on the 12-string. Some people are much more conscientious, or maybe they're just a little overzealous about it.

*What sort of pick do you use?*

I like the medium-gauge Herco gold. It's a nylon pick, and I like it because it doesn't break. There's nothing more frustrating than to be in the middle of your song and have your pick break on you. When a pick breaks, it doesn't just snap off, it usually catches on a string and stops your strum in the middle of it. These don't break. They're heavy duty.

*Are you still using the same technique you used on your Rickenbacker?*

Yes—a flatpick and two fingers. My nails are pretty tough; they hold up. If I let them get too long, they'll crack in cold weather. They'll dry out and snap—I'll open a car door and lose a nail. Then I have to resort to fingerpicks, and that really changes everything. They're kind of awkward.

*You're playing banjo again onstage. What sort of banjo do you play?*

It's a composite—a very old Vega rim with an Ode neck. I would imagine that it was put together sometime in the Sixties.

*Do you use the same flatpick and fingers technique on banjo?*

No. I use a thumbpick and fingerpicks on banjo. My banjo playing isn't anything exceptional, I just get along with it. I do mostly frailing in *G*, *G* modal, *G* minor, and *C* tunings.

*Do you see a new band on the horizon?*

I don't really see one right away. I like acoustic music. One of the desires of my heart has always been to be a folksinger. It's so much easier than traveling with a band; it's really a pleasure to breeze into a place with a couple of cases and a suitcase, and there you are. No fuses to blow, nothing.

---

### A Selected Roger McGuinn Discography
**With The Byrds** (On Columbia): *Mr. Tambourine Man*, PC 9254; *Fifth Dimension*, PC 9349; *Younger Than Yesterday*, PC 9442; *The Byrds' Greatest Hits*, PC 9516; *Sweetheart Of The Rodeo*, PC 9670; *Pre-flyte*, KC3218. **Solo** (On Columbia): *Roger McGuinn*, KC 31946; *Peace On You*, KC 32956; *Roger McGuinn & Band*, PC 33541.

# TOM PAXTON

One of the most popular composers of modern folk music, Tom Paxton got his start singing at Greenwich Village coffeehouses in 1960. His compositions were covered by the Kingston Trio, John Denver, Peter, Paul, and Mary and many others. He was, and is, a frequent contributor to *Sing Out!* magazine. Tom still performs in the United States and also in England, where he has been even more popular. He discussed his long career and instrumental techniques in this May 1982 interview in *Frets*.

**By Sherwood Ross**

**D**URING THE FOLK ERA of the '50s and '60s, Tom Paxton was among a handful of stellar artists whose powerful musicianship—combined with social and political messages—struck a responsive chord in the American public. Many of those who made their folk careers ripping at social injustices and the Vietnam War have since slipped from view, or have so changed or electrified their music that barely a trace of their roots remains. But Tom Paxton remains true to his no-frills, solo acoustic calling. "I'm still just a dedicated folkie," he says.

Today, about 25 years since Paxton first played his way into the limelight, his stature as a performing artist remains unchallenged and he still has an avid following both in this country and abroad. Last year he was featured, along with guitarist/singers Odetta, Bob Gibson, and Josh White, Jr. on "Folk Music USA," a special feature on national television's *Sound Stage*.

Born in Chicago, Paxton grew up in Bristow, Oklahoma, in the same part of the state where Woody Guthrie was born. Paxton materialized on New York City's Greenwich Village coffeehouse scene about the same time as did Bob Dylan and the late Phil Ochs, and his work there proved an inspiration for such folk artists as Joan Baez and John Denver.

Aside from his prodigious skills as a guitarist and singer, the 44-year-old Paxton is a noted songwriter

whose prolific output includes the well-known "Rambling Boy," "The Last Thing On My Mind", and "Talking Viet Nam Pot Luck Blues."

• • • •

**W**HEN DID YOU FIRST *become interested in music? Do you remember the first music you ever heard?*

I always liked music. In Chicago, where I spent my first ten years, we had one of those great big old floor-standing radios in the living room. My family had tastes for the light classics, and I remember listening to radio shows like the *Voice Of Firestone, Manhattan Merry Go Round,* and *Fred Waring.* I liked that kind of music very much. I still do have a soft spot for the old chestnuts—like Tchaikovsky's *1812 Overture.*

*What was the first type of music you listened to that relates to what you are doing now?*

Songs by Burl Ives. Before I listened to him, I heard things on the radio that were vaguely folkish, but I didn't know there was such a thing as folk music. All I knew was that it was different from things like Vaughan Monroe singing "Mule Train" or "Ghost Riders In The Sky." Then I began to hear some songs by Burl Ives, and that really appealed to me. I remember getting an extended-play record of Burl Ives singing "The Fox Went Out On A Chilly Night," and "Streets Of Laredo", and I just loved it. I still love those songs.

*I heard that your first instrument was the trumpet. Is that correct?*

Yes. I took up the trumpet in high school, and made first chair. But then I began to get bored with the instrument. I got interested in the guitar through the ukulele. I can't remember how I wound up with my first ukulele, but I've always had this corny streak in me. I still sing "Down By The Old Mill Stream" in the shower. Well, I had this ukulele and went away to church camp and met a few other people who also played. Then I went to military school for a year

when I was in junior high school. My ukulele got smashed in an accident, and the following summer my aunt gave me an old guitar she had in the attic. The action was so high it was practically a Hawaiian guitar. It was impossible to play, but it kindled my interest for sure. I knew the top four strings from the ukulele, and gradually I began to incorporate the bass strings and to learn a chord or two. I think the first song I learned to play was "Streets Of Laredo," followed by "The Fox Went Out On A Chilly Night." They don't have many chords to them.

*How did your playing develop when you went to college?*

I went away to college at the University of Oklahoma, to be a drama major. I got even more interested in folk music and found out that there was a lot of it going on. I began to hear about Folkways Records and Pete Seeger and Woody Guthrie. The first time I listened to a Woody Guthrie record I thought, "My God, this guy's awful. He can't sing at all. He can't play the guitar. This is terrible stuff." I was used to hearing Burl Ives, with his beautiful bel canto kind of voice. But gradually the spirit of Woody Guthrie stated getting through to me, so that by the time I finished college, I was really a dedicated folkie and I had made up my mind that this was what I wanted to try to do. But then I was listening to people like Oscar Brand and the Weavers.

*Having a good instrument obviously is quite important to a performer. When did you finally get a good guitar?*

In my second year of college I asked my mother for a second-hand guitar for Christmas and I got this second-hand Gibson sunburst flat-top. I don't know what model it was—it was a full-size acoustic, and was more of the old country and western style. Someone told me I should put nylon strings on it, and I didn't know any better, so I did—even though it wasn't made for it. It wasn't a classical guitar. I kept those strings right on through college.

*Were you taking lessons from anyone at school?*

There were very few people around who could play the kind of guitar that I wanted to learn. All the instruction books were for playing plectrum, dance chords, and jazz chords; and there were lots of Roy Smeck books. I wanted to learn to play like Ed McCurdy and Burl Ives. They played extremely simple fingerstyle, but none of the books could show me that. I had to slowly work that kind of stuff out myself. About the time I came to New York, I could play in four or five different keys, and I had worked out kind of a nifty little clawhammer kind of thing with my right hand, playing the bass with the thumb, and then just using my first finger. And that stood me in pretty good stead for a while.

*Dave Van Ronk had a big impact on you. How did your association begin?*

When I moved to New York, I took one or two lessons from him and he became—and remains—one of my closest friends. In one hour, he got me into three-finger picking, managed to teach me the alternating bass, and how to use the first and second fingers. After the lesson, I was so excited that I went down to the Gaslight, New York City, where I was working. and in my first set I played one of my then standards, "The Golden Vanity" [*Together In Concert*], which I played in the key of *G*. I played three-finger style—but in the second verse my hand cramped, because it wasn't used to doing that. I thought I would die. I finished the song, although I think I cut a verse or two, just to get to the end of it. Still, that one lesson got me into the kind of guitar I play today.

*You seem to have taken an immediate liking to fingerpicking. How did your interest in flatpicking evolve?*

Through listening to [Ramblin'] Jack Elliot. It was really Jack's touch with the flatpick that intrigued me, and I like the way his flatpicking sounded with folk music. Before that, I had a prejudice against flatpicks: they weren't "folk" to me. But after hearing Jack, I thought, "I'd like to do that too." I think it was his kind of soft-strum flatpicking that influenced me in the beginning, and it still does.

*What type of guitar are you playing now?*

I play a Martin M-38, which is the first non-dreadnought I have ever played. I've always played Martin guitars as much out of habit as anything else, and I've always played dreadnought body shapes. But a few years ago I became dissatisfied with that shape. I began to feel that it had too much bass for me and I investigated some of the other guitars around. I wound up in Matt Ulmanov's shop in New York City, and told him I was looking for something. He said, "Play this," and he handed me and M-36, which is a plainer version of the M-38, and I really liked it a lot. I liked the way it felt and sounded and I liked the relationship of bass right on through to treble. It seemed to be very nicely balanced. So I bought it, and I've never regretted it. I just had to have the action reset a few times—it kept coming up on me. But now it seems to have settled in pretty well. I have a Mark Leaf case for it. I figure that the only way to survive on the road nowadays is to have the strongest case you can reasonably carry. There are stronger cases, but it would take a truck to carry them.

*How often do you change your strings?*

I hate to change strings, and I always leave them on too long. And only when I've embarrassed myself by getting out of tune in a show, do I finally give up and change them again.

*You and your family lived in England for three years. What differences did you notice between the folk music scene there and in the United States?*

In London there are a lot of folksingers who play on the streets or in the subways. They always bash their guitar, though, strumming it or using a flatpick. They beat the hell out it in order to be heard. It doesn't do their guitar playing any good, because all they're learning to do is to bash the hell out of the guitar. I'm afraid that when someone like that gets a chance to play indoors, they tend to bring those habits with them.

*Most of your career has been as a solo performer. Did you ever have any desire to perform in a group?*

The times that I have regretted not playing with a group have been when I just performed with friends informally on stage. I'll think, "Gee, I'd like to have this more often." A group can be tremendous fun. A few summers ago, Bob Gibson and I played together in Chicago at Chicagofest. We played in this great big hall at the end of Navy Pier and the place was absolutely crammed because the star of the night was Steve Goodman. Bob and I went out and sang together. It wasn't so much a duo as it was a song swap—he'd sing a song and I'd sing a song. We also sang some songs together. It was terrific. When something goes as successfully as that went, it has to start you thinking, "Hey, maybe we should do this all the time."

*Have you ever had the desire to make a country album?*

I would feel constrained doing that because my career as a performer interests me a lot less now than it used to. I'm much more interested in the writing, and the avenues that may open up for me. They are much more exciting to me than aiming for a hit record. God knows, I'd take it if it came, but I think it would be more exciting for me to get involved in a really good writing project. What would happen if the album would be successful? Then I'd be honor bound to go out and tour to support it, and I don't want to do that. Those country guys bust their hearts. They're on the road nine months of the year, even eleven months of the year.

*How did you view the future of folk music in this country?*

I think there's a healthy, low-key enthusiasm in folksinging in this country, based around local folklore centers. I think it's going to be harder and harder to earn a living at it, though. If someone is young and starting out, it's going to be hard to find places to play and people to pay you. But that's not going to stop them. It didn't stop me. The satisfaction has very little to do with money. It's just that I don't recommend it as a quick way to get rich.

---

**A Selected Tom Paxton Discography**

*Complete Tom Paxton*, Elcktra, ELK 7E-2003; *Ramblin' Boy*, Elektra, ELK 7014; *Festival Of Acoustic Music*, Fantasy, FSY 79009; *Greatest Folksingers Of The Sixties*, Vanguard, VSD-17/18; *Heroes*, Vanguard, VAN 79411; *Philadelphia Folk Festival*, Flying Fish, VLF 064; *Up And Up*, Mountain Railroad, MR 52792; *The Paxton Report*, Mountain Railroad, MR 52796; *Together In Concert*, Reprise, RPS 2R-2214; *Even A Gray Day*, Flying Fish, F 280; *Things I Notice*, Elektra, 7403.

# STEFAN GROSSMAN

Stefan has been a leading proponent of traditional guitar forms—blues, ragtime, marches, waltzes, and more—for two decades. He was the student and biographer of the legendary guitar teacher, Reverend Gary Davis. Stefan also founded Kicking Mule Records, to promote traditional music and fingerstyle guitar, and has published numerous guitar instruction books. Today he resides in Italy, producing other instrumentalists, writing, and occasionally performing. This interview dates from the April 1979 issue of *Guitar Player*.

**By Jas Obrecht**

AT AGE 15, STEFAN GROSSMAN began making tri-weekly pilgrimages from Brooklyn to a shack on Claremont Avenue in the heart of New York City's Bronx to take lessons from a legendary bluesman, the late Rev. Gary Davis. He then became a dedicated member of the "Blues Mafia"—a group of researchers intent on rediscovering the great bluesmen who had performed on the race records of the '20s and '30s—where he became close friends with Skip James, Mississippi John Hurt, Son House, Mississippi Fred McDowell, and other great American bluesmen and songsters. Never one to rest on the oars, Stefan then authored several music books that presented these styles to pickers worldwide.

Before moving to Europe in 1967 to live with Eric Clapton (the guitarist was then in the process of co-founding Cream), Stefan gigged with the Even Dozen Jug Band, singers Janis Joplin and Taj Mahal, an early counterculture rock band known as the Fugs, and Mike Bloomfield in the band Chicago Loop. While living in Italy several years later, Stefan decided that there was a shortage of good, instructional guitar records and music, so he co-founded Kicking Mule Record in 1973. With a lineup of artists that includes guitarists Dave Evans, Tom Van Bergeyk, Happy Traum, Duck Baker, Bert Jansch, John Renbourn, and Davy Graham, Kicking Mule has been instrumental in promoting and preserving the best in blues, ragtime, and contemporary picking. In addition to his record producing, personal recordings, instructional writings, and other projects, Stefan kept up his live appearances, performing two world tours with John Renbourn.

Born in New York City in 1945, young Stefan began playing guitar at age nine, when his father bought him an acoustic Harmony f-hole guitar from a Goodwill Shop in New York City. "Then I eventually got an arch-top acoustic Gibson, and I played between ages 9 and 11," Stefan remembers. "I was taking proper lessons, and I learned how to read music. I was playing tunes like 'Tea For Two' out of the Mel Bay books. I got totally disinterested in it by the time I was 11 years old; I was more interested in playing handball and basketball, so I put down the guitar." By the time he was 15, however, Grossman began buying records by blues singer/guitarists Elizabeth Cotten and Big Bill Broonzy, and folksinger Woody Guthrie. He returned to playing the guitar, buying an acoustic flat-top Harmony that was strung with nylon strings. "I got to like the sound of the black people that I was listening to on records," Stefan says, "and after a couple of months I got a Martin 00-21 steel-string guitar.

"At the same time, a friend said, 'Oh you should go up and see this blind man in Harlem called Gary Davis. I went up to Rev. Davis's house on a Saturday. He'd say, 'Bring your money, honey'—$5.00, you got a guitar lesson. I stayed with him for two hours; I was absolutely enamored of him, the music, the surroundings, the experiences. He lived on Claremont Avenue, which is *the* worst block in the Bronx, behind a derelict tenement house in a shack. To him, living there was horrible, probably; it was like rough living to me, and I'm from Brooklyn. In a way it was a really romantic situation.

"I started going up there Fridays, Saturdays, and Sundays, going home at night. I started spending eight to ten hours there at a time, eventually going up with tape machines to record the guitar lessons, trying to document his whole repertoire. I was trying to learn as much as I could. Eventually I went from the 00-21 to a Gibson F-200 steel-string, because that was the guitar Gary Davis was using at the time. For three years I just immersed myself in his music; at the same time I was listening to [blues guitarists] Brownie McGhee and Lightnin' Hopkins records, and starting to collect tapes of old 78s because there were no reissue programs at that point except for the Origin Of Jazz Library releases. So I got to be very intimate with [blues researchers] Bernie Klatszko, Pete Whalen, and other people. I started to learn other music from records, and as I was learning them it also enhanced my experience with Rev. Davis.

"I was learning bottleneck tunes, and I brought a tape up to Rev. Davis and played it for him, saying 'Wow, this is fantastic, isn't it?' He was a very jealous, possessive teacher, and he said, 'Oh, that's nothing.' I said, 'Well, you don't even play bottleneck.' He said, 'That is a cheating way of playing guitar.' So I said, 'If it is so cheating, why don't you play it?' So he called

out to his wife, 'Annie!' Annie brought over one of those big cigar holders made out of metal and he started to play a bottleneck tune. He played it better than anything else I had ever heard. Rev. Davis was always like that—staying two steps ahead. He got very involved with me as my teacher; apparently every few years he would grab hold of one of his students and you would become his lead boy, and he just wanted you to carry on his tradition. His thing was that you weren't allowed to perform in front of people until he'd tell you, because he felt you were taking his reputation onstage. As far as playing goes, he would say, 'Always have the guitar around, and first thing in the morning when you wake up, play that guitar.' It's a great idea, actually."

When Grossman was 18, he formed the Even Dozen Jug Band with guitarist Steve Katz (who later played with Blood, Sweat & Tears), harmonicist/singer John Sebastian, and pianist Josh Rifkin. The group recorded the LP *Even Dozen Jug Band* for Elektra in 1964. At the same time, Stefan became more interested in his work as a blues researcher. "I was involved with a group of friends who were finding these old 78s," Stefan recalls, "and eventually this enlarged into finding the old people who made those records, Some of us had names for each other—Tom Hoskins was called Fang, I was Kid Future, and Katz was Kid Past. And there was Mike Stewart, who was known as Backward Sam Firk, and John Fahey, also known as Blind Joe Death. Also among us was ED Denson, who was known from time to time as harmonica ED.

"We discovered many of the old musicians, and they used to stay at our houses. When I lived in New York or Berkeley, California, I had John Hurt staying with me, or Fred McDowell, or Skip James. I started to learn their music just as intensely as I learned Rev. Davis's music; however, it was much easier and took less time to encompass the repertoire of someone like Skip James, Son House, Fred McDowell, or John Hurt than it was with Rev. Davis's. Rev. Davis's repertoire was immense. I have hours and hours of tapes of him, and I still have a list of tunes I didn't get him to record before he died in May of 1972, things people will never hear now. His repertoire was in the hundreds and hundreds of songs; every song had a distinct, fantastic guitar arrangement, different from the other guitar arrangements."

When Stefan reminisces about the blues musicians he has known and learned from, it is soon apparent that one of his favorites was Mississippi John Hurt. "John was unique, and he was a wonderful human being," he says. "Skippie, Son, Rev. Davis—they were wonderful human beings because they were creative—but they were not as Christ like perfect. If you ask people who knew John, they will tell you he was an angel, but he was not condescending. He was not your black man from Mississippi who was going to bow. He used to say, 'When in Rome, do Rome.' He was a very wise man, a gentle grandfath erly type of person who would sit down and show you the way he was playing. He had a guitar style that students would think is extremely simple, yet it was amazingly perfect. His bass was not always boom-chik, boom-chik, boom-chik, and that was very fascinating. He had a repertoire of about 80 tunes, each one a little gem. And he would get up onstage and rock backwards and forwards with a little smile and play. It wasn't your Delta blues like Son House would play, which is very emotional music.

"John was more of a songster, and a great influence, I think, to guitar players even before his rediscovery. His old 78s were a great influence, and John just gave a certain attitude and feeling that you can imitate him. No one can really imitate Rev. Davis because there is too much happening—it is sort of like going to an opera on the guitar, with your vocal playing counterpoint to three other counterpoint lines on the guitar. John had a more straight-ahead type of music, and this was illustrated by the type of person he was.

"When John was rediscoverd, he began using Tom Hoskin's Gibson J-50, and then when he made his records on Vanguard, he used my Martin OM-45, which was great because it is a fine recording guitar. About a year after his rediscovery, the Newport Folk Foundation said, 'We would like to buy you a guitar.' So we went into Fretted Instruments Folklore Center in Manhattan, and they said, 'Any guitar in the shop is yours.' Fretted Instruments had a Martin 00-42, 000-28 Herringbone, and other very fine vintage instruments. John picked a guild, a nice, simple, Sunburst Guild that was the same size as a Martin 00-42. When it came to picking a guitar as a present, John wasn't going to take advantage of the situation at all. Just a nice, simple guitar.

"John eventually got uncomfortable with the people fighting for control of his recording, and so he moved back to Mississippi. He died in his sleep one night, which also, to me, symbolized John Hurt. You know, if there is a God, what a nice way to let someone die. You are an old person, and you die in your sleep, just pass away. That was the way John was; he came in gently, left gently."

Another artist Stefan spent a good deal of time with was Fred McDowell. "I don't ever think of him as a primary blues source, either as a singer or a guitar player," Stefan says. "I think he's fantastic, mind you, but his music is more of a bridge—the old Delta blues, as well as Blind Willie Johnson material from Texas, updated in rhythm and feel until it's like music of the '40s and '50s. I think a lot of people today can get into it because there's a certain rhythmic quality that's sort of modern. He used to use a half-inch piece of bottle on his little finger, a fingerpick on his right index finger, and a thumbpick on his thumb. He would get into a very distinct sound. He was great fun to party with. He was totally unlike Skip James who was a very aristocratic professor of his music; he had ideas on music that are incredible. Skip was very

intense, a philosopher. Also, he thought his music was *it*, just like Rev. Davis thought *his* music was it. Skippy presented his music as being like the finest, which is fascinating, because very little of it is really Skip James. Most of Skippy's songs were learned from Henry Stucky, who was *the* man in his town, Betonia, Mississippi. He was also very possessive of the people he was teaching.

"Son House was totally different from all of these guys, He was into drinking. On the day [blues researcher] Dick Waterman brought him into New York, Son was uptight, and he was playing a guitar he wasn't comfortable with. He was looking for a National, but what these guys really wanted were old Stellas. The big-body Stellas were just not around, because they sort of disintegrate—they were cheaply made guitars. So I said to Son, 'I have a National—it's yours, take it.' I just gave it to him as a present. Dick couldn't believe what happened next. Son took the guitar and started playing tunes that no one had ever heard him do. Then he went to a club and sat down to play. He slid a note down to start "Levee Camp Moan" [out of print], and when his slide went up to the twelfth fret, his head whipped back and his eyeballs went straight into his head; all you saw was white. A vein popped out from his forehead, and this voice started to sing The Blues. I had heard a lot of *blues singers* before, but I had never heard someone *sing the blues*. It was an incredible experience. Every time I heard Son it was like that, except when he was drinking so much he was on the floor. There is a lot of technique and a lot of very important guitar sound in what he does."

In 1965 Stefan released his instructional *How To Play Blues Guitar* LP. Impressed by the album, producer Paul Rothchild invited him to play with Taj Mahal and Janis Joplin. At the time Stefan was 21 and living in Berkeley, California. "I was playing with another acoustic player named Steve Mann, who was a first-rate guitarist," he says. "Rothchild had the idea that Janis's and Taj's voices would go well together; they were ignoring any contractual problems. The four of us just jammed and it was phenomenal, because Janis had a very gravelly voice, and Taj's is very smooth. We were going to try and get a drummer and bass player, and rehearse for three months and make a record. When I went to New York three months later, I was told it was impossible to do it, because Janis was getting to be real popular and Taj was signed to some record company. And I said, 'Oh, shit—I'm broke.' So I was walking down the street in New York, and Mark Silber, who owns a guitar shop, told me that the Fugs needed a guitarist. So I saw [Fugs lead singer/author] Ed Sanders and I said, 'You need a guitar player?' He said 'Yes, are you crazy?' I said, 'Yes, I'm crazy.' He said, 'Good, you have a job.' I had to go out and buy an electric guitar."

Stefan played with the Fugs from September 1966, until January 1, 1967, buying a Fender Telecaster and a Gibson Les Paul to use in the band. "They were a

**Stefan established Kicking Mule Records to help other guitarists get recorded and to spread the music he likes best.**

crazy band, and businesswise they really sucked," he says. "They wouldn't pay musicians for sessions, and they really got nasty. So I left and joined a group called Chicago Loop. I was with them for four months, hanging out with people like Mike Bloomfield. They were a very good pop-to-blues band, and we toured with [singer] Mitch Ryder after he split from the Detroit Wheels."

In April 1967, Stefan avoided the draft and finished four music books that he had already outlined. With this work behind him, he left for Europe. "When I went to England the only friend I had there was Eric Clapton. I met him when I was in Chicago Loop. I stayed with Eric, and we played a lot together. I learned a lot about left-hand technique from Eric, stuff I've employed in fingerpicking guitar. He has a fantastic vibrato, and his phrasing is phenomenal— I've never been able to duplicate it. Peter Green and Jeff Beck were also playing great guitar then; I was much more impressed by these electric players than their American counterparts, except, of course, for Jimi Hendrix. I personally thought the two finest electric guitarists at the time were Jimi and Eric. I always preferred Eric's playing, and I was amazed because Eric was very much in awe of Jimi Hendrix's playing. I could understand where Jimi came from in a way—it was a very American energy, the anger.

"I only think of Hendrix as a blues player, just as Eric's a blues guitar player. Eric used to say he would play blues guitar and just change the background, and the critics would just change the category. All of Eric's guitar playing is blues guitar, period. And the way he played—you can say no one can play better than him, but it's not that he is playing better; it's just that he's doing it right. People can try to imitate Lightnin' Hopkins, and Lightnin' plays very simple, but who can play like him? It's perfect; it's just right.

Stefan began playing the folk scene in London, where he met Bert Jansch and John Renbourn. "I enjoyed being able to perform as a soloist," he says, "so I started combining that with writing the other books I wanted to write. I was in England for almost two years; it was raining a lot and I wanted to travel, so I traveled from Sweden down to Spain and France and Italy. I really enjoyed Italy, and I met a girl there and we eventually got married. Italy is like the northernmost point of Africa, meaning it is very isolated. It was great to do tours and come back to Italy, but after a while it got bad being isolated from other musical ideas and creative people. So I moved back to England in 1977. The result of living in Italy, though, was the founding of Kicking Mule Records.

"I was trying to continue to be creative with my own pieces, but I wanted to hear other people's music as well. I would meet guitar players on the road, but they didn't have any records. So I wanted to start a record company that would have music that I would like to listen to, and that would also have tablature booklets so I could learn how to play the material. It would also give me a chance to make my records available in America. I talked to ED Denson—he was one of the original founders of Takoma Records—and about a year after we spoke about it, we started Kicking Mule with records by people like Ton Van Bergeyk, who was a 20-year-old computer engineer in Holland and one of the finest ragtime and swing fingerpicking guitarists. And we had Peter Finger from Germany, Dave Evans from England—these are all major guitar players that people would not know about unless we exposed them. Other people we recorded were more well known, like John James and Happy Traum. My favorite musician is Art Rosenbaum, who plays a 5-string banjo and just perspires music. I still think the best record we ever did on Kicking Mule was Art's first album, *5-String Banjo.*

"The way Kicking Mule is set up now, I essentially handle the European side and ED the American side. I handle most of the A&R and production work, and now we also have a Japanese office."

Stefan's favorite acoustic guitar is his Martin OM-45. "They made them from 1930 to 1933, and mine's a 1930," he says. "It is the guitar that was personally owned by [retailer/repairman] Jon Lundberg for years. I had to trade him umpteen guitars for it in 1965. It's a superb instrument—it's so good I have not played it for the last five years because it spoils me, and my compositions become dictated by that guitar. Now I use Prairie States or Euphonons, which are very rare guitars; they are much funkier than the Martin OM-45. I have a mahogany Euphonon, a maple Euphonon, and a rosewood Prairie State. They were all made in the Maurer shop in Chicago from the turn of the century until the '40s. Besides these, I've got tons of other instruments, including pre-War Stella 6- and 12-string guitars that I use for bottleneck as well as regular playing. These Stellas were sold by Sears & Roebuck for an incredibly cheap price.

Grossman favors D'Addario light-gauge strings, claiming that the makers of this product are "very, very conscious of maintaining a high quality." He doesn't use a pick, preferring instead to play finger-style: "I rest my little finger on the face of the guitar, and I use the skin of my finger—I don't use nails at all. I use just the index finger, middle finger, and thumb, basically. Sometimes I use my ring finger. I favor very strongly the index finger and thumb, just as Rev. Davis did."

Methods of making bottlenecks for slide guitar have been experimented with and discussed for years; Stefan has found that the plain old smashing of a wine bottle against a curb is as good as any. "I use the bottleneck on my little finger," he explains, "and it must be about three inches long on the playing side, and about two and a half inches in the back—I put my ring finger behind the back of the bottleneck, and I need a little indentation my finger can rest in. I remember in Denver I was almost arrested one night in the back alley of the Folklore Center breaking bottles, and I couldn't explain to the policeman that what I was doing was a valid exercise! The only other good way I know of making them is to use professional glass-cutting material. The heavier the glass, the better. Glass has a different sound than metal, and a heavier piece of metal will give a richer sound than a lighter piece. The Mighty Mite slide is a good size and weight; you can also go to a car place that has tubing for engines or a place with plumbing tubing and make your own slides."

As a master and teacher of many guitar styles, Stefan is often asked how guitarists can improve their playing. "One way," he answers, "is to read all of my books. I have a tablature system that is uncompromising. But if you really want to learn to play the blues, for example, you have to listen to blues players. No book is going to be able to teach you how to play like John Hurt. You have to listen to John Hurt play. So the tablature system I devised demands that you listen to the music so that you hear the accent, the rhythm, and most importantly, the feeling. I can teach anyone the notes of any of these blues guys; what I can't teach you is how to get their feeling, their soul. You have to listen to and love the music in order to speak it. Unfortunately, most of these guys are dead, but many of their records and tapes are still available. So what you have to do is get records and records and records. If you like John Hurt, remember that he listened to a lot of different music—fiddle tunes, banjo tunes, etcetera. So just keep buying records, and when possible, see the musicians play."

Stefan continues to record, write, and produce other guitarists as well. He says, "There are a lot of influences happening, and I want to be part of it, putting it down in print and on records. We are all learning from each other, and we need this to grow. A lot of guitar players who have big names stopped growing, and you can find their best work years ago. I hate to think of the day when that might happen to me."

---

## A Selected Stefan Grossman Discography

**Solo albums:** *Yazoo Basin Boogie*, Kicking Mule, 102; *Acoustic Music For The Body And Soul*, Kicking Mule, 105; *Ragtime Cowboy Jew*, Transatlantic, 223; *Those Pleasant Days*, Transatlantic, 246; *Hot dogs!*, Kicking Mule, 131; *Stefan Grossman Live*, Transatlantic, 264; *Memphis Jellyroll*, Kicking Mule, 118; *Fingerpicking Guitar Techniques*, Kicking Mule, 112; *Bottleneck Serenade*, Kicking Mule, 121; *My Creole Belle*, Transatlantic, 326; *How To Play Blues Guitar, Volume II*, Kicking Mule, 151. **With others** (On Kicking Mule): Rory Block, *How To Play Blues Guitar*, 109; Ton Van Bergeyk, *How To Play Ragtime Guitar*, 115; Son House, Jo-Ann Kelly, Sam Mitchell, *Country Blues Guitar Festival*, 145; *Stefan Grossman & John Renbourn*, 152; John Renbourn, *Acoustic Guitar*, East World (dist. by Kicking Mule), EWFL 98001.

# MALVINA REYNOLDS

This self-taught guitarist made her mark as a songwriter with tunes such as "Little Boxes," and "What Have They Done To The Rain." Her reputation was established through recordings of her songs by others, though Malvina often performed at folk festivals in the '50s and '60s. She was interviewed by *Guitar Player* in her native San Francisco in April of 1971. With her death in 1978 at the age of 78, America lost a great topical songwriter.

**By Jim Crockett**

**B**ORN AT THE TURN OF the century, Malvina Reynolds has been one of folk music's most prolific songwriters. Best known as the author of such tunes as "Little Boxes," "God Bless The Grass," and "Turn Around," she first came to prominence through her songwriting talents in the '30s and '40s when some of her compositions were picked up by the Almanac Singers. Since then she has appeared at major folk festivals, and her works have been recorded by Pete Seeger, Judy Collins, Joan Baez, Maryanne Faithful, Harry Belafonte, and other prominent performers.

Malvina's songs are topical, focusing on many aspects of society, from the frivolous to the deadly serious. She writes tunes about such national issues as highway encroachment ("Cement Octopus") as well as local matters such as the People's Park battle

in her home town of Berkeley ("Boraxo") and British children who hung on branches to stop construction men from cutting the trees down ("The Lambeth Children O"). Her one song to appear on the charts (in 1964) was the ironic "Little Boxes," a poke at stifling conformity in a suburban tract. Another important composition from the early '60s, the anti-nuclear "What Have They Done to The Rain?" became a favorite with performers such as Bob Dylan and Joan Baez.

Malvina Reynolds once said, "After Woody [Guthrie], I think I was one of the first who was primarily interested in writing songs based on labor and the folk tradition, songs with a social content. I write topical songs because I think they are necessary."

Her awareness of injustice is partly based on personal experience. In 1916, when she was ready to graduate high school, Malvina was informed by one of her teachers that the school administration planned to interrupt the graduation ceremony, and perhaps deprive her of her diploma, on the grounds that her father was engaged in radical political activities. Malvina chose to stay home, and never graduated. Nonetheless, she went on to earn a Ph.D. in literature from the University of California. She wrote her doctoral thesis on a medieval folk tale, and went into teaching full-time. By the late '30s, however, Malvina began to write her traditionally-styled songs, and has since become one of folk music's most inspirational songwriters.

Many people heard *about* her long before they ever saw her perform. For years Pete Seeger would tout Malvina at many of his concerts, and so did Joan Baez. Malvina and Pete developed a close friendship which was to evolve into a number of collaborations on such songs as "Andorra" and "70 Miles" among others. "I would come up with some lyrics I knew Pete would like, and phone him in New York. He'd write them down and a couple of days later would call me to play the new tune over the phone." She has two publishing companies of her own now: Shroder Music to copyright her own songs, and Abigale Music for the ones she writes with Pete Seeger.

Women's liberation has long been a major theme of Malvina's. "Women still belong to the men. They have no time or room to develop their own abilities. You know, it's understood that a man is supposed to have a room of his own. And who can build calluses while washing dishes?" Her interest in the rights of women hasn't developed just with the rise of feminism, however, as her 1956 song "We Don't Need The Men" proves.

Her struggle with the major and minor issues of her time has produced literally hundreds of songs. One of the things that makes her work so readily adopted by the public, is the singability of the songs—which she attributes to her limited knowledge of guitar. She sticks to common "guitar" keys, simple chord structures, and avoids rapid lyrical passages.

"It's too bad that my knowledge of guitar is so feeble," she says. "Because a writer's playing style determines the form of the song. But, maybe that's why people take to them so easily. Because they're so simple."

Part of the reason Malvina Reynolds' guitar technique is so basic is that she came to the instrument comparatively late in life. "I had studied fiddle as a kid," she comments, "but never very seriously nor for very long. Then my family moved from San Francisco to Berkeley and I decided that the academic way of life was for me. That's when I went for the doctorate at Cal."

Malvina was in her forties when she began picking up guitar to accompany herself as she sang her first songs at various hootenannies which preceded the meetings of one organization after another. "It was an old clunk of an f-hole," she recalls, "with a crack in the body." She soon traded it for a better one, and has progressed through a long line of folk guitars.

To indicate how important the guitar is to her songs, even though she isn't a guitarist in the strictest sense, Malvina always turns to it to see if her songs work. "I often write them on piano, but the real test is when I try to play them on guitar." If they are too complicated, they don't get performed. And her record indicates that the more complicated songs don't catch on, anyway. Because she is limited to the 1st and 2nd position on the fingerboard, her songs are always simple enough that even beginning guitarists can play them.

"A good knowledge of music is essential to the songwriter," she maintains. "If you can think in terms of harmonies and rhythms, the lyrics fall into singable patterns." Currently her playing relies on three basic strums: a regular folk 4/4, a blues 6/8 and a traditional waltz played with the thumb and first finger. "But sometimes these three are too limiting," she adds. "I need some more to expand. But I'm too old to start practicing regularly now. Haven't got the patience."

Malvina's songs can be heard on any number of records by other performers, as well as on three of her own: *Malvina Reynolds Sings The Truth*, on Columbia; *Another Country Heard From*, on Folkways; and her latest, *Malvina Reynolds* on Century City with The Byrds, The Dillards and others playing backup.

Oak Publications has released two of her books: *Little Boxes and Other Handmade Songs* and *The Muse of Parker Street*. Her own Berkeley firm, Shroder, publishes her two children's song collections *Feedles and Twoodles for Young Noodles* and *Cheerful Tunes for Lutes and Spoons*.

Over the years, the songs of Malvina Reynolds have had a tremendous influence not only on generations of audiences and admirers but on many other folk artists who have been both enlightened and inspired by the plain-speaking, integrity of her songs.

Has she ever regretted leaving academia for the life of a musician and songwriter? "I'd rather be a songwriter than a college professor," she says. . . "I like to say in my songs what other people are thinking and feeling . . . in their hearts."

---

## A Selected Malvina Reynolds Discography

*Malvina*, Cassandra Records, CFS 2807; *Malvina Reynolds*, Century City Records, CCR5100; *Malvina—Held Over*, Cassandra, CFS 3688; *Artichokes, Griddle Cakes, Etc.*, Pacific Cascade, LPS 7025; *Another Country Heard From*, Folkways, FN 2524. Malvina's records are available from Schroder Music Co., 1450 Sixth St., Berkeley, CA 94710.

# ARLO GUTHRIE

Woody Guthrie's boy grew up in a musical environment. Pete Seeger, Cisco Houston, Bob Dylan, and others were frequent guests at the Guthrie's in the '50s. His personalized, authentic sound bridges the gap between older and newer folk styles. Like his father, music and politics have been intertwined in his career. His song "Alice's Restaurant," used humor to skewer the Selective Service system, and led to great commercial success in the late '60s. Arlo was interviewed about his music in May of 1979 by *Frets*.

## By Marty Gallanter

STRONG PERSONAL commitments are the inspiration for much of Arlo Guthrie's music, just as they were with his father. The times that a person lives in usually color how other people label what he does," Arlo says. "Most of my songs, in some way or another, are dealing with morality as opposed to politics. Alice's Restaurant was a *moral* play, not a *political* one, but in 1967 that particular morality had political overtones. I'm not a political writer or singer; I'm a person singing who has had a particular kind of instruction in morality from my parents and other people."

"Alice's Restaurant" was the song that thrust Arlo into the popular spotlight in the late Sixties. The song led to his first album, which subsequently became a gold record, and its story was turned into a motion picture.

"I started making it up in 1965," he recalls, "and by the time 1967 rolled around, a little, diddly tune had turned into a half-hour story. I went to the Newport Folk Festival, and I played it one afternoon for a few hundred people—who got very excited. We ended up closing the festival with it, and by that time there were 20,000 people, or so, who were very excited, and *that* excited some record people. So we went in, and for $3,500 made ourselves an album."

After that, Arlo seemed to be everywhere. He was at Woodstock, New York, for the famous 1969 festival there, and was included in the album that documented the event. At about the same time he bought his mountainside farm in Berkshire County as a place where he could retreat from the world, relax, think, and write new material.

To the public he might have seemed an overnight success, yet Arlo's career had actually started a long time before. Born in New York City on July 10, 1947, he was the eldest son of famous folksinger/songwriter Woody Guthrie, the "Dust Bowl Balladeer;" but Arlo was in the sixth grade before he was aware of his father's fame. Woody's mother had succumbed to Huntington's Chorea, a hereditary nerve disease, when Woody was 13, and Woody himself was hospitalized with the disease in 1954. He never left the hospital, and he died in 1967.

Though Arlo never saw his father perform, he grew up surrounded by music. By the time he was in high school he was an accomplished musician.

"When I was a senior in high school I'd already been playing in New York, in the Village," he recalls. "In those days—the Sixties people had started to recognize the value of folk music. I was very familiar with a lot of different styles after listening to a lot of the old-time folk singers and hearing their songs, long before I heard the songs from the Kingston Trio. I started to go down to some of the coffeehouses and bars and just play for the fun of it. That's when I got a sneaking suspicion that, if I wanted to, I could continue doing it and earn a living. But I felt the pressure of finishing school, going to college, and getting a decent job. I went to Europe the summer after graduation and played music on street corners and in folk clubs for a couple of months. Then I came back to the States and went to college in Montana. They were playing Bob Dylan songs on the radio, and that's when I decided I should try making music my career. I mean, after all, if they were playing Dylan on the radio in Montana, of all places, I figured folk music must really be selling and I should at least try to earn a living at it."

After six weeks of college, 18-year-old Arlo went back to New York City. Out of cash and owing a little money to several friends, he took a job with Harold Leventhal, the New York City folk producer and promoter who was later to become Arlo's personal manager. "I worked in his office just sort of delivering insane pieces of paper to people who really didn't need them," Arlo recalls.

At the time, Leventhal managed Pete Seeger and Judy Collins, worked on shows with Bob Dylan and Joan Baez, and was generally considered the central figure of the New York City folk music scene in terms of production and management. Arlo, bored with his job and conscious of all the important folk music people wandering in and out of the New York office,

decided it was time to go out and allow music to be his way of making it in the world. Most of the people who passed through Leventhal's office were intimately familiar with Arlo's famous father. Pete Seeger, in particular, was an old family friend and to them Arlo's desire for a career of his own came as no surprise. Interestingly, though Woody had a direct effect on the careers of people like Pete Seeger and Jack Elliott, he was only an indirect influence on the career of his eldest son.

"I never actually saw Woody perform anywhere," says Arlo. "I didn't even know he was a well-known singer until I changed from a public school to a private school in the sixth grade. I went to a 'progressive' school and they were all singing his songs. I was absolutely stunned and shocked that somebody knew the words to Woody's songs. I was the only one there that didn't. That's when I decided I'd better go home and learn them; I was embarrassed that I didn't know them, and everybody else did. It wasn't that the other kids realized that I didn't know the songs—I could fake the words well enough in choir to get by. I felt the pressure from inside. Besides learning the songs, I also became able to learn words and music when I needed to. Woody was responsible for me picking up those skills; but it was his music, not him personally."

However, it *was* Woody, personally, who started Arlo on the music trail by buying him his first guitar. The occasion was Arlo's sixth birthday. Another family—friends and neighbors of the Guthries—asked Woody if he would pick up a guitar for their daughter as well, and Woody bought two Gibsons for $80.00 each. In 1953 that was more money than either family earned in a week, and the expensive instruments caused quite a scene when Woody brought them home. He offered to return the guitars and buy cheaper ones, but he said, "I tell you, though, if you want a kid to play the guitar, you'd better buy him a good one 'cause a cheap guitar sounds cheap and a kid can tell. He won't play it, and that'll be the real waste of money."

The families relented and the youngsters were allowed to keep their high-priced instruments.

"I guess what he said proved out right," Arlo notes. "Both of us are still playing, and I still own that old Gibson."

Arlo is also the custodian of Woody's instruments. The family placed them in his care after Woody died. "They're not mine," Arlo says. "They belong to the family, but since I'm the one in the family who plays, I get to take care of them. I play them every once in a while, but they don't go out for public performances."

Musical influences on the young performer were wide and varied. Arlo remembers a lot of people, so many that he hesitates to mention names for fear of leaving some out. I've been influenced by all kinds of people for different reasons, and not just musically either," he states simply. "I think I've always been more influenced by personality than by musical

**When Arlo's whimsical anti-draft ballad, "Alice's Restaurant Massacree" was first broadcast on WBAI in New York City, the radio station was deluged with requests.**

ability. Often the music comes second."

To Arlo, those musical personalities blend into one long line of traditional American folk music, and it becomes difficult to separate the influences. "I was listening to one of my albums, and I realized that a lot of it sounds familiar. I wondered what I would do if someone said, 'Well, that sounds like so-and-so.' The only thing I can say is that it's the same tunes that other people have used over and over—the same musical themes. All the people that I'd been influenced by borrowed their tunes from the same sources. The difference has been their personalities."

Arlo refuses to concern himself with "commercially acceptable" labels for the music he plays. "It's all folk music," he says. "That's what I call what I do. It all comes out of the same tradition. Personally, I think that rock and roll and disco are folk music too. I play a lot of different instruments on the stage, acoustic and electric, and try to fit the instrument to what I'm doing. Obviously, when I'm out in the woods my favorite wouldn't be an electric guitar; but when I'm on the stage and have all the juice I need, then I want to be heard. I still prefer to play amplified acoustic instruments, but sometimes the tune just calls for an electric, or sometimes my hand just gets tired on the acoustic guitar, or sometimes the monitor is bad and I can't hear myself, so I pick up an electric and just wail away for a while. I can't get stuck in a pattern. It wouldn't be fair to the music."

Arlo is very concerned about the progression within a topical tune from the motivating political events to the general moral issues. The theme, he feels, always needs to be timeless, even when the issue itself is part of a passing scene. This concept is as important in Arlo's philosophy of living as it is in his approach to writing songs.

"I think a good example of someone who couldn't translate his political action to its moral application was Phil Ochs," Arlo says. "Once the cause is removed, once the fad dies away, you have to be left with something for yourself and it has to give you meaning. If it can't sustain you, then you have no purpose and you can end up in the same bucket that he did. [Phil Ochs, the topical singer/songwriter and social activist who earned the sobriquet "The Kipling of the New Left," committed suicide in 1976.] We're all prone to feel, from time to time, like we don't belong in the world. I try to find my purpose for being in the world, and to see to it that my purpose makes it worth the effort. That means transcending the political issues of the moment and moving toward something that's a lot more lasting."

An outspoken opponent of nuclear power, Arlo was at Seabrook, New Hampshire, in June 1978 when 20,000 people gathered to protest a nuclear power plant there. He has been an active participant in Pete Seeger's favorite project, the Hudson River Sloop *Clearwater*. Arlo sees environmental issues as being far deeper than the news reported in the papers. Even fresh from the events of the Three Mile Island

nuclear plant accident in Pennsylvania, he preferred to approach the matter from another perspective.

"One of these days we have to realize that we are just like any other country in the world," he said. "Like water, culture flows to even itself out. In time, we're going to find ourselves on a more even basis with the rest of the world. The Russians, the Chinese, and the Latin American peoples are going to have to have a little more, and some of the Western nations are going to have to get along with a little less. The real question is, when are we going to become more conscious of how much we waste? Most of the world can't afford that kind of waste. Are we going to start making good things so the rest of the world can afford to buy them, or are we going to continue to live with false security, with ignorance, and have things forced on us? The attempts to build nuclear power plants and export nuclear power plants are just futile efforts to use technology to try to hold back that natural leveling between us and other societies. It isn't going to work, because it isn't natural."

At an everyday level, Arlo sees a parallel in the instrument world. "It's the same thing with guitars," he says. "Years ago they were made differently. After all, doesn't everybody spend a lot of time looking for an old Martin or an old Gibson? But if you go to the factory and ask them why they sound different, what the difference is, they'll tell you that there isn't any. But they do sound different. Who buys a new acoustic instrument now and expects that in 20 or 30 years it's going to be a classic piece? No one—at least no one I know. Anyone who wants a real special guitar goes out and looks for one that's already 20 or 30 years old. What's going to happen to all today's

junk guitars in the future? A lot of companies are going to go out of business, 'cause the time is over when we can afford to make 20 guitars and hope that one of them is going to last. We can't afford to manufacture or purchase junk anymore."

In Arlo's philosophy the political, economic, and social issues relate back to the overall moral question, and everything relates back to his music. "I'm not saying that it will bring peace and happiness; I'm not even saying that all of this should happen," he says, "but I think that it's going to happen. So my songs have to do with what kind of a person you have to be to live in a world like that. Who do you have to be to do the things we need to do? You've got to have courage. You've got to be organized when organization is called for, and be an individual when being an individual is called for. Above all, you've got to have some fun, or the whole thing just isn't worth it. I'm real happy to be a part of what I see coming."

The folk tradition, through the centuries, has always been more than just music-making. In it there is a history of crafts and a history of political and social involvement; and both went right along with the making of music. Musicians made their instruments, or had them made by friends; and composed their own music, or adapted and sang what other friends taught them. They combined all their skills and used them within the social movements of their times. In our more complex and economically sophisticated society, Arlo still sees an extension of that tradition; and because of that extension he sees some promising signs.

"I think the greatest thing out of all of this is that more and more individuals are making guitars personally," he says. "Even just ten years ago, there were only a few individuals making acoustic instruments—

not many at all. And those who were doing it weren't making a whole lot. But now there's a bunch of these people, and the instruments they make sell. You can't find anybody who has built a whole lot of good guitars who still has them around; they've all been sold—and not cheap, either—to people who are willing to pay for a good guitar. Maybe it means waiting a little while longer, not being able to buy right away, but that's the way it's going to have to be."

Arlo's principal guitars are both Martins. He uses a Buffalo pickup (formerly made by the Group 128 company in Waltham, Massachusetts, and no longer available) in addition to miking his instruments. "The instruments I use in the studio are determined by the song," he says, "but in general, for my kind of songs particularly, the acoustic guitar I use for recording is an old D-18. I took it on the road for about ten years. I had it refinished so much and fixed up so much that eventually the wood just got so thin—even though the sound was terrific—that I couldn't afford to take it out, because I knew it would get broken. About five or six years ago my wife picked up another Martin, a D-41, which I now play on the stage—and which I assume will get sufficiently cracked and worn and so forth so that the only place I'll be able to play it will be the studio."

Arlo isn't too particular about his strings, as long as they're bronze. He says they don't stay on his guitar long enough for brand considerations to matter. "I use cheap, bronze strings," he says simply. "I change strings so much when I'm on the road that it doesn't matter which kind I use. I change them almost every night, or every other night; so there is no great string for the road—you have to change 'em all. I usually change strings the day of a show, then do a sound check with them, and that's it. I don't worry about

**Although Arlo is primarily known as a singer/songwriter, he has roots in traditional guitar styles and is an accomplished flatpicker.**

breaking them in."

Arlo has had the bridges on some of his guitars modified so that the ball ends of the strings are held by the bridge itself instead of being secured by the pins in the bridge-pin holes. Arlo, who notes that the arrangement is similar to that on classical guitars, says he likes it because it "spreads the sound more." Much of his custom work was done by California builder/repairman Porfirio Delgado, of Candelas Guitars, who retired several years ago. "He built a few guitars for me," says Arlo, "including a beautiful, *beautiful* 12-string that I still play. I had a few of his guitars that I traveled with for years, when I was still on my own. I didn't want to waste time tuning or worry about breaking strings, so I'd just bring along extra guitars."

No longer a solo act, Arlo usually performs with his long-time backup band, Shenandoah. Before joining forces with the group back in the fall of 1975, Arlo had often used the services of Linda Ronstadt's backup band, Swampwater. Arlo recalls. "Linda and I worked together a lot back in those days, and we shared the band. The problem was that they didn't work unless Linda or I worked. When she left that scene for a while, they started working with me; but economically it wasn't really feasible because I didn't work enough for them to support themselves."

Arlo found Shenandoah virtually in his own backyard. "They're all from this area, up in the Berkshires," he says. "A couple of the guys were together in a band called Quarry, which played at Woodstock, but I didn't even know them then. I met some of them during the folk years; the father of David Grover—David plays lead guitar and does a lot of the vocal arrangements—was the head of the Berkshire Folk Music Society for ten years, and those are the same kind of people I first started really playing for when I was in school back in '64. When the band finally became Shenandoah, it was playing at a local bar about a mile down the road from me. I just went in to hear them, and the thought struck me that, with a little work, they could play the same circuits I was playing, and it would be a big help to me to have a group backing me that was already a working band—maybe they weren't making a great living, but at least they were surviving. I asked them to play a benefit for me, one we were doing in the area, and they said they would; and then I asked them to play a couple of tunes with me at the benefit, and it worked out well enough, without any rehearsal or anything, that we agreed to rehearse and go on the road." Shenandoah first recorded with Arlo on his album *One Night*, cut not long afterward.

Although he feels that working with a band has

cost him a certain degree of intimacy with his audiences, he prefers having company on the road. "There is less personal communication with an audience," he says, "but the reason I really like working with the band is that being out on the road by yourself can get to be real lonely. It's a very weary, lonely life, and I'm not interested in pursuing a weary, lonely existence; so I bring along a band—not just for sound, but to bring friends who play."

He says that being with a band has had a definite effect on his playing. "They've made it a lot worse," he laughs. "I don't have to work nearly as hard. I *used* to be a good guitar player. As far as technique goes, the biggest influence for me was probably Clarence White trying to imitate Doc Watson. You couldn't just say Doc Watson's playing—I like it modified."

The early Sixties' commercial "rebirth" of folk music paved the way for great artists like Pete Seeger, Mississippi John Hurt, and others. The same popular movement laid the groundwork for the careers of such new, younger, acoustic folk performers as Bob Dylan, Judy Collins, Joan Baez, and Arlo Guthrie. Arlo's view of what has sometimes been called the "current expanding acoustic scene" is not as broad as the views of some other observers. Arlo focuses on a smaller portion of it, one which shows signs of developing into something enduring.

"The vast majority of people interested in music are interested in electric music," he says. "It's not because of the music itself. It's because of the advent of the *event*, of being at a place where that kind of music is played—the big, 30,000-person concerts. Acoustic music is something else, with another kind of draw. It's the act of getting together, of having a good time. The fact that there's nothing good on TV is helping to create a scene of people who are making their own acoustic music. The more people get interested in a world that's more than a place to just live and die in—a world they can sort of transfer on to their kids and to others—the more people will get interested in acoustic music. Acoustic music provides you with a personal, emotional experience. It provides you with a real close friendship with other people in a way that those big events just can't. The more people want to take part in that kind of world, the more people will be interested in acoustic music.

"My first love has always been acoustic instruments, for that reason. My mom used to say that she didn't care if I was a professional or if I was working, 'cause I could always sit around the house and play music. That's the kind of feeling that acoustic music provides."

---

## A Selected Arlo Guthrie Discography
(On Reprise): *Alice's Restaurant*, 6267; *Amigo*, 2239; *Arlo Guthrie*, 2183; *Hobo's Lullaby*, 2060; *Last Of The Brooklyn Cowboys*, MS4-2142; *Washington County*, 6411. *Best Of Arlo Guthrie*, Warner Brothers, K-3117; *Tribute to Woody Guthrie*, Warner Brothers, 2W-3007; *One Night*, Warner Brothers, BSK-3232; *Bitter End Years*, Roxbury, 300 (out-of-print); *Festival Of Acoustic Music*, Fantasy, 79009.

# DAVID GRISMAN

Mandolinist David Grisman was part of a new generation of bluegrass musicians who participated in the Greenwich Village folk scene in the early '60s. In the '70s his group, the David Grisman Quintet, established a unique sound—fusing acoustic jazz, and bluegrass—that has come to be known as "Dawg" music. Since this article was written for *Frets* in 1979, David's influence has grown. The group has headlined at jazz, folk, and bluegrass festivals in the United States, Europe, and Japan, and David has recorded with many of the biggest names in jazz, folk, and pop music.

**By Dan Forte**
(Additional material supplied by Dix Bruce)

**W**ITH SO MUCH unimaginative, derivative music pouring out of the radio 24 hours a day, it is refreshing when a truly original musician comes onto the scene.

To call the music of mandolinist David Grisman "original," and leave it at that, would be a colossal understatement. The development of a new musical movement within an existing idiom is a rare enough occurrence; creating an entirely *new* form of music, which is what Grisman has done, is a monumental achievement.

None of the hyphenated hybrid categories (jazz-rock, folk-rock, etc.) collectively known as fusion or crossover can pigeonhole what Grisman has been cultivating in recent years. The antecedents are numerous and well in evidence, but still don't describe or define the music—unless you want to call it bluegrass-jazz-Gypsy-rock-Middle-Eastern-Hebraic-folk-classical-Grisman. And even then, the most important element, Grisman himself, would be the hardest to pinpoint.

What people have been calling it thus far is "Dawg" music, after Grisman's nickname. *The David Grisman Quintet* album, released in April of 1977, definitely opened a few ears. *Billboard*, listing it as a recommended LP in both the jazz and pop categories, described it as "fire-breathing acoustic string music that fuses the emotional freedom of rock to the tight precisions of bluegrass to create something new and unique in contemporary instrumental groups." *Billboard's* concluding remark was "Best cuts: all of them." As of this writing, album sales have passed the 100,000 mark. *The David Grisman Quintet* is now second in all-time sales for an independently released acoustic LP. Only Leo Kottke's *6-& 12-String Guitar Instrumentals*, issued in 1971 has done better.

Because so much attention has been focused on Grisman the band leader and innovative composer, his accomplishments as a superb instrumentalist have been almost overlooked. But performing was the trade Grisman learned first, and for years he was what he describes as "the hot mandolin player in the second generation New York City bluegrass scene."

By age 18, only two years after discovering the mandolin, he was producing the album *Red Allen, Fred Wakefield, And the Kentuckians*, and playing on his first LP as part of the Even Dozen Jug Band, with a cast of "future all-stars" that included Stefan Grossman, Maria Muldaur, Steve Katz, and John Sebastian. A year later, his group, the New York Ramblers, won the award for best bluegrass band at the prestigious Union Grove contest in North Carolina.

To date, David Grisman has appeared on more than 45 albums, with such stars as Linda Ronstadt, Bonnie Raitt, James Taylor, Judy Collins, Martin Mull, Tom Paxton, the Pointer Sisters, and the Grateful Dead. He has been a key member in several short-lived but innovative bands, including Earth Opera (with Peter Rowan), Muleskinner (with Bill Keith, Richard Greene, and the late Clarence White), and Old And In The Way (with Vassar Clements and Jerry Garcia).

Grisman has been acclaimed by critics as well as by such musical peers as Stephane Grappelli, Doc Watson, and Bill Keith, who wrote in the liner notes to his *Something Newgrass* album, "I've had the plea-

sure of playing music in several different contexts with David during a friendship spanning almost fifteen years, and his unequivocally eclectic style never ceases to amaze me."

Born March 23, 1945, in Hackensack, New Jersey, David was exposed to music at an early age. "My father was 47 when I was born, and earlier he had been a professional trombone player," he says. "My mother was an art teacher, but she also played the piano. Piano was my first instrument, beginning when I was seven. My father died when I was ten, and I sort of slacked off—he'd kept me practicing. I didn't have the discipline to go home and practice my lessons."

At ten, David and his mother moved to Passaic, New Jersey, and by the age of 16 he was caught up in the folk music boom of the early 1960s.

"I got interested with two friends in school, Fred Weisz and Jack Scott," he recalls. "We quickly progressed from emulating the Kingston Trio to being into the New Lost City Ramblers in about six weeks or so. Jack had an FM radio, so he was in touch with the *Oscar Brand Show*, which had Roger Sprung playing banjo. One day Jack came back from New York with a record called *Mountain Music Bluegrass Style*. He put on a cut called 'White House Blues' by Earl Taylor, and it just totally flipped me out. It was so fast! We just played it over and over. I was ripe to hear that sound—not so much the mandolin at first, but as I started listening to more records the mandolin sounded really neat."

Around this time, David met noted folk music enthusiast Ralph Rinzler, who played mandolin with the Greenbriar Boys. "Fred, Jack, and I wanted to start a folk music club at school," Grisman recounts, "so we asked our English teacher, Elsie Rinzler, if she would be the advisor. She said, 'Oh, I have this cousin named Ralph who is really into folk music.' Ralph came to class one day with his mandolin, guitar, and banjo, and gave a demonstration—it just blew me out. He was the first guy I saw play a mandolin who affected me."

Grisman was soon hanging around Rinzler at every available opportunity. "We just started bothering him," he laughs. "He was a ticket agent for BOAC airlines at the time, so he'd get home at around midnight, and we'd go over there [*laughs*]. He'd play for us or play tapes of Bill Monroe. Some of it was too strong for me at first, but I started developing taste real fast. At first Bill's voice was too high for me. And his records had more fiddles on them, and I rebelled against that, because my initial flash was the mandolin and banjo—I liked those kinds of sounds. But on August 8, 1961, Ralph took me to see Bill Monroe perform, and it all changed; I loved his voice. But I had to see it come out of a real human being."

Following along wherever Rinzler went proved to be the best education the three aspiring bluegrassers could ask for. As Grisman puts it, "Ralph was always trying to turn us on to the real stuff—which is what he's always been into and still is. He'll get around to

The David Grisman Quartet in 1981. (Left to right)
Violinist Darol Anger, bassist Rob Wasserman,
David, and guitarist/mandolinist Mike Marshall.

discovering me in a few years; in about 30 years Ralph will show up on my doorstep with his Nagra tape recorder [*laughs*]. We worshipped him. We'd sit at rehearsals of the Greenbriar Boys with our mouths open. I remember when Ralph brought Clarence Ashley and Doc Watson back from North Carolina; he discovered them and later managed Doc and Bill Monroe for awhile."

By this time David had been noodling around on his first mandolin, a Kay model he got for $16.00 in New York City. "It was a really crummy mandolin," he admits; "I didn't know a thing about it. I worked out 'Woody's Rag' from a Weavers record where Pete Seeger played it. But it was so alien to me, I figured it all out on one string [*laughs*]. Then Ralph came over and showed me that I had to go on to the next string. I never took formal lessons from him—I probably should have—but I just hung out and he showed me a lot of stuff."

Soon Grisman was making his own hitchhiking journeys to ferret out that "high lonesome sound."

"In 1963, during Easter vacation from school," he recalls, "I made a pilgrimage to Washington, D.C., to meet Frank Wakefield. I'll never forget it. It was this *tiny* little bar, and he and Red Allen were sitting at the table in front of the stage, drinking beer. I just walked right up to Frank and introduced myself and told him I played mandolin. He just took me home with him! Frank was a huge influence on me."

The boys' folk music club soon progressed into a bluegrass band, the Garret Mountain Boys. Eventually the Garret Mountain Boys recruited Steve Mandel, who later played guitar to Eric Weissberg's banjo on "Dueling Banjos" in the movie *Deliverance*. The group then merged with a rival bluegrass band, the Downstate Rebels, to become the New York Ramblers. In 1964—with Grisman on mandolin, Winnie Winston on banjo, Gene Lowinger on fiddle, Eric Thompson on guitar, and Fred Weisz playing bass—the Ramblers went to North Carolina and won the Union Grove competition.

"We won first prize of the whole contest, World Championship Bluegrass Band," David states proudly. It's like the Olympics of bluegrass. We mainly wanted to play there, but the way to play was to enter the contest. We played several tunes, one of which was 'Rawhide.' Unfortunately, they didn't have a mandolin category in those days."

During this period Grisman was studying English at NYU. Living in an apartment on Thompson Street in Greenwich Village, he became a part of the seminal folk music scene that was developing there in the early Sixties.

"I don't know what I was doing at school," he admits, "because I was a bluegrass mandolin player first; that was my existence. We used to play at Gerde's Folk City every Monday night, Hootenanny Night. We had a good following. We all started hanging out in Washington Square. Bob Dylan and those guys were there, too—I used to see Dylan walking down the street. But I didn't really appreciate that singer-songwriter sort of music, because those guys were just singing songs and not tuning their guitars. I'd rather listen to Roscoe Holcomb. I was into the real thing, *real* folk music—like Clarence Ashley. I could walk down the street to Ralph Rinzler's house and hear the greatest Doc Watson stuff that ever was. I'd spend entire afternoons listening to Ralph's collection of tapes."

Despite his purist sentiments, it was with some of these young New York folkies that Grisman cut his first record, *The Even Dozen Jug Band*. He recounts, "Stefan Grossman was friends with Peter Siegal, and we were all sort of friends, but we were into different areas of music. I was really into bluegrass mandolin and Stefan was into blues guitar, but we were both hanging out in Washington Square, along with everybody else. So Stefan put together a jug band for this album, with himself, Steve Katz, John Sebastian, Maria D'Amato [Muldaur], me, Fred Weisz, Peter Siegal, Joshua Rifkin on piano, Danny Lauffer on jug, and a guy named Bob Gurland who would imitate a trumpet with his mouth."

Even though Grisman was playing bluegrass almost exclusively, he was already beginning to incorporate some of his own ideas. "I was just back in New York," he notes, "and I heard a tape of an unreleased album by the New York Ramblers. There are tunes on there like 'Fannie Hill,' which I still play, and I noticed there's a little part in there where I played a solo with only bass accompaniment—it just went into this other zone. I think I always had a certain streak of wanting to do something with that kind of music. But first I had to get a grasp of something to hang on to, so I really studied Bill Monroe and Frank Wakefield. I got into sounding more like Bill Monroe than anybody *should* sound."

Besides providing David with the basis of his early mandolin style, Monroe and Wakefield also instilled in him the value of writing his own songs. "That's something I consciously tried to do," he explains, "because I noticed that Bill and Frank wrote. My first composition was 'Cedar Hill,' which we still play. I patterned it after a song of Frank's called 'Leave Well Enough Alone.'"

A virtual trademark of Grisman's recent work, his penchant for minor keys, dates back to before he began playing the mandolin. "In synagogue, I remember certain melodies," he says. "I've always been attracted to minor melodies and Hebraic music. I've always liked sad music, and there are a lot of sad melodies in the Jewish faith. Some people have said that the minor sound sort of defines my style, but I've written a lot of tunes in major keys, too—like 'Janice' and 'Dawg's Bull' [on *Hot Dawg*]—and some of my most recent pieces—which I've yet to perform—are more away from tonality."

Grisman continued to move upwards in his succession of mandolins, eventually acquiring a Gibson F-5. "Ralph Rinzler had reworked his F-5," he recalls,

"so I tried to do it to my A-Junior. I regraduated and refinished it, and one night there was a loud snap, and the top caved in [*laughs*]. So I put a huge lug nut inside it to prop the top up, and it acted like a tone bar—it was actually louder. Then I made the big move and got together $150.00 and bought an F-4 that had belonged to Mike Seeger. I had that during the latter part of the Garret Mountain Boys and the New York Ramblers. I eventually sold it and bought a 1951 F-5 for $325.00. But it was real garbage; it had a mahogany neck and didn't even have black and white binding! I had it reworked and doctored up and sold it for $475.00. In 1965 I bought a 1920s Lloyd Loar Gibson F-5 from Harry West for $550.00."

In 1967 David made his first deliberate move away from bluegrass and with Peter Rowan formed a rock outfit called Earth Opera. "Pete had left Bill Monroe," he recounts, "and I wanted to form a bluegrass band with him and maybe Bill Keith and Richard Greene. But in 1967 there was no place for bluegrass. There wasn't anything like *Frets* or *Pickin'* magazine—and I could have used that stuff back in 1962 [*laughs*]. Players like me are cropping up now, but we were happening back then. We were sort of the lost generation in that whole evolution. There was Ralph Rinzler's generation and people like Bob Yellin, John Herald, Mike Seeger, and Roger Sprung before us, but my generation of bluegrass pickers never continued what we started. Anyway, Pete Rowan was on sort of a reactionary trip after leaving Bill Monroe's band, and Bill Keith and Richard Greene were in the Jim Kweskin Jug Band, so Peter and I got together and started doing some songs he'd written as an acoustic duo. Then we decided to put together sort of a rock band. Looking back on it now, I think we should have stuck with the acoustic duo. We got a contract with Elektra Records, and they set us up with Simon And Garfunkel's manager, who sug-gested that we be an acoustic duo. But we decided we wanted to have a band [*laughs*]."

It was with Earth Opera that Grisman finally found a use for the mandocello he'd bought in 1964. [*A mandola is tuned a fifth below a mandolin; a mandocello is tuned an octave below a mandola.*] "I figured if I was playing a different kind of music, like Earth Opera, it would be fitting to have a different instrument. I was attracted to mandocello because no one else played one. I got my Gibson K-4 model for $300.00 then, which was sort of a fluke. I electrified it with a Johnny Smith pickup mounted in the fret-board—I had some frets taken out. I used fuzztone with it and everything."

Grisman, Rowan, and a few others thought of themselves as the "bluegrass dropouts." Grisman however, stayed in touch with the bluegrass world, even though he was living in California and getting more deeply involved in his own music.

In 1972, David and some of the other "dropouts" formed a sort of rock-bluegrass outfit, Muleskinner, which produced an LP by the same name. The band consisted of Grisman on mandolin, Rowan on rhythm guitar and vocals, Richard Greene on violin, and Bill Keith on banjo, along with the guitarist some have called the greatest flatpicker of all time, the late Clarence White.

"Clarence was the greatest, as far as I'm concerned," declares David. "I spent a week in 1964 playing with him in the Kentucky Colonels. They were in New York, playing at the Gaslight, and Roland White's wife was having a baby, so I subbed on mandolin. That was the best bluegrass band I ever played in—it was Clarence, Roger Bush [bass], and Billy Ray Latham [banjo]. One of my big regrets of my musical life is that they asked me to go to Chicago with them the following week and I didn't go.

"The thing I loved about Clarence's playing,"

**Grisman has functioned almost as the musical godfather of the New Acoustic Music scene. Many ex-members of his bands, such as Tony Rice, Darol Anger, Rob Wasserman, and Mike Marshall have gone on to establish successful solo careers.**

Grisman continues, "was the way he would mess with time; he'd play a whole bar ahead or behind. He also played real light and delicately. When he died, I thought that was just gone forever, but Tony Rice [the Grisman Quintet's guitarist] has that spirit and that awareness of time. He's the only other cat who does. I mean, people can learn the notes or licks, but that's not really what Tony has done. He's got the same *feel*, that attitude. I always dreamed of doing some of my own songs with Clarence, but it just seemed too remote. I got to do one, 'Opus 57,' on *Muleskinner* [out of print, to be reissued on the Ridge Runner label]. See, I could never get guys to *learn* stuff like that."

Although the members of Muleskinner now represent the cream of the progressive bluegrass at its beginning and the album has become a collector's item, Grisman admits, "I never really liked the record that much. There was so much music that could have come out of Clarence in two hours, but we were doing these songs. An interesting thing, by the way, which isn't mentioned on the original album jacket, is that Roland White played mandola on the intro to 'Opus 57.'"

The next group Grisman and Rowan played in, Old And In The Way, also featured bassist John Kahn, Vassar Clements on fiddle, and Grateful Dead guitarist Jerry Garcia playing 5-string banjo. "I had met Jerry," David reminisces, "at a Bill Monroe show in West Grove, Pennsylvania, in 1964. I made my first trip to California a year later and stayed at a house in Palo Alto where Eric Thompson was living, along with [bassist] Phil Lesh, Garcia, and all the guys in the Grateful Dead—at that time called the Warlocks.

"In 1973," he continues, "we were all living at Stinson Beach. One day we were sitting in Garcia's living room and he said, 'Let's pick some bluegrass.' We started playing in clubs like Paul's Saloon, and for Jerry it was his musical outlet—but Pete Rowan and I could use the hundred bucks, you know [*laughs*]. Jerry was, of course, a big name, a big entity, so I wanted him to call the shots—because, let's face it, I'd already played in hot bluegrass bands in 1966. And Old And In The Way wasn't a tight band, because those guys were out of shape and Jerry doesn't like to rehearse. We got Richard Greene to play fiddle on a few gigs, but he was in another band, so we called Vassar Clements, who I'd never met; he was like a legend to me. After a while I decided to devote more time to my own music. A live album was released after the band dissolved."

Grisman's next group began even more casually than Old And In The Way and never even recorded. But the Great American Music Band (originally the Great American String Band) finally gave David a platform for his original compositions as well as some jazz playing.

"A gig came up at the Great American Music Hall [in San Francisco]," he recalls, "which was supposed to be Richard Greene and Vassar Clements, each with his own band. Richard asked me to play with him, so we got Eric Thompson on guitar, Sandy Rothman on banjo, and Bing Nathan on bass. Some promoter got a local group called Skunk Cabbage to back Vassar, and on the afternoon of the opening night both bands played a radio show. After Skunk Cabbage heard us play they said, 'We can't play with Vassar; he belongs with you guys.' They were honorable enough to do that. So they opened the show for us, and we had Richard *and* Vassar and called it the Great American Fiddle Band. The second night Jerry Garcia played banjo, and Sandy Rothman switched to guitar. Bing Nathan couldn't make the second night, so Taj Mahal played upright bass. Another musical friend of mine, [guitarist] David Nichtern, who wrote 'Midnight At The Oasis,' had been interested in my stuff—to the point where he'd make cassettes of the songs and learn them. So he showed up the second night and knew all the tunes—played right out of the audience.

The group eventually settled with Grisman, Greene, guitarist John Carlini, bassist Joe Carroll, and singer/guitarist Ellen Kearney.

While David was playing with the Great American Music Band he was also teaching mandolin at the Family Light Music School in Sausalito, California. Coincidentally, the day after the school fired him over a disagreement, he received a phone call from none other than Bob Dylan, asking for mandolin lessons.

"He had a blonde F-4," explains Grisman, "and he wanted to learn all about it. He took the three-day crash course. I showed him some basic fingering exercises and some chords; we listened to Charlie Monroe records. One day he hung out for about 13 hours. The third day, he came back and had written a song on the mandolin, which is probably what he wanted to learn."

The following week, the Great American Music Band was playing at Los Angeles's famous Palomino Club, opening for Bill Monroe. "Dylan was real interested in Bill Monroe," says David, "so I told him about the gig. So here we are playing our new music at a gig opening for Bill Monroe. After our set—Bill had come in after we'd started—I was out in the parking lot and Richard Greene came out and said, 'I just saw Bill Monroe, and he ignored me. I stood next to him for ten minutes and he didn't acknowledge my existence.' See, not only had Richard played in Bill's band, but Bill had always praised him—he's still complimentary towards him—but this night he was giving him the cold shoulder. I said, 'Well, he ain't gonna do that to me.' We were tight; he used to call me up onstage; I named my son Monroe Grisman; he'd once even said he wanted to manage Pete Rowan and I. He was into me when I was playing successor to the throne. So I went inside, and I'm standing in the doorway to the dressing room, wondering if I should go say hello or what, and all of a sudden who shows up but Bob Dylan with Robbie Robertson. He says, 'I really dug the set. Hey, I want

**David Grisman (below) lists Andy Statman, Mark O'Connor and Jerry Douglas, among the important New Acoustic musicians.**

to meet the man!' so here I am about to be possibly snubbed by Bill Monroe, and I have to introduce Bob Dylan to him. Suddenly Bill turns towards me, sticks out his hand, and smiles. He was real impressed when I introduced Dylan to him; they sang 'I Saw The Light' together backstage."

While still teaching at Family Light, Grisman met future Quintet member Todd Phillips. "He was my ace student," the leader boasts, "and we got into playing with two mandolins." The rhythm-and-lead-mandolin sound became an essential element when the David Grisman Quintet was finally formed in late 1975.

Phillips, who played bass on *The David Grisman Rounder Album*, became second mandolin in the group, with Darol Anger on violin, Bill Amatneek on bass, and Clarence White's apparent successor, Tony Rice, on guitar. "I met Tony cutting Bill Keith's *Something Newgrass* album in Washington, D.C.,"

remembers Grisman. "We picked a few tunes, and Tony asked me what I was up to, so I played him a tape of the Great American Music Band. I put on 'Dawgology' and after about ten seconds of it, he said, 'That the greatest music I've ever heard.'"

Tony recalls that day: "We were compatible right there on the spot; I liked his playing and he liked mine. When I heard a tape of his Dawg music, with Richard Greene and [guitarist] John Carlini, that idea really appealed to me—playing without vocals and without a banjo. I figured I could play this stuff—after a little training. As it turns out, I didn't get any training; I had to do it myself [*laughs*]. We kept in touch, and finally I left J.D. Crowe And The New South to see if David and I could get something going. I moved out to California about four months after I'd first heard his music."

With the formation of the David Grisman Quintet, Grisman got to really flex his jazz chops. "The very first jazz record I got turned on to," he states, "was a very obscure record called *Bass Ball* on Philips by a bassist named Francois Rabbath—just bass and drums. Then I got *A Love Supreme* by John Coltrane and *Eric Dolphy At the Five Spot* in around '67, and started becoming a jazz freak. Of course, I already had a couple of Django Reinhardt-Stephane Grappelli records. I began to see that jazz was a category of music where it was *all* good; it was a style of music where you *had* to be good to play it. I admire all those guys: Jim Hall, Bill Evans, Charlie Parker, Duke Ellington, McCoy Tyner, Wes Montgomery, Oliver Nelson, Oscar Peterson, Dizzy Gillespie, Charles Mingus, Keith Jarrett, Sonny Rollins . . . ."

But in spite of Grisman's love of jazz, he views his own music as a form of classical music. "The style I'm trying to play in," he explains, "has a lot of elements that aren't jazz. I think I like the idea of classical music; that is, composing something that's fixed, and playing it every time. It's working on the idea of the execution; the music is already written out, so it's just the interpretation. Of course, there's a lot of improvisation, too. That's one criticism I've encountered; one jazz critic accused us of working out our solos. That's not my total approach, writing out solos, but any musician develops the same kinds of ideas no matter how many times he plays the same song. I had the opportunity on the last album to hear Stephane Grappelli play maybe five takes of the same song— and nobody's schizophrenic enough to play a totally different solo every time. I think there's a tendency among jazz buffs or critics to expect that to be good it always has to be different and spontaneous. But, you know, spontaneity is just part of existence; there are other things, such as thoughtfulness. Classical musicians devote their whole lives to areas such as expression and articulation. That's valid too."

The main thing that differentiates Grisman's Dawg music from the bluegrass he used to play is probably the chord voicings. Mike Marshall, a 21-year-old mandolinist from Florida, who recently moved to

California and is now playing second mandolin in the David Grisman Quintet, observes, "When I first started trying to learn the stuff on the Quintet album, I had to have David relay some of it over the phone, because it's quite different from just bluegrass, which I'd been playing for about six years. The chords are completely different. In bluegrass you have three or four certain chord forms of majors and minors and that's about it. They're called 'chop' chords, and they're real punchy. In Dawg music, you play more like a barre chord, and you use more colorations, like 6ths and minors. And David has it worked out so that with two mandolins one plays low register and one plays high. He uses three-finger chords a lot, so that between the two you form a six-note chord."

Grisman explains further, "When you start using different chords and progressions, minor 7ths to dominant V7 chords, you have to eliminate something, since you only have four [paired] strings. I've found that on the mandolin, the color notes seem to be more important than playing the roots, because you're usually playing with other instruments that can supply those notes."

Although he keeps on hand a number of method books from which he practices such things as scales and arpeggios, Grisman improvises mostly in terms of melody. "It's hard for me to just take something out of a book and throw it into my playing," he says. "I like to learn the different scales and try to adapt them to something in my style, rather than just play something right out of the book."

David's main instrument today is a 1927 Gibson F-5 he bought from Matt Umanov in New York City. Also included in his collection are the K-4 mandocello, a 3-point F-4 (pictured on the front cover of *The David Grisman Rounder Album*), a Gibson H-4 mandola, a Gibson solidbody electric 4-string mandolin, and a Japanese Blue Bell.

Trying to pinpoint the advantages of the F-5, Grisman reflects, "F-5s are loud, and they have a certain tone quality that's kind of penetrating. In a bluegrass situation, it's the only mandolin that'll really cut through a loud banjo and fiddle; another model will get swallowed up. I think the most important thing in a mandolin is balance. Some mandolins are bright, others are bassy; some have good high strings, some have good low strings. But to find a mandolin that sounds the same on all the strings is pretty hard."

Grisman has made a few modifications on his Gibson: "I removed the pickguard and the tailpiece cover and end-pin," he says. "I took all the weight off of it, which wasn't much. I had another fingerboard built for it, then I put on a third fingerboard which

was given to me by Mike Apollon, [vaudeville mandolinist] Dave Apollon's son. It's an old Twenties F-5 fingerboard that was a spare of his father's. I've also had the neck slimmed down."

David strings his mandolins with custom-gauge D'Addario phosphor bronze sets. High to low (*E, A, D, G*) they are: .011, .015, .026, and .041. His picks are tortoise shell, "but not so stiff that you can't bend them. They're about the size of a guitar pick, like a Fender—with one point and two rounded edges—but I like to use the rounded edge."

Among his favorite mandolin players, David lists, "Hugo D'Alton, who's an English classical mandolinist; Buck White; and of course, Bill Monroe, Frank Wakefield, and Jessie McReynolds. Right now Ricky Skaggs, Sam Bush, and Jethro Burns are really playing some contemporary mandolin. Jethro pioneered the whole idea of jazz on the mandolin. He's an inspiration to any mandolin player worth his salt. Another fine mandolinist is Tiny Moore from Sacramento [formerly with Bob Wills And His Texas Playboys], who plays electric 5-string. I produced an album with him and Jethro for Kaleidoscope. I think on a technical level Sam Bush has the most going for him of just about anybody. One of my ex-students whom I'm really proud of is Andy Statman, who came to me when he was fourteen or fifteen—I was seventeen. He's one of the most progressive players around. Also, Mike Marshall is hot stuff."

David had an opportunity to use several mandolin players and other fine instrumentalists on a recent film project, the soundtrack for the movie *The King Of The Gypsies*. He got the assignment after producer Federico DeLaurentis happened to hear the David Grisman Quintet album at a Tower Records store in Hollywood. On several pieces in the score, Grisman augmented a 56-piece orchestra by adding mandolins, mandolas, and mandocellos to the various string sections. Musicians present on the soundtrack include: guitarist Tony Rice, John Carlini, and Diz Disley; violinists Stephane Grappelli and Richard Greene; bassist Ray Brown; and mandolinists Andy Statman and Mike Marshall. Guitarists Tony Rizzi and Tommy Tedesco also contribute mandolin parts.

This is the fourth movie David has scored, the previous three being *Big Bad Mama, Capone,* and *Eat My Dust.* "One of my fantasies," the mandolinist muses, "is to put out an album called 'Good Music From Bad Movies.'" The soundtrack for *The King Of The Gypsies*, the most challenging film product Grisman has yet worked on, is, in his words, "my conception of Gypsy music. I played it for a real Gypsy lady, though, and she got goosebumps."

## A Selected David Grisman Discography

**Solo albums:** *Hot Dawg,* A&M Horizon; *The David Grisman Rounder Album,* Rounder, 0069; *Acousticity,* Zebra Acoustic, ZEA365. **With others:** *The David Grisman Quintet,* Kaleidoscope, F-5; *Muleskinner,* Warner Brothers, BS-2787; *Old And In The Way,* Rounder, RX 103; *Grappelli, Stephane/David Grisman Live,* Warner Brothers, BSK-3550; *Quintet '80,* Warner Brothers, BSK-4369; *Mondo Mando,* Warner Brothers, BSK-3618; *Mandolin Abstractions,* Rounder, 0178; *Here Today,* Rounder, 0169.

# NEW ACOUSTIC MUSIC

Borrowing from traditional swing, jazz, and bluegrass, New Acoustic Music is the most original new instrumental style to evolve in many years. Its proponents include musicians as diverse as Irish bouzoukiist Andy Irvine and "spacegrass" guitarist Tony Rice. *Frets* interviewed mandolinist David Grisman and banjoist Tony Trischka for their views on New Acoustic Music in February 1984. Grisman's various bands have been a training ground for so many top solo artists—such as Tony Rice, Mark O'Connor, Mike Marshall, and Darol Anger—that he could be called the Miles Davis of New Acoustic Music. Tony Trischka has carried the melodic banjo style, which he absorbed from Bill Keith, into challenging areas of free jazz and other experimental styles.

**By Jim Hatlo**

"NEW ACOUSTIC MUSIC"—even among its leading practitioners, you won't find agreement on what properly comes under that umbrella. Mandolinist/bandleader David Grisman probably is considered the archetypal New Acoustic musician, yet he is one of the artists least comfortable with the label.

It is easier to be clear about where the name comes from than to be clear about what it means. "New Acoustic Music" formalizes a concept that has been around at least since 1979, when banjoist Tony Trischka—writing the liner notes for the first album of his former pupil Bela Fleck—used the term "nouveau acoustic music" in describing the material on Fleck's innovative *Crossing The Tracks*. Three years later, Grisman opted for the variation "acoustic nouveau" as he penned the notes for Fleck's sequel, *Natural Bridge*.

"Nouveau" never quite caught on, but the idea stuck. It was former Grisman Quartet violinist Darol Anger, who in 1983 fired the first deliberate shot aimed at making New Acoustic Music a household word.

Not only did he sanction the name, he even designed a catchy logo to go with it. Anger's efforts weren't purely art for art's sake. Necessity—specifically, economic neccessity—helped birth the plan.

Anger and other New Acoustic artists were keenly aware that for years, record stores—and the industry at large—had been perplexed over how to classify this new music. In three different stores, the same album might be filed under three different headings. As a result, people who wanted New Acoustic Music had a hard time finding it—and people who didn't know what it was weren't likely to learn. A Dec. '83 issue of *Billboard*, for example, listed the new release *David Grisman's Acoustic Christmas* under "Jazz/Fusion."

The situation wasn't helping sales. Anger theorized that a recognizable identity would give the genre more clout in the marketplace, and give New Acoustic Music artists and fans a flag around which to rally.

Though the campaign is still young, it is gaining ground. So far, at least one record label has adopted the designation. But there have been some skirmishes within the ranks on what belongs inside the New Acoustic Music camp, and what is beyond the pale. Mainstream jazz lies outside, as do the older forms of "progressive" bluegrass. So does another contemporary phenomenon, "Windham Hill music"—so named because of the record label closely associated with that impressionistic "urban-folk" style, which tends to emphasize mood and texture over melody. But beyond that, the borders of New Acoustic Music tend to blur.

To shed light on what New Acoustic artists perceive their rightful turf to be, David Grisman and Tony Trischcka took part in a free-ranging interview on how the style evolved, and on what sets it apart from other kinds of music.

·  ·  ·  ·

**Y**OU'VE BOTH INDICATED *that you think the term "New Acoustic Music" is a mixed blessing for the people who play it. Granted that it brings a very diverse style of string music into sharper focus for outsiders, where does it fall down as a label?*

**Grisman:** I could argue a lot of points about what "New Acoustic Music" means. First of all, what does "new" mean—recent? Modern? If it's modern, then maybe the music of Schoenberg or Stravinsky might be more modern than either my stuff or Tony's stuff. And they did that years ago. If it's just "new," then pretty soon it's going to be dated, because all the new music is old in a few years. "Acoustic"? Well, I noticed Tony has an electric bass in his band, and I have used electric guitar on records, so maybe that lets us out. "New Acoustic Music" is good as far as it goes, but the words tend to specify other things that might not fit in that category.

*Which is why you coined your own name for your music.*

**Grisman:** Right. I call it "dawg music." It's an anti-name name. People used to ask, "What do you call your music?" I figured if I just had this generic term, I could lay it on them and we could go on to the next question. If I'm pressed, I tend to say, "What I do is acoustic-string instrumentals—mainly original compositions."

**Trischka:** I ran into that, too. People would say, "What kind of music do you play," and I'd say, "It's sort of coming from bluegrass, and it has a little jazz in it, and a little punk, a little rock, a little classical," and so on. It would be easier to say, "It's New Acoustic Music," instead of saying all that.

*You think the term helps people relate to the music better.*

**Trischka:** Partly, "New Acoustic Music" is a marketing ploy, a way to educate the public and sell records. But it's also a stylistic rallying point. The drawbacks surface when you ask, "Who really *plays* New Acoustic Music?" I suppose our band, Skyline, plays New Acoustic Music; but at the same time we have vocals. Are there vocals in new Acoustic Music—or do you define it as purely an instrumental style? What about a group like Eclectricity, out in the Midwest? They do kind of Middle Eastern stuff along with everything else.

*Are there some things all the groups have in common?*

**Trischka:** I've thought of New Acoustic Music as having had at least some connection with bluegrass and folk, originally, but even that is a little limiting. I think the one thing that characterizes New Acoustic Music—in a general way—is that we don't put any limits on what can be done. In other words, we don't say, "Oh, I couldn't play Chick Corea's 'Spain' with bluegrass-type instrumentation"—as Bela Fleck did on *Crossing The Tracks*—"because that's a jazz tune." Or we don't say, "I wouldn't play an Irish tune, because my background is bluegrass." I think one important characteristic of New Acoustic Music is *experimentation*, not accepting someone else's idea of limits.

*What about the musicians who set the New Acoustic Music ball in motion? Who were the earlier players without whom your music, as it is today, wouldn't have happened?*

**Grisman:** It's hard to categorize like that,

because there are always a few who get left out. Jethro Burns would be on the list. Django Reinhardt and Stephane Grappelli would be two more. Of course, Bill Monroe; and Flatt And Scruggs. I think Chubby Wise inspired Vassar Clements, Bobby Hicks, and Benny Martin—who also are on that list. It's hard to name everybody, because there are musicians who never get real famous, but influence somebody else—like Arnold Schulz, a black guitar player who influenced Bill Monroe, but never recorded.

*Do people like Jethro Burns or Vassar Clements overlap into New Acoustic Music today—or are they one step removed?*

**Trischka:** In my opinion, they're a step removed.

**Grisman:** I'm sure Jethro's heart and soul is in jazz standards—the popular standards that he knows a billion of, like "Deep Purple" or "Sophisticated Lady." Vassar is a genius, but he's also sort of a chameleon. He first showed up in bar-type country bands. When he plays with great bluegrass musicians, he plays great bluegrass.

**Trischka:** His newest record is going to be country music, with some singing.

**Grisman:** He's a good singer. But I think that the difference is that the younger people in New Acoustic Music have got an idea for the whole shebang: They're creating their own context, and finding a new place to put all their energy.

*Besides the players who laid the groundwork for New Acoustic Music, were there others who were inspirations?*

**Trischka:** There are a lot of people, and it would be hard to come up with a complete list on the spur of the moment. I can get a lot of inspiration from [keyboardist] Chick Corea or [saxophonist] John Coltrane. I can listen to a Corea record and get inspired by his creative impulse; I'll want to go out and write

15 tunes—not necessarily in the Chick Corea style, but because my interest gets flowing just from listening to him. [Guitarist] John McLaughlin did that for me for a while, too. John Coltrane has, [saxophonist] Eric Dolphy has; [saxophonist] Charlie Parker's music still does that for me. [Bassist] Charles Mingus does that for me. Those are all jazz guys, of course. Today I listen to the Police sometimes.

**Grisman:** I see the big simlarity in all these musical influences is that a percentage of it is *improvised*—which I think is a twentieth-century phenomenon. And these improvisations have been preserved on records; whereas, though they say Bach improvised, we don't have a record of that. The musician who has that impulse to play spontaneously is sort of going to make up his own way of playing. I think that's the underlying thing that connects all these influences together.

**Trischka:** That's why bluegrass is a good place to start, because it's an improvisatory music. And if you're a Scruggs-style banjo player, but you have ears to hear different things outside bluegrass, then you'll start drawing on those other sources of music. Like, I can't sit down and play one or two Charlie Parker solos note-for-note; but his music *has* inspired me to go off in a certain direction. I'm sure you've been influenced by these players, though not necessarily in a literal sort of way.

**Grisman:** Well, there were a lot of guys who played complicated and fast. But I keep getting drawn back to the guys who can do it all in just a few notes. The late Ben Webster, a great tenor saxophone player who was with Duke Ellington's band for a long time, is one of my favorites.

**Trischka:** When you say you're drawn to the guys who can do it all in a few notes, I can sort of see there may be some truth to the suggestion that there's a "California school" and a "New York school" in New Acoustic Music.

**Grisman:** Really? I can't. And I'm from New York originally, so where do I fit in?

**Trischka:** I think that the major musical statements you've made have come since you moved to California. I guess the way I see it is that, if you listen back to the "New York school" players like Andy Statman, Kenny Kosek, and Stacy Phillips, and compare that with your music, you guys have always been really interested in time and tone. I mean, that's been a prime thing with you.

**Grisman:** And you guys back East have been like, more adventurous.

**Trischka:** Yeah, that sort of thing. The time and tone might not always have been there in the same way.

*How do you mean "adventurous"?*

**Grisman:** That New York crowd will play anything! [*Laughter*] Their music has got more of what I'd call intellect—sort of an intellectual humor; maybe cynicism, too. Take a guy like Matt Glaser: He likes to make bluegrass tunes into jazz standards!

"The one thing that characterizes New Acoustic Music," says Tony Trischka of the group Skyline, "is that we don't put limits on what can be done." (opposite page) David Grisman.

**Trischka:** Andy Statman is definitely the king of that. You could say he's coming from an intellectual point of view. But going back to what I was saying, in Breakfast Special we all gravitated together somehow, and you folks gravitated together out here—you found the guys who could make your particular statement with you. And you can hear it in what's happened to your present band members, when they do their own recording, or with alumni from your band. When Tony Rice does his New Acoustic-type records, I can still hear elements of your music—I mean, there's a thread there. Not that he's playing dawg music, but that thread is running through it. I do think there's a thread that holds together what you guys are doing.

**Grisman:** I don't want to stop people from playing like themselves. Maybe I did unify their outlooks initially, to fit my concept. I mean, if *you're* arranging, then I think you'll get the kind of results you want out of the musicians that work with you. Ultimately a certain type of musician will gravitate toward composing his own music, and that's after he's done a certain amount of learning from whoever inspired him. As to a difference between a California sound and a New York sound, in New York there may be more anarchism. In other words, everybody is coming from a slightly different place. Not chaotic, but more eclectic.

**Trischka:** We really do split up in pretty different directions. Andy Statman is doing klezmer music, Russ Barenberg is doing calypso music—I'm totally generalizing, but it's true that Andy really went in one direction, Russ really went in another direction, and I'm doing my music, whatever that is.

*As an example, how would you distinguish between the different music produced by the two guitarists you mentioned, Tony Rice in California and Russ Barenberg back East?*

**Trischka:** They've both gone into jazzy terrain, but at an obvious level, Russ is playing more calypso-oriented music. It's maybe not as fast and scintillating as some kinds of jazz. And he goes for that beautiful tone, playing real clean. He also goes for more inventive rhythms than a bluegrass musician would play. I've always thought of him as what I'd call a "non-lick" player. Back in the days when we were in Country Cooking, when he came up with a break it was really original. He wouldn't fall back that much on what he'd done before. As for Tony Rice, he has a style of his own, which I think has gone more in the direction of harmonic experimentation. Tony has more bluegrass in his roots, I'd say; but he also plays with a more rhythmic feel than you find in straight bluegrass.

**Grisman:** When I met Tony, the first thing that occurred to me was—and I mean this in a very complimentary way—" Wow! Clarence White is still alive!" Because I never heard anybody else play that way, with those kinds of acute syncopations. Clarence had a very unique thing, a certain precision and defi-

nition, and Tony is still the only guy I've ever heard who can do that; although Tony projects more than Clarence White did—he has a bigger sound. Tony will still tell you that his A-B-C's are *tone* and *time*. Those are the fundamental things I appreciate about him. I look at Tony as a link in a very special chain. I'd agree that the core of his "space-grass" style of music is experimentation.

*What about the scene in the South, with people like Sam Bush and the New Grass Revival?*

**Trischka:** Sam comes from a number of different places. Just in his fiddle styles you have old-time, bluegrass, and rock. But I think the "newgrass" sound originally came from taking rock and roll tunes and doing them in a bluegrass style—and vice versa.

*If someone were to ask you for a crash listening list to get acquainted with New Acoustic Music, who would you put on it?*

**Grisman** I'm not going to say anything about my own records. I like Mark O'Connor's record, *False Dawn*; I think it's a fantastic album, very unique. I think Andy Statman's *Flatbush Waltz* is maybe my favorite out of the whole bunch. It really moved me—it's the only one I ever laughed and cried over. Jerry Douglas' dobro records are great; he's an amazing talent.

**Trischka:** Bela Fleck's *Natural Bridge* is a real strong recording; so is his *Crossing The Tracks*. I think Russ Barenberg's albums are important, *Cowboy Calypso* and *Behind The Melodies; Cowboy Calypso* was the one that really jumped out, for me. And we've already mentioned Tony Rice and the guys in your band, David.

*Any other East Coast albums besides Baren-*

*berg's, and of course, your own, Tony? What about the material by Fiddle Fever, with Ken Kosek and Matt Glaser?*

**Trischka:** That's a good question. I was just thinking about them. For me, that's borderline. They're a great group, but for what we're talking about, I think they're a little more rooted in tradition. You know, there's a record out by [banjoist] Marty Cutler—*Charged Particles*. It's got the spirit of what we're calling New Acoustic Music.

**Grisman:** I heard a tape of it and I was impressed. There's a great version of "Blackberry Blossom" on there. He's got a lot of electric stuff on some of the tunes, so I don't know how that fits into New Acoustic Music. Maybe we should call it "New String Music," because I think what we're really talking about is people who play string instruments.

**Trischka:** I think another important thing about this style is that it isn't calculatingly commercial. The whole premise is really just to do your own thing.

**Grisman:** I'm trying to make my music as appealing as I can, but if I wanted to be *commercial* I'd go out right now and buy the top ten albums in the country, and figure out which rhythm section to hire for my next record. I'd get a whole bunch of guest singers on there and I'm sure I could sell a whole lot more records, and Warner Brothers would be happy. But I wouldn't feel comfortable. I wouldn't feel that I was doing what I was really about. Basically, this is something I can do artistically, and that's why I'm out to try to develop it. I've turned down a lot of things in my career that would have led to vastly more economic success.

**Trischka:** What sells today is not acoustic music—it's generally electric music. So it's hard to get a hit doing what we do, because this music is hard to sell. Our band is in a little different spot

because we have vocals, and you have more of a chance with that than with just instrumental music, because people can relate to vocals more. I don't have any other ideas on how to widen our appeal—if I did, I'd be using them!

**Grisman:** You need somebody out there helping you sell your music. You definitely can't do it alone. If some Texas millionaire wanted to make you a TV ad for Skyline, you'd be selling records. Nothing gets sold to the masses unless a lot of money is put into it.

**Trischka:** There are two ways New Acoustic Music could be a bigger success: You either get someone who is going to pump a lot of money into it, and make it happen: or you get someone who is already doing the music and happens to get popular. I think one reason why there is New Acoustic Music as a recognized style at all is because of your success, David. You're not the Beatles, but you're a rallying point. You're someone who is successful who is doing this, with your film work and your TV appearances, and so you are visible. And that's good for New Acoustic Music.

**Grisman:** Well, thanks; and if the label "New Acoustic Music" helps the style succeed, helps spread the word, then I'm all for it. But if it just leads to more prejudice and snap judgements, then let's go back to calling things "Skyline" music and "dawg" music, and not worry about categories. I have to agree with Duke Ellington that there are only two kinds of music: good music, and bad music. The main thing is to appreciate something, to get exposed to it. Categorizing a style isn't going to make it worthwhile. It's only worthwhile if it has something going for it. We shouldn't be concerned with getting people interested in music because it's "acoustic" or "new"—we should get people interested in music that is *great.*

---

## A Selected New Acoustic Music Discography

**Darol Anger**, *Fiddlistics*, Kaleidoscope, F-8; *Tidelines*, Windham Hill (dist. by A&M), C1021. **Russ Barenberg**, *Cowboy Calypso*, Rounder, 0111; *Behind The Melodies*, Rounder, 0176. **Jethro Burns**, *Tea For One*, Kaleidoscope, F-14; *Jethro Burns*, Flying Fish, FF-042; *Back To Back* (with Tiny Moore), Kaleidoscope, F-9. **Vassar Clements**, *Vassar*, Flying Fish, FF-232; *The Bluegrass Sessions*, Flying Fish, FF-038; *Nashville Jam*, Flying Fish, FF-073. **Cloud Valley**, *Cloud Valley*, Outlet. **Jerry Douglas**, *Fluxology*, Rounder, 0093; *Fluxedo*, Rounder, 0112. *Eclectricity*, Redbud, 1003; *Language Of The Heart*, Flying Fish, FF-281. **Bela Fleck**, *Crossing The Tracks*, Rounder, 0121; *Natural Bridge*, Rounder, 0146. **Matt Glaser** and **Kenny Kosek**, *Hasty Lonesome*, Rounder, 0127; *Fiddle Fever*, Flying Fish, FF-247. **Stephane Grappelli**, *Grappelli/Grisman: Live!*, Warner Brothers, BSK 3550; *At The Winery*, Concord Jazz, CJ-139; *Vintage, 1981*, Concord Jazz, CJ-169. **Richard Greene**, *Ramblin'*, Rounder, 0110; *Blue Rondo*, Sierra, SR 8710. **David Grisman**, *David Grisman Quintet*, Kaleidoscope, F-5; *Hot Dawg*, A&M Horizon, SP731; *Quintet '80*, Warner Brothers, BSK 3469; *Mondo Mando*, Warner Brothers, BSK 3618; *Dawg Grass*, Warner Brothers, 1-23804. **Bill Keith** (with Tony Trischka and Bela Fleck), *Fiddle Tunes For Banjo*, Rounder, 0124; (with others) *Mud Acres*, Rounder, 3001. **Mike Marshall** (with Darol Anger), *The Duo*, Rounder, 0168. **Bill Monroe**, *The Classic Bluegrass Recordings, Vols. 1 & 2*, County, CCS 104/105; *Master Of Bluegrass*, MCA, 5214. **Mark O'Connor**, *Markology*, Rounder, 0090; *On The Rampage*, Rounder, 0018; *False Down*, Rounder, 0165. **Tony Rice**, *Backwaters*, Rounder, 0167; *Acoustics*, Kaleidoscope, F-10. **Peter Rowan**, *Medicine Trail*, Flying Fish, FF-205; *Texican Badman*, Appaloosa, AP010. **Andy Statman**, *Flatbush Waltz*, Rounder, 0116; (with David Grisman) *Manolin Abstractions*, Rounder, 0178. **Trapezoid**, *Three Forks Of Cheat*, Rounder, 0113, *Now & Then*, Flying Fish, FF-230. **Tony Trischka**, *Banjoland*, Rounder, 0087; *A Robot Plane Flies Over Arkansas*, Rounder, 0171; (with Skyline) *Late To Work*, Flying Fish, FF-261. **Frank Wakefield**, *Frank Wakefield*, Rounder, 0007; *End Of The Rainbow*, Bay, 214. **Tim Ware**, *The Tim Ware Group*, Kaleidoscope, F-13; *Shelter From The Norm*, Varrick (dist. by Rounder), VR014. **Rob Wasserman**, *Solo*, Rounder, 0179.

# EPILOGUE

The path travelled in this book, from John Lomax's collection of cowboy songs to the pop ballads of Gordon Lightfoot, or from early southern string bands to the latest fusion of bluegrass and bebop, parallels the urbanization and suburbanization of America. Once brought to the city, the music and its performers rubbed shoulders with dozens of different cultures, becoming more heterogenous in outlook, and urban and commercial in their concerns.

In the process, what we call folk music has been forever altered. To the dismay of some it has gone from being mainly a source of diversion and self-entertainment for ordinary people to being one small arm of a many-tentacled music industry. And the "folk" part of that industry is quite healthy. Dozens of independent record companies are prospering by serving specialized folk markets. Clubs that present folk and acoustic music artists are generally drawing better crowds than they have in many years. Newsletters and magazines aimed at folk musicians, from autoharpists to old-time fiddlers, abound. In New York, Folk City recently threw a party to celebrate its 25th anniversary, drawing old and young fans alike. One new folk-revivalist group, a latter-day reincarnation of Peter, Paul, and Mary, called the Washington Squares, dress like Maynard G. Krebs-era beatniks and play rock clubs and punk venues across the country. Significantly, they also lend their talents to publications like Broadside, carrying on a 35-year-old tradition of musical and political activism.

Just as rock music periodically returns to its rhythm & blues roots for regeneration, various folk music traditions, from calypso and reggae to Celtic and mariachi, continue to feed into the mainstream of popular music. But if a big Folk Revival were to happen tomorrow it might not resemble anything that has come before. If music is a product of environment, then certain forms of folk music may be gone forever. It is not likely that there are any more undiscovered Leadbellies being raised in the bayou country, or more young farmboys like Bill Monroe huddling around the radio to hear the Grand Ole Opry on a Saturday night.

Over time perhaps all folk music moves uptown, has its rough edges sanded smooth from contact with the upper classes, and ends by becoming art. Years ago Charles Seeger wrote an essay, "The Folkness Of The Non-Folk And The Non-Folkness Of The Folk" which discussed in part, how those who preserve folk art are not "the folk." The true folk have no use for folk art, at least not any that is self-conscious enough to call itself that.

Which may be why the name "folk" is rarely used today by the musicians who make the music. They are too busy concentrating on learning their discipline, expanding musical boundaries, and having fun.

Reading the stories of these musicians again, I sense the enormous love they have for their art, and how being a musican is never really an expression of nostalgia for them, nor a desire to preserve every single nuance of an obscure musical tradition. Whether today's young folkie is playing bluegrass or country, or Celtic, or blues, or some exotic fusion of ideas lifted from many cultures, the music is its own motivation and reward. And that's the way it should be.

—*Phil Hood*

# ABOUT THE AUTHORS

**Michael Brooks** is a photographer and journalist. He was formerly a Managing Editor of *Guitar Player Magazine*.

**Dix Bruce**, the former Editor of *Mandolin World News*, is also the author of a mandolin instruction book.

**William J. Bush** is a writer and advertising executive in Florida.

**Helen Casabona** is the Editor of GPI Books and has worked with several publishing companies. In addition, she is a bluegrass guitarist and mandolinist, and a frequent contributor to *Frets Magazine*.

**Jim Crockett** was formerly the Editor of *Guitar Player Magazine*. Today he is President and Publisher of GPI.

**Art Edelstein** is a Vermont-based freelance writer and photographer whose work has appeared in dozens of publications. He is also a contributing editor to *Victorian Homes Magazine*.

**Dan Forte** is an Assistant Editor of *Guitar Player Magazine*.

**Marty Gallanter** is a freelance writer and photographer who has worked closely with the Clearwater Project.

**Rick Gartner** is an Assistant Editor of *Frets Magazine*.

**Alice Gerrard**, one of the foremost performers of traditional music for many years, was a founding member of The Strange Creek Singers, with her ex-husband, Mike Seeger, Hazel Dickens, Lamar Grier, and Tracy Schwarz.

**Doug Green** is a past President of the Country Music Foundation. He is best known as the leader and guitarist of Riders In The Sky, a western band that appears frequently on The Nashville Network.

**Mark Greenberg** is a Vermont-based writer, and a producer of radio shows.

**Jim Hatlo** is Special Issues Editor of *Frets Magazine*.

**Phil Hood** is the Editor of *Frets Magazine*.

**Mark Humphrey** is a freelance music writer and radio show producer. He is a regular contributor to *Frets*, *The LA Reader*, and many other publications.

**Alanna Nash** is a music writer based in Louisville, Kentucky.

**Jas Obrecht** is an Assistant Editor of *Guitar Player Magazine*.

**Sherwood Ross** is a folksinger, writer, and public relations expert in New York.

**Jon Sievert** is a writer, and also staff photographer for *Frets* and *Guitar Player Magazines*.

**Roger Siminoff** is the author of several books and Director Of Operations of GPI. Previously he was Editor of *Frets Magazine*.

**Robert J. Yelin** is a writer and also a jazz guitarist, with several albums to his credit.

# ARTIST INDEX

*Read these other distinguished music books compiled by the editors of Guitar Player, Keyboard, and Frets magazines.***

##  MASTERS OF HEAVY METAL
**Edited by Jas Obrecht**

"Goes to the eye of the hurricane," (Portland, Oregonian). "Fascinating!" (Newark Star Ledger). For fans and players of the immensely powerful, hugely popular, hard-core rock and roll style: intense, high-energy, guitar-dominated. Including serious, informative interviews with Jimi Hendrix, Eddie Van Halen, Jimmy Page, Randy Rhoads, Judas Priest, the Scorpions, and others. Profusely illustrated.
Paperback/$8.95   0-688-0293-X

## ROCK KEYBOARD
**Edited by Bob Doerschuk   Forward by Keith Emerson**

The first major book to document and celebrate thirty years of rock and roll keyboard history; the creative genius, the incredible personalities, the technical development. From boogie-woogie ancestry to the most sophisticated electronic synthesizers. Including exclusive interviews, true history, and astute analysis of Fats Domino, Little Richard, Jerry Lee Lewis, Al Kooper, Leon Russell, Booker T. Jones, Elton John, Billy Joel, Michael McDonald, David Paich & Steve Poracro, Brian Eno, Thomas Dolby, and others. Photos throughout.
Paperback/$12.95/0-688-02961-2

## THE BIG BOOK OF BLUEGRASS
**Edited by Marilyn Kochman   Forward by Earl Scruggs**

Bill Monroe, Lester Flatt, Earl Scruggs, David Grisman, Ricky Skaggs, and other popular bluegrass artists offer practical tips on playing, with note-by-note musical examples, plus valuable advice on technique and performance. The history, the greatest players, the genuine art of this authentic American commercial country folk music, more popular than ever today. Over 100 rare photos and over 50 favorite songs.
Hardcover/$24.95/0-688-02940-X
Paperback/$12.95/0-688-02942-6

##  GUITAR GEAR
**Edited by John Brosh**

A definitive guide to the instruments, accessories, gadgets, and electronic devices; the tremendous variety of both basic and sophisticated equipment that has become so crucial to the creative fulfillment of today's guitar player—how it works, how it's made, how to choose what's right for you.
Paperback/$15.95   0-688-03108-0

## THE ART OF ELECTRONIC MUSIC
**Compiled and with Commentary by Tom Darter**
**Edited by Greg Armbruster**
**Forward by Dr. Robert A. Moog**

The first definitive book: the creative and technical development of an authentic musical revolution. From the Theremin Electrical Symphony to today's most advanced synthesizers. Scientific origins, the evolution of hardware, the greatest artists—including Tangerine Dream, Vangelis, Keith Emerson, Wendy Carlos, Jan Hammer, Kraftwerk, Brian Eno, Thomas Dolby, and others—in stories, interviews, illustrations, analysis, and practical musical technique. From the pages of *Keyboard Magazine*. Completely illustrated.
Hardcover/$25.00/0-688-03106-6
Paperback/$15.95/0-688-03106-4

From your bookstores or directly from the publisher.

**QUILL**
A Division of William Morrow & Company
105 Madison Avenue
New York, NY 10016

**To subscribe, write GPI, 20085 Stevens Creek, Cupertino, CA 95014.